ŔOSITA FORBES

The Secret of the Sahara: Kufara

by
Rosita Forbes

The Long Riders' Guild Press

www.thelongridersguild.com

ISBN No: 1-59048-101-1

To the Reader:

The editors and publishers of The Long Riders' Guild Press faced significant technical and financial difficulties in bringing this and the other titles in the Equestrian Travel Classics collection to the light of day.

Though the authors represented in this international series envisioned their stories being shared for generations to come, all too often that was not the case. Sadly, many of the books now being published by The Long Riders' Guild Press were discovered gracing the bookshelves of rare book dealers, adorned with princely prices that placed them out of financial reach of the common reader. The remainder were found lying neglected on the scrap heap of history, their once-proud stories forgotten, their once-glorious covers stained by the toil of time and a host of indifferent previous owners.

However The Long Riders' Guild Press passionately believes that this book, and its literary sisters, remain of global interest and importance. We stand committed, therefore, to bringing our readers the best copy of these classics at the most affordable price. The copy which you now hold may have small blemishes originating from the master text.

We apologize in advance for any defects of this nature.

TO

AHMED MOHAMMED BEY HASSANEIN
IN MEMORY OF HOURS GRAVE AND GAY, BATTLES
DESPERATE OR HUMOROUS, OF SUCCESS
AND FAILURE IN THE LIBYAN
DESERTS

INTRODUCTION

BY SIR HARRY JOHNSTON

THE OASES OF KUFARA

VERY nearly midway between the great mountains of Tibesti (which rise to over eleven thousand feet in height) ; the plateaus of Fazan; the mountainous 'island' of the Cyrenaica; the oases of Western Egypt, and of Dongola; lies the still mysterious region of Kufara, visited and described by Mrs. Rosita Forbes, the author of this book.

She has been seemingly the second explorer of European birth to accomplish this feat; for although the Kufara district was first placed on the map with no great incorrectness of location by Friedrich Gerhard Rohlfs, after his journey thither in 1878-9, he was—as Mrs. Forbes shows—the only European of his party to reach these oases, and his stay there was very short.

Apparently he only revealed, only realised by sight or information the salt lakes at Buseima and a rather problematical 'Erbelma' (qy. Erbayana, Erbelna?) to the south-west; and either he did not see, or he did not record the more important sheets of salt or brackish water in the comparatively large Kebabo oasis or collection of oases.

These lakes of Kebabo stand at an average elevation of about fourteen hundred feet above sea level, an elevation which was divined or calculated hurriedly by F. G. Rohlfs, but more accurately determined by Mrs. Forbes and her Egyptian fellow-traveller, Hassanein Bey. By these later figures the altitude above sea level of the Kebabo Oases may prove to be slightly lower than in the

estimation of the older maps (1614 feet). Still it cannot be much less on the lake levels than fourteen hundred
feet; therefore in considering the problems it is not possible to attribute the Kebabo oases, the villages of Kufara
to anything more than the site of a largish lake in pre-
historic times which sent its waters flowing west into the
great Wadi al Fardi, the course of which seems to have
passed through Taiserbo to Jaghabub and thence past the
oasis of Siwa into the Nile near Cairo.

The Libyan Desert through which Mrs. Forbes
travelled, starting from Cyrenaica and returning to
Egypt, is classed by her and by most other persons with
the Sahara; which properly speaking lies to the west of
a long chain of peaks, ridges, and tablelands grouped in
its central section under the name of 'Tibesti', the mountainous country of the Tu, Teda, or Tibu (Tebu or Tubu)
peoples. But it would almost seem for reason of its
past mammalian fauna as though we must distinguish
between the Sahara and the Libyan Deserts, just as for
similar reasons we do not extend the name of 'Sahara' to
cover the sandy and stony wastes of Arabia. The true
Libyan Desert—almost a more awful region of desolation than the Sahara west of the Tibesti mountains—
would seem in ancient human times, fifty thousand, a
hundred thousand, two hundred thousand years ago, to
have been the western area of the Nile basin. Its mighty
rivers, their courses still traceable, fed by the almost
Alpine range of Tibesti, by the vanished rain from the
plateaus and ridges of Wanyanga and Darfur, flowed
towards the Nile between its nascent delta and Kordofan.
Its mammalian fauna and to a lesser degree its flora differed in some important particulars from that of the
Sahara (then possibly much covered by shallow lakes and
inland seas); and still more from the beasts and trees of
true West Africa or Central Africa. The White

Rhinoceros or a nearly allied form of it has left fossil remains in Algeria and is still found within the equatorial Nile basin. It has penetrated south along the eastern side of Central Africa, but it does not appear to have passed into the Congo basin or to have reached the regions south of Algeria or west of Tibesti and Darfur. The 'Black' Rhinoceros with the pointed lip has pushed westward to the lands round Lake Chad and into the basin of the Shari, but seems never to have travelled as far westward as the Niger or ever to have been found in true West Africa. No zebra or wild ass, so far as we know, ever left Algeria or the Nile basin to enter the Chad or Congo regions. Many antelopes have in the near past and present ranged between Mediterranean Algeria on the north-west, the equatorial Nile basin, and southern most Africa, but have not appeared in the western half of Africa.

The region therefore into which plunged the author of this book, with the concurrence and assistance of an educated Egyptian of Al Azhar University, has been of great interest to all students of Africa. Rohlfs's visit had almost become legendary and at best its reports were fragmentary and inconclusive. The Kufara oasis was the half-way house between the mysterious and recalcitrant Negro kingdom of Wadai and the Mediterranean coast. Wadai was the last of the great Negro States of Central Africa to come under European supervision and control. But even after Wadai—to the great benefit of North Central Africa—was conquered by the French, and its slave trade abolished, the oasis of Kufara remained for a few more years a legendary district, perhaps mainly created by the excited imagination of a thwarted German explorer, who had already crossed Africa from the Mediterranean to the Benue and the Niger, but who had scarcely penetrated to this secret land of water and palm trees in the centre of the Libyan Desert than he had to leave it.

We now realise from the work of Mr. Harding King in 1913 and from Mrs. Forbes's book, with its admirable photographs and both vivid and circumstantial descriptions, what this series of oases, salt lakes, and underground fountains means in the middle of the Libyan Desert. It is one of the vestiges of a formerly well-watered country ten, twenty or more thousand years ago. It was a more habitable region possibly at a distance in time not exceeding five thousand years. To it came, long ago, when the intervening desert was much more traversable, clans of the Tu, Tebu or Tibu people, nowadays the dominating population of Fazan and Tibesti. A few Tebu—one or two hundred—still linger in Kufara on sufferance, the semi-slaves of the Zwiya Arabs. The author is able to give her readers an admirable photograph of one of these lingering Tebu of Kufara.

Who and what are the variously named Tu, Teda, Tibu, or Tebu tribes? They are seemingly of considerable antiquity, the Garamantes of Herodotos and the Romans, the Tedamansii of Claudius Ptolomæus, the Alexandrian geographer of the second century. They represent one of the numerous races between the White man and the Negro, but in their purer and more northern extension they are a people with a preponderance of white man stock. The skin is dark-tinted and the hair has a kink, a curl about it; but the physiognomy is that of the Mediterranean peoples, except for the occasionally tumid lips. They do not indeed differ very much in appearance, facially, from the Hamitic peoples of North-east Africa; but their language is utterly dissimilar. With this and that corruption, change, and deficiency, it has become the speech of Bornu (Kanuri), Kanem, Ennedi, northern Darfur, Tibesti, Tummo, and southern Fazan.

Commerce even carries its dialects into Tripoli. But this Tibu-Kanuri group of tongues has no discernible connection with any other African group and is utterly dissimilar in syntax and in word-roots from the sex-denoting Hamitic, Libyan, Egyptian and Semitic languages of North and North-east Africa. Neither does it offer any point of resemblance with the Nubian group, with the Niger families, with Songhai or Fulfulde. It is rather hurriedly called a 'Negro' tongue, which explains nothing. There seem to have been many pre-Aryan, pre-Semitic, pre-Hamitic forms of speech generated by the White man in Europe, North Africa and Western Asia, which, like the original language-impulse of the Bantu and Semi-Bantu, were introduced into Tropical Africa and subsequently adopted by the Negro, who was at all times so easily influenced by the White invader. The Tibu speech seems to have been one of the several distinct groups of tongues (Fula may have been another) spoken in North Africa before that region was invaded from the east by the Hamites and from the North-west by the Libyans. It was pushed southwards into Fazan and thence extended across the Libyan Desert to the oases of Kufara.

But though ranking themselves as 'white men' or at any rate as a racial type much above the Negro, the Tibu were not quickly on the White man's side in religion. The ancient Garamantes became Christian only a short time before the Moslem invasion of Tripoli; and were possibly not Islamized until the eleventh century. Probably the Tebu of Kufara were of some vaguely Pagan faith when their oases were invaded by the Zwiya Arabs of Fazan two or three hundred years ago. As they only had spears and arrows to defend themselves against the invaders who were armed with guns, they were soon conquered, semi-enslaved, and coerced to adopt the Muslim faith. They seem to have possessed camels of what is known as the

Teda or Tibesti breed, taller, stouter, clumsier in form than the dromedaries of the north.

On this point hinges a good deal of interesting argument. Was there a native camel, a wild species of the genus *Camelus* in North-east Africa before the domesticated camel was introduced from Arabia and Palestine into Africa at an uncertain period coincident with the downfall of the independence and glory of Ancient Egypt —say three thousand years ago? A wild camel, very near in form to the Arabian species, is found fossil and sub-fossil in Algeria. It must have lingered there till the arrival of Man who possibly aided in its extinction. Were there wild camels similarly lingering in the Teda, the Tibesti country and in Somaliland and Galaland down to quite recent times? And have they contributed to the formation of the domesticated camel stock of Africa?

The Zwiya conquerors of Kufara opened up relations with the Sudan, with Ennedi, Wadai, and Darfur; and on the north with Cyrene and its Mediterranean ports. Their oases obtained wealth and importance by becoming a halfway-house between Eastern Europe and Central Africa, and grew rich during the eighteenth and nineteenth centuries over the trade in ivory and Negro slaves. The importance of the Wadai-Kufara road for camel caravans increased greatly during the second half of the last century because, meantime, Algeria and Tunis had become more or less controlled by Europe. Egypt was likewise supervised, constantly watched by European powers in regard to the Slave trade. Even Tripoli and its sea-faring trade in slaves was hampered by surveillance from Malta.

Turkey, however, was left pretty much to herself after the Berlin Conference of 1878, for motives of international jealousy. She strengthened her hold over Cyrene and likewise garrisoned Crete, not far away. So that long after the Sudan slave trade had been closed in all

other directions by British and French action it remained
alive and active by way of Wadai-Kufara-and-Benghazi,
till, in 1912-1913, Italy took Tripoli and Cyrenaica from
the Turks and resumed the former protectorate of the
Roman Empire in this direction.

Then—as Mrs. Forbes relates—the followers of the
Senusi Brotherhood found themselves in lively conflict
with a modern-tempered European power, and had—
eventually—to come to terms with Italy.

Mrs. Forbes tells us or reminds us of the main facts
and changes in Kufara history: its occupation at an unknown and probably distant date by the Tibu people, who
may have dwelt there when the surrounding deserts were
much less arid, and when the oases and their lakes were
considerably larger. They may have been there while
the Pharaohs reigned in Egypt and before the domestica-
tion of the camel. Then she alludes to the conquest and
occupation of Kufara by the Zwiya Arabs, who seem to
have come from the eastern part of Fazan, especially an
oasis named Leshkerre. Before their coming the Tibu
inhabitants seem to have called 'Kufara' (which in Arabic
means, 'unbelievers', 'heathen') by the name of Tazerr;
and in a valuable Appendix the author relates the subsequent history of these oases when they came under the
influence of the Senusi dynasty.

The statements in this Appendix may be in all points
accurate, but it might be interesting to the reader to give
an alternative version derived from earlier French and
British writers. Some of this information was noted
when the present writer was Consul General in Tunis, and
had commenced studying the results and aims of the teaching emanating from the Senusi confraternity, his attention having been drawn to this movement in Muhammadanism as far back as the 'eighties of the last century, by
the influence of the Senusi missionaries on Nigeria.

The first Senusi teacher was born at or near Mastaghanem on the coast of western Algeria towards the close of the eighteenth century. He was styled—for short, as he had a wearisome array of names—Muhammad bin Ali bin as-Sanusi. [Because there is no *e* in the Arabic language you will find a world-wide conspiracy to use that vowel in the transliteration of Arab names. There is likewise no *o,* so that *o* is thrust into or before Arab names of persons, countries, and mountains in their European rendering with an unaccountable vehemence of contrariety].

Like so many Arabs and Berbers in the history of North Africa he was a religious enthusiast, and like all such in every faith he was willing to die or to doom to death in defence of his unprovable religious dogmas. He resorted to Fez for his theological studies and worked at the so-called university in that Moroccan city till he was past his thirtieth year. He then felt inspired to preach reform in Islam, and to that end set his face westward, expounding his tenets first in Algeria (about to be distracted by the French entry), then in southern Tunis and Tripoli. At last he reached Egypt and enrolled himself as a student at the great Muhammadan university of Al Azhar in Cairo. But his tenets, when he expounded them, were pronounced to be heretical, so he journeyed on to Mecca, seeking further instruction.

At this religious capital of Islam he met among other pilgrims and enquirers a remarkable personality, Muhammad ash-Sharif, a Negro prince from Wadai who in 1838 became supreme monarch or Sultan of that remarkable country in the heart of Africa. A great friendship grew up between the white-skinned Berber (for though claiming to belong to an Arab tribe, the first of the Senusi leaders was obviously of Berber stock) and the black skinned Wadai prince, which affected for seventy years or more the relations between the Senusi sect and the central Sudan. But after the departure of the Wadai prince the relations between Muhammad bin Ali bin as-Sanusi and the authorities of Mecca became more and more difficult; and though the Senusi leader founded monasteries in western Arabia he thought it better to leave that land of orthodoxy and return to Africa.

He settled first—about 1844—near Derna in Cyrenaica.* This region, once in far-back, pre-historic times a huge island, had, together with Morocco, become the only portions of North Africa where Islamic developments were unfettered. Yet even here, in the next decade Turkish enquiries (after the anxiety of the Crimean War was over) irked the first Senusi; so that in 1855 he moved from the vicinity of Derna to Jaghabub, an oasis on the undefined borderland between Egypt and the Tripolitan Pashalik. Hither he brought his two sons, born in 1843 and 1845. They were named Muhammad ash-Sharif and Muhammad al Mahdi, and according to most authorities Muhammad ash-Sharif was the elder. Mrs. Forbes, no doubt on good authority, reverses this order and puts forward the Second Senusi—Muhammad al Mahdi—as the elder and all along the rightful heir.

The story related to me and preserved in several books is that one day at Jaghabub, not long before his death in 1859, the First Senusi put his young sons to the following test of faith. He pointed out a tall palm tree near the mosque and ordered them to climb up it and then, putting their faith in God, to leap off it to the ground. Muhammad ash-Sharif shrank from the test; his younger brother had faith, climbed up the tree to near the fronds, and then dropped to the ground and was not hurt. Him, therefore, his father designated as his eventual successor.

Whether or not this was a true story and whether or

* He is said to have paid another visit to Mecca in 1852.

no the Second Senusi was the younger son of the First,
he succeeded to his father's position, after a short interval
of 'regency' conducted by trusty councillors; though there
seems to have been no ill-feeling between the brothers.
Under Muhammad al Mahdi, the Ꝺeco ,enusi, the
political movement took great amplitude. ʀiis emissaries
spread far and wide over Negro and Negroid Africa.
Houses of teaching and prayer were founded in Senegal,
in western Nigeria, in Hausaland and above all throughout the Tibu countries, Wadai and northern Darfur, as
well as in Fazan, Tunis, and Algeria. A little vague
hostility was shown towards France, but not more than
towards Turkish rule, and the feeling among the Senusiya
was rather in favour of the British. When the other
Mahdi, Muhammad Ahmad, the Dongolese destroyer of
the Egyptian Sudan, strove to enter into close relations
with Muhammad al Mahdi at Jaghabub his overtures were
snubbed very distinctly.

Unknown to himself, no doubt, the Berber blood in
the Senusi leader's veins ranged him against violent attacks on civilised states. He did his utmost to prevent
the Arab fanaticism of the Middle Nile from spreading
to Egypt, or to Wadai and Bornu. His growing influence over Turkish Africa attracted the interested attention of Abd-al-Hamid, Sultan of Turkey. In 1889,
the Second Senusi leader was visited at Jaghabub by the
Pasha of Tripoli escorted by an imposing force. This
visit and other actions of Abd-al-Hamid caused the Second
Senusi perturbation. Accordingly in 1894, he transferred
himself and his funds and band of officials to the Kufara
oases, whither pursuit by Turkish troops would be very
difficult. From this safe retreat he intensified his relations across the Desert with Wadai, Kanem, and Darfur.
In 1900 the Second Senusi pope (as one might by now
call him) moved his headquarters from Kufara to a rocky

stronghold named Geru, in the district of Dar Gorani in western Wadai. He did this partly in furtherance of an unfortunate opposition to the French conquest of these perturbed regions in the very heart of Africa. The Senusi dynasty · never enlightened enough to perceive the wickedness of the Slave Trade, and it resented the efforts of the French to put down the shocking slave raiding of the Wadai Muhammadans.

The French armies however were victorious, and the Second Senusi died of disappointment in Wadai.

The Third in succession was the son of his brother, Muhammad ash-Sharif and was named Ahmad ash-Sharif. He was chosen by the confraternity because the sons of Muhammad al Mahdi were deemed to be too young for the cares and responsibilities of this Pope-like position. Ahmad ash-Sharif re-established his capital at Kufara, but in spite of his recognition as supreme head of the institution attempts were made by the confraternity to ignore the death of the Second Senusi, to announce that he was travelling on secret business, that he would one day return to resume the supreme power vested meantime in his nephew. It is possible this fiction was set about by those who were led to distrust the wisdom of Ahmad the Third Senusi.

Ahmad apparently decided that the Brotherhood should offer unstinted opposition to the French in Central Africa, and that they should ally themselves with the Turkish Sultan whom his grandfather had derided and opposed as an effete and heretical ruler. Between 1902 and 1909, Senusis were fighting the French advance on Wadai and contiguous countries. In 1910 Turkish troops advanced for the first time beyond Fazan into the Tibesti mountains and Borku. But in the following year they were withdrawn northwards to oppose the Italian invasion of Tripoli. Sayyid Ahmad ash-Sharif, the Senusi leader, joined Turkey after the outbreak of the Great War in 1914 and in 1918 had to flee to Constantinople in a submarine, as Mrs. Forbes relates. Thenceforth she becomes the sole historian for the time being of the Senusi family, and according to her relation we see that Idris, son of Muhammad al Mahdi, and grandson of the First Senusi teacher has become the fourth ruler of his family and has been accorded by Italy and Britain the title of a Prince (Amir). His domain is now recognized as covering the inner region of Cyrenaica between the Egyptian frontier on the east, that of Fazan on the west, of the coast region of Cyrene on the north and approximately on the south of the 20th degree of N. Latitude. Jedabia as marked on Mrs. Forbes's map is very near the Mediterranean coast, and Zuetina, also referred to, is actually a seaport which is to be the outlet of a hoped-for Sudan trade coming from Wadai. Whether this important outlet is intended to come within the Sharifian domain of Sayyid Idris is not quite clear: it hardly seems likely that at present Italy would allow a quasi-independent Arab power to attain to a port on the Mediterranean between the provinces of Cyrene and Tripoli.

Italy of course retains from an international point of view the suzerainty over the Senusi Prince, whose access to the Mediterranean she could not permit to be abused or allow it to shelter a revival of the slave trade, practised so long by the Turks, and at no time denounced by the followers of the Senusi.

Somewhat similarly to the action of Italy since the conclusion of the War, the British have been striving to create an independent or nearly-independent Arab state in Mesopotamia; they have evacuated Persia (though it is still threatened by the Russian Soviet) and they are endeavouring to recreate a wholly independent congeries of Arab States in Arabia, especially in the case of the Hijaz, the Domain of Muhammad and the region in which he was born, lived, and worked.

What will Islam do for the world of civilisation in return? Will it give up, once and for all and completely, the age-long attempt to maintain slavery as an institution, to override and enslave the Negro, to persecute the Christian, the Jew, and the harmless pagan? Will it cease to despise true Science, and encourage unfettered education? For a century or two after the Arab conquests of Spain and Mesopotamia, education took great strides, and the civilisation of the Old World was really somewhat advanced. Then followed a heart-breaking Muhammadan reaction, as bad in its effects as Byzantine Christianity. Under the Turks, more especially, Islam was made the cover for a disastrous check to learning, to investigation, to mastery over the planet and its resources. Muhammadanism became the rallying ground for the enemies of Civilisation. Its teaching became and has remained incredibly puerile and futile. Compare the curriculum of Al Azhar with that of British, American, French, German, Italian, Austrian or Spanish universities! The author of this interesting story seems content and hopeful as to the progress of Senusi teaching. I, having traced the downward course of so many Muhammadan movements, split always on the rock of Education, reserve my opinion, and meantime distrust all Islamic agitation.

H. H. JOHNSTON.

July 25, 1921.

PREFACE

I FEEL this Libyan story needs a few words of explanation, for owing to the peculiar circumstances in which it was undertaken it is not the usual consecutive and comprehensive book of travel compiled *after* the return of an expedition wherein the traveller is able to review the journey as a whole. Reading such works, I have so often found myself asking, "And then what happened?" or "I wonder what he felt at the moment?" Well, this is a very simple account of "what happened next." In no way does it pretend to be a scientific record of exploration, for, owing to the ever urgent necessity of secrecy and disguise, the use of most instruments was an impossibility.

The spirit of the story changes with the mood and the method of its development. It was written in so many odd ways at so many odd times—under a scented sage-bush in the sunset while the slaves were putting up our tent, or huddled inside a flea-bag when the nights were very cold. Sometimes, when life was exciting, it was scribbled on a camel under the shelter of a barracan! Twice, at least, the last chapter according to all human calculations was completed in the hope that the tattered copy books would somehow find their way back to civilization and the fate of the expedition be known up till its last moments. It is a daily record of success and failure, of a few months in an alien world, showing how much of that world's spirit was absorbed. Because, in real life, the big things and the little things are inextricably mixed up together, so in Libya at one moment

one worried because one's native boots were full of holes,
at the next perhaps, one wondered how long one would
be alive to wear them.   This book records the former
mood as well as the latter, because both at the time were
equally important.

Naturally such an impossible, illogical journey leaves
one indebted to so many people that it is difficult to pick
out those to whom one owes most.

I have dedicated the story of our adventures to my
co-explorer Ahmed Bey Hassanein, for his knowledge of
the Senussi acquired during his secretaryship to the Talbot
Mission in 1916 was invaluable to me, and he was the
loyalest of my allies throughout the expedition.   His tact
and eloquence so often saved the situation when my
Arabic failed, and we laughed and fought through all our
difficulties together.

Long before my Kufara expedition merged from impossible dream to probable fact, many officers stationed
in the Western Desert lent me their knowledge of the
Senussi oasis, gathered from careful conversations with
Beduin sheikhs and merchants, while from Khartum,
El Fasher and Cairo came maps and route reports which
were most useful.

I now know that we might have benefited exceedingly
from Rohlfs's most careful and valuable writings on the
subject of his North African travels, but unfortunately
we only possessed his "Kufra," which does not attempt
much description of the oasis he was the first European
to visit, confining itself chiefly to the relation of the
story of the destruction of his camp and the break-up of
the expedition.   In a Journal of the African Society the
great German explorer gives the exact bearing on which
he marched from Jalo.   Had we known this at the time
we might have arrived at Taiserbo in spite of the error

in the extent of vegetation marked on the map.* We
picked up the traces of Rohlfs's journey at Buseima,
where some of the inhabitants remembered him as
Mustapha Bey. At Hawari several sheikhs told us stories
about his adventures there and at Buma, but at no point
could we find any trace of Stecker having visited the
oases. On the contrary we were categorically assured
by Sheikhs Mohammed el Madeni, Bu Regea and Sidi
Omar at Buseima, and by Sheikhs Musa Squaireen,
Mansur Bu Badr, Musa Gharibeel and Sidi Zarrug at
Hawari that Rohlfs had no other European with him.
Stecker was the surveyor of the party, and in view of
the difference in the position he assigned to Buma and
that which we believe it to occupy, we made the most
exhaustive inquiries as to the personnel of the German
expedition; but while we collected much intimate information concerning Rohlfs, all evidence offered us
stated positively that he was not accompanied by Stecker
at Hawari, Buma, or on his return journey to Buseima.
On these occasions he was always described as being
"with his cook, Ali, and a big horse."

The gracious reception accorded me by H.E. the
Governor of Cyrenaica, Senator de Martino, made me
regretful that I could not stay longer in his admirable
colony. To him, to General di Vita and the Cavaliere
Queirolo, head of the Ufficio Politico at Benghazi, I
owe my delightful journey to Jedabia and a store of
invaluable information regarding the country to which
they most kindly facilitated my visit.

To any reader it will at once be evident that, after
the generous help of the Italians in Cyrenaica, the whole

* On the Egyptian survey map (2,000,000 series) 1912, re-issued 1915, the green
area of Taiserbo vegetation runs across longitude 22° and touches latitude
26°. It will be seen from the map of our route that we marched across this
angle without finding Kusebeya or any trace of vegetation.

success of the expedition depended on the good will of the Emir Mohammed Idris es Senussi and of his brother, Sayed Rida. It is absolutely impossible for any European to set foot into Libya without the permission of the Emir or his wakil. We were welcomed by the Sayeds with a hospitality that reminded us of the Arab greeting to a guest, "All that is mine is thine." Whatever we asked for was given us, multiplied a hundredfold. Sidi Idris and his brother were so prodigal of their generosity, so unfailing of their help, that we shall feel eternally their debtors.

Since surprise has been expressed that we should have met with any opposition in Libya once we were provided with Sidi Idris's passport, I should like to explain that we had no permit from the Emir himself. The letter referred to throughout the book was merely a casual, personal letter expressing his willingness to receive us. We had, however, a passport from Sayed Rida authorizing the Sitt Khadija, a Moslem working for the good of Islam and the Senussi, and A. M. Bey Hassanein to visit the country. This document insured us the most hospitable welcome from the official classes in spite of the plots of the Bazama family and of Abdullah, to which plots alone I imagine we owe the adventures of our journey.

Because of the good will of the Sayeds we found many friends and allies in their country, notably Mohammed Quemish and Yusuf el Hamri, who accompanied us through 1,000 miles of desert till, somewhere east of Munasib Pass, we fell into the hands of the Frontier Districts Administration, and thereby hangs a tale, for so few of us in England know for how much she is responsible abroad!

Egypt is like a tadpole, her head the Delta, and her tail the long curving valley of the Nile. Therefore, of all countries, she is the most vulnerable of attack, and never could she defend her own borders! Mohammed Ali subsidized the sheikhs of the Wilad Ali to police his frontiers. Before the War the Egyptian Coastguards built their forts along the Mediterranean and Red Sea shores and pushed their outposts south into the deserts, but during the War a far more efficient force sprang into being. Nowadays the Frontier Districts Administration, a kingdom within a kingdom, is responsible for the safety of "all country not watered by the Nile" between the Sudan and the Mediterranean, the Red Sea and Cyrenaica. The territory is divided into four Provinces, and under a Military Administrator in Cairo, Brigadier-General Hunter, C.B., C.M.G., the governors and officials combine the complicated duties of protector and judge, guide, instructor and friend to the tens of thousand Beduin who might at any time prove a thorn in the flesh of Egypt. This exceedingly capable organization, or such portion of it as officiates in the Western Desert, took charge of us before we reached Siwa, and to them, especially to Colonel MacDonnell, Governor of the Western Desert, and to Colonel Forth, Commandant of the Camel Corps, we owe more than it is possible to acknowledge in a mere preface.

In fact, I find myself unconsciously including in a long list of indebtedness the fact that, having written their names far and wide across the Eastern Sahara, they had fortunately for me, temporarily omitted Kufara from the itineraries of those swift dashes into the wilderness which habitually add a couple of hundred miles or so to the known chart of Africa!

One name is always connected with theirs, because it appears on so many desert routes—that of Dr. Ball, F.R.G.S., the Director of the Desert Surveys of Egypt. Encouraged by his sympathy and experience, we brought

PREFACE

him our rough notes and drawings and from them he compiled the map of our journey. I think, therefore, that my readers' gratitude should be nearly as great as my own!

ROSITA FORBES.

Abu Menes,
March, 1921.

CONTENTS

LIST OF ILLUSTRATIONS

THE SECRET OF THE
SAHARA : KUFARA

THE SECRET OF THE
SAHARA: KUFARA

CHAPTER I

WE ENTER ON THE GREAT ADVENTURE

THE great adventure began at Jedabia, 190 kilometres from Benghazi as the crow flies. It is only a group of scattered sand houses, with the mysterious windowless walls of the East, flung down on a wide space of white rock and sand, yet it is the home of the great Senussi family. We arrived there on November 28, 1920, having come by divers methods across the stretch of stony desert which lies to the southwest of Benghazi, the capital of Cyrenaica. It is an almost deserted country of flat reddish sand, sprinkled with rocks and tufts of coarse grey grass which provides food for rare camel caravans and fuel for the Beduin fires. There are no made roads, but rough tracks link the scattered Italian forts, manned by companies of stalwart Eritreans and irregular Arab levies. To the south, the *altipiano* rises in a faint line of purple cliff which catches wonderful reflections in the setting sun. Otherwise the vista is intensely monotonous save for an occasional encampment of Auwaghir. Unlike the solid black "beit esh shar"[1] of the Syrian or Algerian nomad, their tents are of the poorest description, made of patched sacking of various grey-brown shades; they are very low-pitched, so that even in the centre one cannot stand upright.

In the dry season, wherever there are wells, may be

[1] A glossary of Arabic words and phrases used in the book will be found on p. 337.

1

seen congregated flocks of sheep and goats and herds of camels numbering many thousands. After rain, however, so much water lies out on the rocky ground that the animals can drink wherever they like, so the country presents its most deserted appearance.

Benghazi is a little white town lying on the very edge of the Mediterranean breakers, unprotected by harbour or mole. Famine and disease considerably reduced its population during the War and the suqs are almost deserted. An occasional donkey with scarlet tassels and a load of fresh dates passes down the Sidi Shabi where European stores and native booths stand side by side. A few camels come in from the country half buried beneath huge sacks of grain. In the evening there is a mustering of bearded merchants at the little café by the mosque, while contemptuous Askari in scarlet tarboushes and swinging capes stroll by, smoking Italian cigarettes, but the life of the town is confined to the European quarter containing the hotel and the Government offices.

The biggest of the white, Oriental-looking buildings is Government House, with a double line of great Moorish arches decorating its imposing façade. So different from the windowless dwellings of Jedabia with their discreet high-walled yards, yet it was there that I first saw Es Sayed Mohammed Idris bin es Sayed el Mahdi es Senussi, the man whose power is felt even beyond the boundaries of Libya and Cyrenaica. The Italians and the Senussi had ratified a few days before the provisional treaty of 1916 and there were great festas at Benghazi in honour of the newly made Emir, who was spending a few days in the capital on his way to Italy to visit the King.

There had been an official reception and down the broad steps moved the black mass of Italian uniforms splashed with the vivid blue of their gala sashes and the glint of their gay-ribboned medals. Foremost came the Governor, Senator de Martino, in the green and gold uniform of a Knight of Malta, and General Di Vita, with his splendid rows of decorations. Between them walked a figure which dominated the group and yet gave one the impression of being utterly remote from it. Robed all in white, in silken kaftan and trailing burnus, the rich kufiya flowing beneath a golden agal, with no jewel or embroidery to mark his state, Sidi Idris came slowly forward leaning on a silver-handled stick. An Italian officer murmured in my ear, "Give him a longer beard and he would be the pictured Christ!" He was right. The ascetic leader of one of the greatest religious confraternities in the world had the strange, visionary eyes of the prophets of old. His long face had hollows under the cheek-bones. The lips were pale and the olive skin almost waxen. He looked out, under a broad brow, dreamily, far beyond the pageant prepared in his honour, to realms even more remote than his own untrodden deserts. Thus might the Nazarene have walked among the legionaries of Rome!

The following day I met the Emir at a dinner which Omar Pasha gave in his honour. Before the other guests arrived we conversed, I in faltering Egyptian Arabic, he in the classical language of the Hejaz. In the same flowing white robes he sat in a great chair at the head of the room and in a long line beside him sat the ekhwan who were to accompany him to Italy. They were a picturesque sight in their multi-coloured robes of ceremony. Prominent among them was the General Ali Basha el Abdya, a delightful bearded personage with a complete set of gold teeth, which touch of modernity contrasted oddly with his crimson kaftan and splendid dark burnus bordered with silver. Beside him sat the

venerable Sharuf Basha el Ghariam, who had been the
teacher of Sidi Idris and was now his most trusted
councillor. His jerd was a sombre brown, and the end
of it covered his head over a close-fitting white ma-araka,
but his kaftan, with long embroidered sleeves, was vivid
rose. He had a kindly, serious face and seemed much
more interested in his surroundings than the others.

I stumbled over my words of formal greeting, expressed in the unaccustomed plural, wondering whether
the man who looked so infinitely remote and uninterested
would even listen to what I was saying. The brooding
eyes softened suddenly and a smile that was veritable
light flashed across his face. If graciousness be the token
of royalty, then Sidi Idris is crowned by his smile! For
such a look the Beduin prostrates himself to kiss the
dust the holy feet have pressed! Thereafter we talked
of my journey and he blessed me in his frail voice,
smiling still and saying, "May Allah give you your
wish!" I tried to tell him of my love of the desert, of
how I was happiest when, from a narrow camp bed, I
could look at the triangular patch of starlight beyond the
flap of my tent. "I, too," he said, "cannot stay more
than a month in one place. Then I must move, for I
love the *scent* of the desert." It is true there is a *scent*
in the desert, though there may be no flower or tree or
blade of grass within miles. It is the essence of the
untrodden, untarnished earth herself!

We dined gorgeously on lambs roasted whole and
stuffed with all sorts of good things—rice, raisins and
almonds—and on strange, sticky sweetmeats that I
loved and bowls of cinnamon-powdered junket and,
best of all, the delicious thick Arab coffee, but the Emir
ate little and spoke less. The Senussi law forbids
drinking and smoking as also the use of gold for
personal adornment, so after the meal glasses of sweet

tea flavoured with mint leaves were handed round to
the solemn ekhwan, who took no notice whatever of
their fellow guests, consisting of the Governor, the
general, the captain of the light cruiser which was to
carry the Senussi to Italy, and myself. Omar Pasha
made me sit beside the Emir, who suddenly turned to
his venerable followers, "Come and salute this lady,"
he said, and instantly, with the unquestioning obedience
of children, they clambered up from their low chairs
and moved in a body towards me. "Aselamu Aleikum"
they murmured gravely as they shook my hand without
raising their eyes, but giving me the Moslem salutation
to a Moslem!

Benghazi was *en fête* those days. There were so many
ceremonies—a review, a great dinner in the Governor's
palace in honour of Italy's new ally—so I did not see
Sidi Idris again till the last night of his stay, when there
was a general reception which brought streams of Arab
notables as well as Europeans to witness the fireworks
from the wide verandas of His Excellency's dwelling.
I saw the Emir standing aloof from the chattering crowd,
his ekhwan near him, and wondered what he thought
of us all. Half the guests were of his own race and
creed, yet not here was his real kingdom, but among
the ten thousand Beduin who spring to horse or camel
at his word, among the hundred thousand pilgrims who
learn the law from his zawias! We stood together on
a wind-swept balcony and looked down at a wild dance
of Abyssinian soldiers. A thousand black figures, each
bearing a flaring torch, gyrated madly in the moonlight,
yelling hoarse songs of victory and prowess. The three
things a man may be justly proud of in Abyssinia are
killing a lion, an elephant or his enemy! The fantastic
dance we saw might celebrate one or other of these
achievements. Gradually whirling into tempestuous

circles, the soldiers flung their torches into flaming piles in the centre and their chaunt rose stronger on the wind. Sayed Idris was pleased: "You will see ceremonies like this in my country," he said, "but there will be no houses. You will not miss them."

The moment the last gun, announcing the Emir's departure for Italy, had been fired, Hassanein Bey and I climbed into the car most kindly lent by the Government. When he first consented to accompany me to the Libyan Desert, where his knowledge of the language, religion and customs was invaluable to me, Hassanein Bey assured me that he came for a rest cure. Later on he assumed so many characters that it was somewhat difficult to keep count. He was always the Q.M.G. of our little expedition and he used to produce macaroons at the most impossible moments from equally impossible places! He was a chaperon when elderly sheikhs demanded my hand in marriage, a fanatic of the most bitter type when it was necessary to impress the local mind, my Imam when we prayed in public, a child when he lost his only pair of primrose yellow slippers, a cook when we stole a bottle of Marsala from the last Italian fort and chased a thin hen till, in desperation, she laid an egg for our *zabaglione!* He also made the darkest plans for being a villain and murdering anyone who interfered with our affairs, and I nervously listened to tales of sudden disappearances in the Sahara.

However, on the day of our departure from Benghazi he was distinctly subdued, for, on looking at our piles of camp kit and my two very small suit-cases, I had suddenly noticed several exceedingly large and heavy leather bags. With horror I demanded if they were all absolutely necessary to his personal comfort. "Yes, really!" he assured me. "They are only actual necessities. As a matter of fact they are half empty. I

thought they would be useful for putting things in."
The words were hardly out of his mouth when one of the
opulent-looking cases, slipping from the Arab servant's
hand, burst open and deposited at my feet a large bottle
of "Heure bleue" bath salts, several packets of salted
almonds and a sticky mass of chocolates and marrons
glacés, together with a pair of patent leather shoes
and a resplendent Balliol blazer. Words failed me!
"Necessities!" I stuttered as I marched towards the
camion to see that the heaviest cases of provisions were
not put on top of the rather fragile fanatis intended for
carrying water.

Ten minutes after leaving Benghazi the white town
with its slender minarets had disappeared into the sand,
and our camions crawled like great grey beetles over a
sunlit waste, with here and there a line of camels black
against the horizon. It was the season of sowing and
the tribes were scattered far and wide, planting the barley
that would suffice for their frugal life next year. Here
and there, as we went farther inland, a stooping figure,
in close-wound white jerd, pushed a plough drawn by a
camel, while a friend guarded his labours, rifle slung
across his back. Sometimes a rare traveller on gaily
caparisoned mule, his coarse brown jerd flung over his
head and hiding the scarlet sederiya beneath, gave us
grave greeting, "Marhaba!" "Bien venu!" We spent
a night at Soluk, where the wells had attracted a
great flock of sheep, black and brown, numbering about
a thousand. The following day we rode the thirty kilometres to Ghemines on wiry Arab horses with mouths
like iron beneath the wicked curved bits, and high-
pommelled saddles mounted on black sheepskins. Three
irregulars of the Auwaghir band accompanied us, generally galloping round us in circles by way of showing off
their horsemanship.

A small encampment of some half-dozen tents lay beside our path, so we turned in to see if they would make us tea. At first they refused because I was a Christian. Then a woman in striped red and yellow barracan, with a heavy necklace of carved silver, came out to inspect us. "It is all right," she said to the others. "She is a nice little thing and she has a Moslem with her"—this in appreciation of Hassanein Bey's white brocaded kufiya. They spread a scarlet camel's hair rug for us to sit on, but they were not really convinced of our good faith. My companion began asking the men if they had made the pilgrimage to Mecca. "Not yet," said the oldest wistfully. "What is written is written. If Allah wills it, I shall go."

We were rapidly making friends when a fierce-looking individual with a hard weather-beaten face and stern eyes appeared. He carried tea and sugar, but bargained for them violently, thinking we were both the scorned Nasrani. When we told him we knew Sayed Idris, he laughed in our faces. "Our lord Idris is travelling," he said. "Would you like to see a letter from him?" I asked. Awe showed on all their faces, and their eyes followed Hassanein Bey's every movement as he pulled out the somewhat crumpled envelope from his pocket. They read the superscription reverently, and then one by one kissed it with passionate earnestness and gravely pressed it to their foreheads. They returned it in complete silence. Without a word the atmosphere changed. The fanatic looked at us with humble yearning. The old man's eyes were glazed. We knew that we could have told these three men to get up and follow us to an unknown destination and they would have obeyed with unquestioning, ungrudging faith. "Sidi Idris has gone to visit the King of Italy," I said. "He has been made an Emir." They accepted the statement indifferently.

How could a mere king confer honour on the man whom Allah himself had distinguished above all others living? As we remounted the old man kissed my hand with tender eyes, murmuring, "Inshallah ma temut illa Islam," and we galloped away amidst the wild "Ulla-la-een" of the women and children.

Ghemines to Zuetina meant 120 kilometres in a camion over a very bad sandy track, but that night I slept in a tent for the first time for six months. There was a wonderful starry sky with a full moon, and a Senussi sheikh rode into see us on a splendid grey horse with a scarlet saddle. The high pommels back and front and the wide stirrups were of silver, and the purple-tasselled bridle was heavily embossed with the same metal. Sayed Mohammed Hilal es Senussi is a cousin of Sidi Idris and a brother of the Sayed Ahmed es Sherif who fled to Turkey at the end of the War. A kindly, cheerful personage, he apparently had cut adrift from the stern rules of his order and found charm in a semi-European life. His language was so full of rhetorical flowers that I found it difficult to understand, but he lent me an excellent horse for the journey to Jedabia. He also requested me to deliver to his cousin, Sayed Rida, a poetic epistle which began, "Oh freshness of my eyes, may Allah bless your morning with peace and joy."

The sand dunes of Zuetina gave way to a flat, colour-less waste tufted with grey brushwood. As we turned our horses' heads inland tiny jerboas scuttered into their holes at our approach, and occasionally a great hawk wheeled above our heads. Otherwise there was no sign of life save one solitary horseman in white jerd on a white horse and a boy sitting on a pile of stones playing an odd little tune on a wooden flute. Our grey Arab mounts were tired when at last we mounted a low rise and saw before us a fringe of patched Beduin tents. It was the first step on a long journey. Everything was uncertain. There were so many difficulties to be surmounted, but we felt that now, at least, the last trace of Europe lay behind us. We breathed more freely. We both loved the desert and the dwellers therein, and we felt that they must understand and respond to our sympathy. I turned to Hassanein Bey as the sandy track ran between the blind mud walls that I had seen in so many countries. "I feel as if I had left behind me the last shred of civilisation. The simplicity of life is beginning to impregnate me. I believe that old Beduin's blessing has bewitched me. When we leave the desert I shall be a Moslem."

We sent to ask if Sayed Rida el Mahdi es Senussi, the brother and wakil of Sidi Idris, would receive us and we waited for an answer at the edge of the suq, where grave, bearded men, with the wistful eyes of those who look at far horizons, stood in white-robed groups. A few camels lay beside piles of grain, but otherwise the wide open spaces between the square walled-in yards, where were Arab houses, were deserted. The banner of the Senussi family, a silver crescent and star on a black ground, floated over two of the houses and the protesting roar of laden camels came from one of the larger enclosures, for Sayed Safi ed Din, cousin of Sidi Idris and brother of the banished Ahmed, was travelling to the interior the following day with the whole of his family and sixty beasts of burden.

A soldier of the Arab guard brought us news that the Sayed would receive us at once and we dismounted in one of the windowless yards before the door of a big white house. We were ushered into the usual Arab reception room with a stiff row of crimson brocaded chairs and sofas round the walls and a table covered by a beautiful embroidered satin cloth in the centre. Sayed Rida came forward to meet us with a reflection of his brother's smile. One liked him at once. One appreciated instantly his warm kindliness and hospitality. Sidi Idris is a mystic imbued with the aloof dignity of another world, but his wakil is young, spontaneous and sympathetic, with a very simple, unaffected manner. He offered us immediately a house to live in while we were in Jedabia and put at our disposal a cook and two other servants. He made me talk Arabic to him and corrected my mistakes with his broadest smile. Sweet tea, flavoured with mint, appeared in delightful, painted glass cups, and I soon felt as if I had known our host for years. He was amused and interested in our divers journeys. He made plans to show us a falcon hunt. He wanted to give us instantly anything from horses to dates. In fact, I felt that I was in the presence of a magician who could wave his wand and produce the wish of my heart! In appearance Sayed Rida is large and imposing with a round, olive face and very dark eyes, soft as velvet, which crinkle up humorously as he smiles widely, showing strong white teeth. He wore a black jelabia under his striped silk jerd, snowy white, and a rolled white turban above a red ma-araka. Arab hospitality is famous throughout the world, but we left the dignified presence of Sayed Rida feeling almost overwhelmed at his gracious welcome.

Our temporary home fascinated me. A solitary door pierced the mysterious expanse of yellow wall made of sun-dried blocks of sand of all sizes and shapes. One passed through a small roofed court to a wide sunlit yard whose high walls ensure the complete privacy of an Arab family. Hassanein Bey had a small room at one end and I a great high chamber, hung with texts from the Koran. We were a kingdom to ourselves, for there was a well just under my window, charcoal in an outhouse and a large yard beyond where we could have housed camels and horses. As it was, we stored our simple outfit in it, for the evening was dry and fine. We knew from the beginning that we must travel light and that our final success might depend on our capability for riding fast and far. We might have to leave all our luggage by the way and, disguised as Beduin camel-drivers, slip away in the night into the uncharted land where none may follow.

Thus, besides our sacks of rice, tea and sugar—the two latter intended for gifts to Beduins who helped us on our journey—we had only a single fly tent, eleven feet by eight feet, which could be divided into two by means of a canvas curtain, a waterproof ground-sheet and a couple of beds which rolled into our immensely thick, wool-lined sleeping sacks, a small army canteen that was so heavy that we had grave doubts as to its eventual fate, a canvas washing basin and a shamadan case complete with vast supply of candles, for I foresaw burning much midnight wax over note-books and maps. We had reduced our provisions to the minimum which would support human life for four months, such as coffee, tins of army rations, slabs of chocolate, tins of cocoa and milk already mixed, bully beef, vegetables to avoid scurvy, and malted milk tablets, but the daily ration was absurdly small, for we trusted to supplement it with dates and rice.

By the light of Hassanein Bey's electric torch we picked our way back over flat white rock and sand to Sayed Rida's house to dine. This time we found our host accompanied by Sayed Safi ed Din, "the little warrior," as he is called among the tribes. He is a boy with a vivacious, pale face, a charming manner and a ready wit. He is intelligent and, far more than the others, he is interested in the ways of Europe. "I think we should get on well," he said, "for you are as curious about me as I am about you!"

The memory of that dinner will haunt me for a long time, for it consisted of twelve courses, of which eight were meat in one form or another. We began eating at seven-thirty and at ten-thirty the beautifully scented tea with sprigs of mint made its welcome appearance. During these three hours we ate soup, chicken, hashed mutton, slices of roast mutton, aubergines stuffed with sausage meat, fried chops, shoulder of mutton cooked in batter, ragout of mutton with vegetables, stuffed tomatoes, boiled mutton with marrow, savoury rice and sweet omelette. It can be easily imagined that the feast left us a little silent and comatose, but not so our host. He was literally brimming over with kindness and forethought. I was suffering at the time from a severely dislocated foot, which had not been improved by the long ride, and I was obliged to hobble in one shoe and a swollen native slipper by the aid of a stick. Sayed Rida slipped away for a minute in the middle of the meal and when we left the house, lo and behold, a horse was waiting for me outside the door! His kindliness was as simple and natural as his whole bearing. We asked him if he travelled much and he replied, "I have not time. I have so much work. You know it is just like planting a garden. Everything grows and grows till one's time is full!" This from the Emir's wakil, whose word was borne across half the deserts of the world, to Nigeria, to the Sudan, to the outposts of Morocco, to the doors of the "House of Allah" (Mecca).

I remember opening my shutters that night to a flood of moonlight as clear as the day. A faint myrrh-scented breeze, icy cold from the Sahara, came in, and I wondered whether it had blown over the unknown oasis

we hoped to reach. We had had a long talk that evening
of past difficulties and future plans. In Italy Kufara
represents the goal of so many hopes, in Cyrenaica the
ambition of so many daring young political officers, that
it is difficult to realise that in England it is an unknown
name. The sacred place of the Sahara, the far-off oasis,
six hundred kilometres from Jalo, which in itself is seven
days' rapid journey from the outskirts of civilisation,
is spoken of with awe and longing in Benghazi. "I
will tell you a great secret," said the Italian major who
had spent a couple of days with Sidi Idris at Jaghabub,
and had therefore penetrated many hundreds of kilometres farther into the interior than any of his compa-
triots, "Some day I want to go to Kufara. No one has
ever been there except Rohlfs, forty years ago, and he
saw nothing—nothing at all!"

Without going deeply into the story of the Senussi
confraternity, it may be explained that their founder,
Sidi Mohammed Ben Ali es Senussi, preached his doctrine
of a pure and ascetic Islam from Morocco to Mecca, but
his teachings met with their greatest success in Cyrenaica,
where the Beduin had almost lapsed from the faith of
their fathers. Rapidly his zawia spread along the coast,
and his authority was acknowledged by the Sultan of
Wadai, who made him responsible for the caravans
traversing the great deserts of Wadai, the Fezzan and
Lake Chad. Thus the stern beliefs of the Senussi
spread with every caravan that went into the interior.
Mohammed Ben Ali, so holy that he never unveiled his
face to his disciples, so honoured that his followers
prostrated themselves to kiss his footprints, died at
Jaghabub in 1850 and left to his son, Mohammed el
Mahdi, the leadership of one of the greatest and fiercest
religious confraternities in the world. Their laws were
harsh—for even smelling of smoke a man might lose his

right hand! Their hatred of the infidel was fanatical.
They ousted the Zouia and Tebu from their ancient
homes in Kebabo and established impregnably their holy
of holies in this oasis which nature herself had protected
by surrounding it with a belt of mighty dunes and two
hundred and fifty miles of waterless desert.

Kufara, the Kebabo of old, lies some six hundred
kilometres south, faintly south-east, of Jalo. It is the
heart of the Eastern Sahara and the centre of its trade,
for the only big caravan route from the Sudan and Wadai
to the north passes through it, yet the journey is so difficult that none but the strongest caravans can attempt it.
From the well at Buttafal, a day's journey south of
Jalo, seven hard, waterless days bring the traveller to
Zieghen, where there is a well, but no fodder or oasis.
After that he must continue another five days, two of
which are through dunes, before he reach Hawari, the
outskirts of the Kufara group, sometimes considered by
the Arabs to be a separate oasis because it is divided
from the main group by a chain of mountains. This is
the main route and the easiest. It continues to Wadai.

To the west of this track lie three other oases. The
first, Taiserbo, is also seven days' waterless journey from
Buttafal and it is rarely approached, for it has neither
civil, religious nor commercial importance, but its Tebu
ruins might make it of interest historically. Some
hundred and fifty kilometres beyond in a south-westerly
direction is Buseima, which is famous for its dates, for
which caravans sometimes visit it, and still farther south
lies Ribiana, to all description a lawless spot from which
come the marauding bands which make the neighbourhood of Buseima exceedingly dangerous.

Of course, all this information was acquired at a later
date. When I arrived at Jedabia I knew less than
nothing of Libyan geography. I did not know that the

principal villages in Kufara were Jof, the seat of government, and Taj, the holy of holies of the Senussi faith.
I did not know that mountains and lakes, fields of
tamarisk and acacia, peaches, grapes and figs were to be
found in this Garden of Eden lost amid the impenetrable
sands, between the Dakhla Desert to the east, untraversed
by Europeans, and to the west the trackless waste
stretching to Uau Szerir at the edge of Tripolitania, to
which remote prison some of the unfortunate survivors
of the Miani column were sent as prisoners. To me,
Kufara was almost a mirage. It represented the secret
which the Sahara had rigidly guarded for so long against
Christian eyes. The tragic story of Rohlfs' ill-fated
expedition fired my enthusiasm to reach this centre of
the world's most fanatical confraternity, the unknown,
mysterious country untrod by foot of stranger, be he
Christian or Moslem.

Having regard to the amazing difficulties of the
journey and the almost maniacal hatred with which
strangers are regarded, it is natural that, with one possible exception, no European should ever have been able
to reach the sacred cluster of zawias and morabits at Taj.
A French prisoner spent some time in Kufara during the
war; he was sent there from Uau Szerir by order of
Sayed Ahmed. Over forty years ago a German explorer
made a very gallant attempt to solve the mystery of
the far-off oasis. In 1879 the Kaiser Wilhelm I sent
a scientific expedition to Libya consisting of four men—
Rohlfs, Stecker, Eckhart and Hubner. It was backed
by the whole power of Turkey. It carried magnificent
presents from the Emperor. It was laden with cases of
silver and gold. Hostages were held at Benghazi, while
Rohlfs led his party to the southern deserts. He left
Jalo on July 5 with a hundred camels and a large
escort of Zouias mounted on horses, including several

THE EMIR IDRIS ES SENUSSI

THE AUTHOR AS A BEDUIN SHEIK

sheikhs, the principal of whom was Bu Guettin. He accomplished the amazing feat of reaching Taiserbo in four and a half days, by riding nearly twenty hours out of the twenty-four. In his most interesting book on his North African travels, which has unfortunately not been translated into English, he suggests that Taiserbo may have been the site of the original Tebu sultanate, as he saw ruins which might possibly be those of a castle or stronghold at Diranjedi. He continued his southern course by way of Buseima, till he reached Hawawiri, where he was persuaded by a friendly sheikh, Korayim Abd Rabu, to camp in an outlying palm grove to avoid any friction with the villagers, who refused to allow the Nasrani to enter their country.

The plucky Teuton describes the gathering outside his tent and the long discussion as to whether he and his companions should be murdered or not. The day following, August 14, they were induced by Bu Guettin and the treacherous Zouias, who were fanatically opposed to the presence of strangers and greedy to share the spoils of so rich a caravan, to leave Hawawiri and, skirting the oasis, to isolate themselves in Boema, the loneliest and most deserted spot in the whole group. Rohlfs apparently agreed to this plan because the neighbourhood of any of the main villages was dangerous. He had to oppose the combined hatred of the ekhwan and pupils of the zawias, religious fanatics, the villagers who jealously guarded the privacy of their country and the passing caravans of pilgrims and merchants. After being held a prisoner for nearly a month in this lonely camp, in daily fear for his life, he was helped to escape by his original friend, Korayim, who took him by night, with his three companions, to his son-in-law's camp, somewhere in the neighbourhood of Zuruk. That very night the German's camp was attacked and looted. Every

single note-book, map, drawing and scientific instrument
was destroyed, so Rohlfs was unable to attempt much
description even of his journey up to Hawawiri.

In the book which he calls "Kufra" he devotes a
chapter to his perils and battles in that inhospitable oasis,
but, after his rescue by Korayim, whose son we met at
Taj, his narrative becomes very disjointed. He was
moved to another place before being allowed to leave the
oasis. He himself thinks it was Jof, but from his
description of the journey this seems impossible. He
spent another fortnight under the surveillance of Korayim
—he tells us that he was not allowed to move without
a guard of twenty rifles—during which he seems to have
confronted every form of extortion and threat with calm
and intrepidity. On September 27 he left the oasis with
Korayim, who took him all the way to Benghazi, where,
unfortunately, the sheikh died. Consequently there is a
legend that Rohlfs poisoned him. With experience of
the greed of our own escort, I came to the conclusion
that the grateful German probably gave him too much
of his own cherished stores and the Arab over-ate!

After this ill-fated expedition no alien presence cast
a shadow on the sanctity and isolation of Kufara till
Sayed Ahmed sent his prisoner there. Many attempts
were made from Siwa to pierce the first barrier of dunes,
but in vain. The secrets which Rohlfs had so nearly
solved remained wrapped in the mirage of the great
deserts and Kufara was still a legend more than a fact.

The amicable relations at present existing between
Italy and the Senussi, and the genuine friendship of
Senator de Martino and Sayed Idris made it easy for
us to reach Jedabia as the guests of the former's most
hospitable Government, but thenceforth it was left us to
fend for ourselves. We could not take our kindly hosts
of Benghazi into our confidence, as they would have

been aghast at the idea of a young woman venturing alone
into a territory as yet unexplored. The agreement that
had just been signed with Sidi Idris gave them control
of the whole of Cyrenaica, thus assuring a future of great
prosperity to the colony, but it left the great Libyan
desert from Aujela to Jaghabub, with Kufara still another six hundred kilometres to the south, in the hands of
Sayed Idris as an independent ruler under Italian
protection.

A most humorous complication added immensely to
our difficulties. Hassanein Bey, having been secretary
to the Italo-British Mission which arranged the treaty
of 1916 with the Senussi, was promptly suspected of the
darkest Pan-Islamic designs. For a week at Benghazi
we lived in a state of suspense. Intrigue was in the air
and everyone suspected the motives of everyone else. If
a camion broke down, we decided that we were not to be
allowed to reach Jedabia. If Hassanein spoke to a
Beduin, using the Moslem salutation, the eyes of our
so-called interpreter would almost pop out of his head
with interest and dismay. Relays of kindly individuals
took the utmost interest in our history, plans, ideas and
belongings. We were "pumped" until we could not think
of anything more to say; and we, in turn "pumped"
every hospitable and amiable individual who politely
and indifferently asked us our destination! At times we
must have worn such strained and agonised expressions that I wonder we were not suspected of Bolshevism
at the very least. The most amusing part of the business was afforded by the spies who constantly surrounded
us and who were so thrilled with their own importance
that I used to have daily fights with Hassanein Bey to
prevent him playing delightful little comedies to excite
them still more.

However, once Jedabia was reached we felt happier.

The open desert lay before us and the lure of the great tracks south! Somewhere far beyond the pale mauve line of the horizon lay the secret of the Sahara, the oasis which had become the goal of every explorer, from the enthusiastic coastguard officers who dreamed of forcing a trotting hajin through the sands, to the governments whose camions and light-car patrols had failed to pierce the waterless drifts. The masked Tuaregs, those lawless riders who threaten the lumbering south-bound caravans, bring strange tales of a white race, blue-eyed, fair-haired, whose women live unveiled with their men. Legend has attributed its home to the mysterious oasis whose position varies according to the whims of the map-maker. "Inshallah" I breathed to the stars and the winds!

CHAPTER II

PLANS FOR THE FLIGHT

I WENT to sleep beside a glassless window opening into an empty yard, after wondering whether we should be able to buy necessary food in the suq, or whether we should have to break into our hoarded provisions. I woke to a busy scene and rubbed my eyes in amazement. In one corner was a white bell-tent, from which came the smoke of a charcoal fire. In another was tethered an excellent horse with a European saddle. Half a dozen servants appeared occupied in preparing an immense meal. I called to Hassanein Bey: "Where on earth did you get all this?"

"*I?*" he replied, bewildered. "I? It is all from Sayed Rida. Do you realise that that horse is going to stay here for you to ride whenever you like, that the tent is a fully equipped kitchen and that you've got a cook and I don't know how many servants besides? You mentioned you liked dates last night. Well, a huge sack arrived this morning, *and* meat, *and* bread, *and* tea, *and sugar,* and heavens know what beside. We are the Sayed's guests and for the Lord's sake don't say you like anything else, or it will arrive here within an hour!"

He paused for breath, while I gazed at him helplessly. When one has come from an Italian colony one is used to hospitality, for, from the Governor downwards, everyone was amazingly kind to us, but this was overwhelming. I felt that a whole garden of floral rhetoric would not adequately express my gratitude.

21

We rode out through the deserted stretches of flat white rock and sand to see great herds of camels being watered. Bronze figures, nude but for a scarlet loin cloth, shouted and sang with monotonous rhythm as they let down goatskins at the end of a rope and heaved them up brimming to pour their contents into rough troughs. A white morabit and single palm marked the centre of a cluster of sand-coloured houses. Otherwise, the buildings were scattered over a broad expanse with a straight line of the suq booths in the centre. We created so much sensation in the latter that I decided that my grey riding coat and felt hat were out of place. We told Mustapha, a resplendent individual belonging to one of the irregular bands, whom the Political Officer at Benghazi had kindly lent to us, to go and discover someone who wished to sell some native clothes. He returned half an hour later with a baffled and at the same time awed expression, in company with Sayed Rida's confident, whose coal-black face looked out from the folds of an immense white kufiya. "You are the Sayed's guests," the latter informed us respectfully. "Anything that you need I will get for you at once." Gravely he offered me a bulky parcel. It contained the most beautiful white silk jerd, striped like the one I had silently admired the previous night, with a green and silver agal, and a kufiya that filled my heart with joy, for it was a subdued blending of all rich colours—purple and rose and blue on a silver ground, with long dropping tassels. There was also a tarboush and a pair of wonderful yellow slippers. Before the faltering words were out of my mouth, Hassanein Bey had pounced upon the yellow slippers. His expression was that of a small child when a much-loved doll has been restored to it. "Hamdulillah!" he exclaimed, and fled, clutching his prize.

I confess to spending a happy half-hour struggling

with the intricacies of the jerd and picturing myself dressed in Sayed Rida's splendid gift offering sweet mint tea to reverend sheikhs. Thereafter we erased any verbs expressive of desire from our vocabulary, but we did not succeed in evading our host's royal generosity. We wanted a couple of small sacks into which to put a week's supply of rice and flour, for once we left Jedabia we should have seven or eight days' journey to the next oasis, and we planned to send the baggage camels ahead and ride light on the fastest beasts we could find. With this intention we again despatched the brightly clad Mustapha to the suq. Ten minutes later he was brought firmly back by the Head of the Police, a stalwart black with a hard, keen face. Our follower was protesting wildly, but to deaf ears, for behind him came the ebony confidant, Haji Abdel Salam. "I will send you the sacks," he told me in the tone of a parent scolding a foolish child. "The Sayed wishes to give you everything you can need." Even Hassanein Bey's eloquence failed him, while I wondered if we were living in one of the tales of the Arabian Nights.

Our peace, however, was short-lived. For the first few days at Jedabia we were in a fool's paradise. All round us lay the desert. It seemed so easy a thing to hire a few camels and a guide and disappear over the rim of the horizon. By the fourth day we had discovered a few of the most important difficulties. Firstly, there were no camels. There had been an excellent harvest. The Beduin was rich and he didn't want to work. It was impossible to explain the exact destination of the caravan, for the Holy Oasis is far beyond the bourne of most camel-drivers' dreams. Secondly, all work had to be done in secret, because the whole of our household were spies with the possible exception of the black cook, Ali. Mustapha had been in the Ufficio Politico and he

dutifully reported the minutest of our doings. The Head
of the Police, the stalwart Mabruk, was also not averse
to Latin gold, so he placed his brother to watch us as
horse-boy and, lest that were not sufficient, he sent us
a mysterious servant whose head appeared suddenly at
the glassless window whenever Hassanein Bey and I were
studying the Koran or writing notes. We were never
able to relax our vigilance for a second. We used to hold
long Arabic conversations on how pleasant we found life
in Jedabia, how we must certainly stay there a fortnight
before returning to Benghazi. We knew that every word
would be overheard and repeated.

Bazaar rumour spoilt our first plan, which was exceedingly simple. We meant to persuade an ekhwan to
accompany us to see some neighbouring village, where
there would be a suppositional marriage or other *festa,*
and from there drift on. We had not reckoned with the
fanaticism of the Moslem. Tales of a wealthy Christian
woman about to travel into the interior spread like a
bush-fire. Mustapha came to me with lurid tales of
throats cut almost within sight of the suq. Sayed Rida
himself explained that no Christian life was safe beyond
the boundaries of Cyrenaica, and that anyone, supposed
to have money was a marked prey for the lawless bands
who swept out of the desert, seized their prey and disappeared into the limitless sands as ants upon an English
lawn. We learnt many things that day. We discovered
that Mannismann, the German, had been killed by his
own Arab guard a few hours outside the town because
he had twelve thousand pounds in gold upon him. We
heard that the Tebu tribes of the group of oases erroneously known as Kufra (really Kufara) have not
entirely submitted to the Senussi rule and, consequently,
still attack any caravans travelling beyond Taiserbo.
"But I don't understand," I said. "Taiserbo is part of

Kufara, isn't it? It is marked so in our maps." "No! No!" replied our informant impatiently. "Taiserbo is gareeb, gareeb [near]. You can go there easily. It is not important. There is no sikka [way]. Kufara is much farther on. The dangerous part is after Taiserbo. If you go to Buseima you may have to fight."

Thereafter we began a laborious, systematic campaign to correct the impression of a rich Christian woman. I discarded my hat for the Sayed's beautiful kufiya. Early and late I could be heard reciting verses of the Koran. I already knew all the obligatory prayers, and took care to perform them minutely. Moreover, we used to wander through the Beduin camps which fringed Jedabia, talking to the women and gradually gaining their confidence. At first we were regarded with the utmost suspicion, which gradually relaxed as we gave them Moslem salutations and told them how happy we were to be living an Arab life among Arabs. If a sheikh, a Haji, came to us, I used to murmur the "Shehada" to him: "Ash hadu illa Illaha ill Allah wa ash hadu inna Mohammedan rasul Allah," upon which he generally blessed me warmly. After a few days I was greeted enthusiastically and introduced to the solemn-faced babies adorned with silver amulets and taught how to bake flat, heavy bread in mud ovens.

It is amazing how perfect is the wireless telegraphy system of the desert. One night, dining with Sayed Rida, I remarked that I was so glad there was no electric light and that I liked the local colouring and primitive lighting effect in Arab houses. This was translated into the bazaar into, "She is a Moslem. She hates all European things. She wants to keep the old customs as our fathers had them."

We knew our campaign had succeeded on the eighth day, when, after the chief spy, despairing of getting a glimpse of us any other way, had brought us as a gift an absurd black bird with a bald head, a brother of Ali, the cook, arrived from his camel's-hair tent. He greeted us kindly and told us that the Beduins were in sympathy with us, that they knew we were Moslems and of their own blood.

Thus we felt we had done something to dispose of the probability of sudden death before we were a hundred kilometres on our way, but all other arrangements lagged intolerably. The most venerable and respected of all the ekhwan, Haji Fetater, who had done the great journey right through Kufara to Wadai, was the one man who could probably help us on our way. He was of the Mojabra tribe and he so loathed the "Nasrani" that he would not be in the same room as a Christian. I do not know whether it was Hassanein Bey's eloquence, or his sudden discovery that Sidi es Senussi himself had prophesied that the English would eventually be converted to Islam that finally induced him to promise to accompany us. "We are all servants of the Sayed. Only if he tells me to go, must I go," he said, but when the prophecy had aroused his enthusiasm, he flung back his splendid grey head. "I will protect her," he exclaimed; "I will take her to Kufara, and she shall kiss the holy qubba and be a Moslem!"

He was eighty years old, but he determined instantly that he would run the whole caravan and generally instruct us in the art of desert travelling. He had caught but a glimpse of me as I was hurried from the house in case my presence therein should pollute him. He can only have seen an exceedingly shy young person, with respectfully downcast eyes, in a pale blue tweed suit huddled on a ridiculously small pony, dangling a swollen foot in a native slipper, but he luckily took it into his head that he liked me. Hassanein Bey rapidly

clinched his acceptance by repeating the "Fatha," the
opening "sura" of the Koran. This is only done on
very important and solemn occasions and it constitutes
at the same time a blessing and an oath.

Even then our kindly host was not satisfied, but
insisted on sending an escort with us, ten soldiers of his
guard, coal-black slaves, under a commander called Abdul
Rahim. He also determined to settle the vexed question
of camels once for all by sending a caravan of his own
to Kufara to bring back some of his belongings and
allowing us to travel with it. To anyone who does not
know the East, it would now appear that things were
successfully settled. Not a bit of it! The soldiers were
at Zuetina, distant 24 miles. The camels were at least
two days' journey away, a matter of 60 miles. They
were vaguely described as being in the region of Antelat,
the house of Sayed Rida's family. Each day we
watched the horizon with anxious eyes. Each day we
counted eagerly every row of black specks that appeared amidst the sun-browned grass and rock, but
neither camels nor soldiers appeared. We had decided
that the caravan should announce its departure for noon
and that in reality the long line of camels should steal
past our door at 3 A.M. A few would be driven round
a convenient wall and loaded hastily with all our outfit,
after which we could mount and be 50 kilometres away
before anyone knew of our departure! We could leave
letters explaining a sudden opportunity and an equally
sudden determination, and send back further notes from
every oasis *en route*.

Unfortunately, it was a race against time, for everyone was growing suspicious at my inexplicable desire to
stay so long in a little mud village on the edge of the
world. Omar, our Government interpreter, was determined to get back to Benghazi for Christmas. The

delightful cavalry lieutenant who was political officer at
Zuetina was naturally bored at having to drive his heavy
camion three or four times a week from his little camp
by the ocean to see what a mysterious Englishwoman
might be doing in the debatable country on the fringe
of civilisation.   As the days wore on they tried by every
means in their power to lure me from Jedabia, but my
exceedingly swollen foot did me good service.   "The
stirrup hurt it so much riding here that I don't want to
risk it again till it is quite recovered," I explained.
They suggested camions, and I assured them I had so
much work to do that I was only too glad of the peace
and quiet of my Arab house to do it in.

It was a ludicrous situation.   Five young people used
to forgather in the house of the doctor to partake of
M. Omar's delicious *zabagliones,* and not one of them
ever uttered one word of truth!   Each felt instinctively
that the other was lying, but none knew exactly how
far he was bluffing or what card he had up his sleeve.
Perhaps we were a little better off than they, for we
knew their game and they luckily had failed to understand ours.   The political aspect was always before their
eyes.   In their anxiety to know whether Hassanein
Bey was plotting a Pan-Islamic empire with the thirty
Egyptian ex-coastguards who had taken refuge with
the Senussi during the war, they overlooked other possibilities.   I think the idea did occur to them that I
wanted to go much farther into the desert than they
cared to permit, but I doubt if they suspected our real
goal.   This used to surprise me immensely at the time.
Looking back, I realise that it would have been very
difficult for them to imagine that the woman they saw
in a panniered frock, with her French hat veiled in
drooping lace and high heels to match the red of her
striped cloak, would metamorphose herself into a Beduin

and attempt a journey which they looked upon as impossible for a European and exceedingly difficult even for an Arab.

We felt that we had one last card to play that they would never suspect—a midnight flight. We were loathe to use it, however. We waited patiently for the camels that did not come, and fenced desperately for time. Luckily our opponents were deceived by the apparent *froideur* existing between Hassanein Bey and myself. We had made a point of disagreeing with each other at every possible opportunity and even retailed our grievances occasionally to sympathetic ears. Suddenly, therefore, they took my companion into their confidence, which made things distinctly easier. Together they used to lay dark plots to induce me to leave Jedabia, where there was no *café chantant* and no "Hotel Nobile!" In spite, however, of this new move, we began to get very anxious. The spies had redoubled their vigilance. There were no signs of camels. Mabruk, the Head of the Police, introduced a person into our house whom he said was an ekhwan from Kufara, evidently intending that we should question him enthusiastically about his journey. We refrained from all mention of it, and the supposed ekhwan was so intensely stupid that one cannot imagine that he could have been much use to any secret service!

This was our position on December 4 when, on our morning's wander round the neighbouring encampments, we saw a line of camels coming in from Antelat. We instantly jumped to the conclusion that they were ours. One of the spies was leading the horse on which I was balanced sideways to protect my lame foot, so we could show no signs of joy, but for a few hours we made happy plans for the freedom of the desert. We had just finished a lunch of rice, dates, mutton and mint tea

when the blow fell. The black wazir arrived in considerable perturbation. Not only was there no news of our
camels or of our soldiers, but our opponents were well
aware that a caravan was starting for Kufara in a few
days' time and that we hoped to travel with it "for a
day or two." Hassanein turned to me with blazing eyes
in a chalk white face. "It's come to a fight," he said,
"and I'm glad." I used to be amused sometimes at
the way he shirked doing the simplest things till the
last moment, but in sudden emergencies the whole
strength and energy of the man flamed out and there
was no one in the world I would rather have beside me.
He grasped essentials rapidly and left me to fill in details.
"It's flight on two camels and the caravan must follow!"
he said. As usual, I started to work out the practical
possibilities while he went to gain further news.

I think I shall always remember that long dragging
afternoon. The wind was full of dust, but I took the
pony and went down to one of the encampments feeling
I simply could not smile. I felt hopeless and trapped
as if a net were closing round me and there was a numb
dead ache at my heart. Nevertheless I could not help
responding to the smiles of the Beduin women who
pressed round me, brilliant blots of colour in their orange
and black, or red and black barracans, with blue tribe
marks tattooed on their foreheads and half a dozen
huge silver ear-rings dangling beneath their plaited hair.
One laughed at my white hands against her black skin.
"You have soap to wash with. We have none," she
said. The lounging white figures in the suq stared at
me curiously as I passed, but did not protest. They
had stoned a "Christian dog" from Zuetina the day
before, but I was the Sayed's guest and therefore
honoured. A dignified sheikh gave me greeting. He
was a Haji and he told me: "We are all under the

Sayed's orders. You may go safely where you like among us, for it is the Sayed's wish." Mustapha listened eagerly. "It is true," he said. "The Sayed is great. All the people fear him. Otherwise they would kill every Christian in the country."

I began to realise the vast problem with which Italy is faced and to admire more than ever the way she is dealing with it. For the moment Europe has no message for the fierce fanatics of Libya, but the fertile *altipiano* of Cyrenaica, only a few miles from the sea, will have a prosperous future. Italian workmen have done so much to build up the prosperity of Egypt and Tunis. There is a wide field opening for them from Zuetina to Tobruk in which their industry and thrift may benefit their own country. Cyrenaica, once the granary of the Roman Empire, will be fittingly colonised by the descendants of those legionaries who left their trace from Cyrene to far-off Misda. The budding colony should have a splendid agricultural future and the friendship between Italy and the Senussi, recently cemented at Regima, should open up the old trans-Saharan caravan routes. The Sultan used to confide his most precious merchandise to the protection of Sidi Ben Ali es Senussi on its long journeys to Wadai. Why should not the same arrangement be made between the Governor of Cyrenaica and the hereditary Emir of the Senussi?

The sun was setting as I left the suq, a blaze of deep, flaming orange that we never see in Europe. The sky was molten in the crucible. I sent away the pony and sat crouched on the sand to watch the glory fade. A camel or two passed like huge distorted shadows across the burning west. A few white shrouded figures went by me with a soft "Bismillah!" I ached for a horse, a camel, anything that would take me away into the wide spaces beyond Jedabia. The strain of suspense eased a little in the evening, for during one of our games of cross purpose at the doctor's house we discovered that our opponents proposed to prevent our accompanying the caravan on the ground that no ekhwan was going with it. Apparently they still did not suspect our ultimate destination, but we were not at all certain that they had not wired for the camions from Benghazi. We sat up late that night in the silent court with the stars above us, and the guardian walls, which I had learned to love, shutting out all eavesdroppers. The spies retired in a body after our frugal dinner and Ali was always thankful to spend the night in the family tent. We decided on a simple but somewhat desperate plan. We felt that we should be allowed only two or three more days in Jedabia without an open fight, and we could not be certain of the twenty camels necessary for the caravan. Therefore we decided to leave practically all our luggage behind and go off in the middle of the night, if possible, with the ekhwan. Our little world would be told next morning that we had gone to visit some of the neighbouring camps and would return in a day or two. To reassure them they would see all our clothes hanging up on their usual pegs, most of our suitcases scattered about the room, our sacks and boxes of provisions stored in various corners, even my camp chair and the table on which I wrote.

On December 6 we did a hard morning's work. After our date and egg breakfast we settled ourselves with a Koran and note-books behind closed doors and said we did not wish to be disturbed. As soon as our retinue had retired to the white bell-tent which served as kitchen we set to work on the provision boxes. We emptied them of their contents and carefully filled them with immense stones which we laboriously collected from an inner court in course of construction. On top we

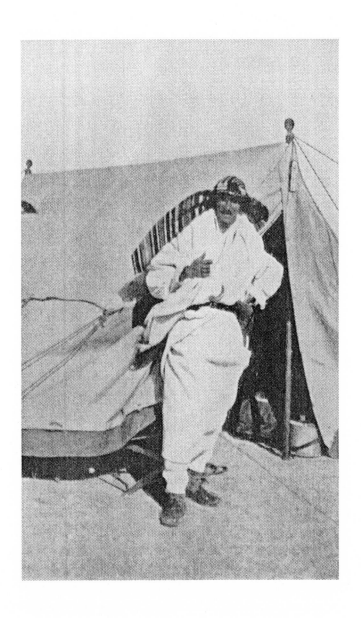

AHMED MOHAMMED BEY HASSANEIN, MY FELLOW EXPLORER

SAYED RIDA ES SENUSSI

put layers of straw and a few tins which could be seen through carefully arranged chinks. We sorted out an extra week's provisions to add to those we had already prepared and the rest we put into big sacks, with the intention of sending these latter at midnight, when the spies were sleeping peacefully, to some place where they could be stored until the dilatory camels arrived and the caravan started. They would then be packed unostentatiously with all the rest of the loads and when we joined the caravan a few days' journey on the way to Aujela we should recover our most necessary provisions. We ourselves, with the tent, two rolls of bedding, a fortnight's provisions and two suit-cases chiefly containing films, medicine, apparatus, candles, soap, etc., would disappear the following night in Beduin clothes.

I confess to feeling a certain pang when I realised that I must leave every single European garment behind except a pair of riding boots and breeches and a woollen sweater. Hassanein said he thought it was carrying realism too far. I understood the reason when, sternly insisting that his one suit-case should hold half the apparatus and only the simplest necessities of life, it disgorged seven different coloured bottles of eau de Cologne and a mass of heterogeneous attire more suited to Bond Street than to the Sahara. I had to superintend the packing lest he ignore the claims of malted milk tablets, towels and woollen underclothing in favour of delicately striped shirts and a lavender silk dressing-gown! We wondered if we should ever see again the garments we left gracefully decorating the walls in order to indicate the imminence of our return, or whether a new fashion would be set in Jedabia!

At lunch time the tailor came to fit my strange garments. It appeared that Sayed Rida wished to give me no fewer than four suits, but I assured him that I wanted only one to be photographed in and to show my friends in England. We finally compromised on two, one of which arrived that evening, an oddly shaped pair of trousers, very narrow at the ankle, made of white calico spotted with green leaves, and a dress like a voluminous chemise of dark red cotton with a blue pattern. We were told that the camels were ready but that the ekhwan was already regretting his moment of enthusiasm. "Will he be ready to start to-morrow at midnight?" "Inshallah!" was all the answer we got. Our plan was so simple, but it depended on two nights' secrecy and secrecy is impossible among Arabs!

However, we pretended not to worry. "El Maktub maktub!" we said, but I caught Hassanein anxiously opening the Koran to see whether a verse chosen at random would prove a good omen. He was delighted because the first one he saw read: *"Nasrun min Allahi wa fathan garib"* ("Victory and an opening out from Allah are near"). I was not very much more composed myself, for on repeating the long formal prayers that afternoon I realised from my companion's horrified face that I was ascribing unto Allah salutations, prayers and —physics! (*Tabiat* instead of *ta-hi-bat.*)

Sayed Rida took us for a drive in his car in the afternoon. There are no roads or even tracks beyond Jedabia, but the sand is hard and smooth. The Sayed thought it would be a good thing to show himself openly with us, and indeed, our fame increased after that drive. When we returned the whole of our household had attired itself in clean white garments and there was an awed moment while they all reverently kissed the Senussi's hand. They dared not approach very close to do it, lest their garments touch their holy master, but it was wonderful to see the worship and homage they put into the act. They were chattels in the hand of the

Sayed. As wakil of Sidi Idris he represented to them, as he does to thousands like them, the mystic being chosen by Allah to direct them. Their lives are his to command. He is their supreme judge as he is their defender and their guide. It is difficult for a European to realise the power held by the Senussi family, for there has been nothing approaching it in Europe. It is a reflection of the temporal and spiritual Papacy at its height. For instance, Sidi Idris might order one of the oldest and noblest ekhwan to start the following day for a two-thousand-mile journey to Lake Chad, and he would obey unquestioningly, without preparation or even surprise. "We are the servants of the Sayed," he would say as he wrapped his burnus round him and prepared to face the waterless sands.

When we decided on flight as the only possible means of leaving Jedabia, we asked Sayed Rida for a guide. He gave us Yusuf el Hamri and Mohammed Quemish and, calling them into our presence, he told them that if anything happened to us, whether by their fault or not, they would die immediately. The men accepted the statement as undoubted fact. Yet as Sayed Rida sat in our only camp chair in my big bare room, drinking sweet tea and eating Hassanein's last macaroons, it was difficult to realise that the fate of a country probably lay in his capable hands. The Sayed might declare a Holy War to-morrow against the infidels, and Islam, from Wajanga to the Mediterranean, might respond, but that afternoon our host talked with the simplicity of a child. We were trying to thank him for his amazing hospitality and for the permission he had given us to travel to Egypt by way of the great desert, which included the loan of camels, guides and an escort of soldiers, besides immense gifts of food and native clothing.

Coming from an Italian colony we had become used

to gracious hospitality, but Sayed Rida's generosity was overwhelming. I have travelled in half the countries of the world; I have been the guest of mandarin and boundary rider, or rajah, Fijian ras and North-West Mounted Police and of every intermediate race and grade, but I have never received such generous, unquestioning welcome as in Beduin countries. Some of the happiest weeks of my life were spent in Syria as the guest of a great Arab prince. I used to think that nothing could match his kindness, but here in Jedabia I found its equal in another descendant of the Prophet, a Sherif of Islam.

We asked Sayed Rida if we could send him anything from Cairo, our thoughts running to a jewel or a gold inlaid rifle. He asked for a green parrot and some gramophone records with a smile as delightful as his brother's.

"You see," he said, "my life is rather lonely. It is not wise that I go out or that I show myself very much to our people. Our family is holy and we must live a secluded life. We may not see dancing or hear singing. Our people would not understand, but sometimes when I am alone late at night I play the gramophone, for I love music very much." A curiously sweet smile illumined his kindly face and he beat time to an imaginary tune with a jewelled finger. "I do not like much noise," he said. "I like the sad, soft melodies best. I think all music should be melancholy."

For a moment he was a child thinking wistfully of a toy and then, as Ali entered bent double with respect over his tray of tea, the Sayed resumed the grave dignity in keeping with his gorgeous clothes—a purple embroidered jelabia under an apple-green silk jubba with a wonderful crimson and blue kufiya stiff with gold thread and having great tassels of gold.

Our busy day closed with a most humorous scene. After Ali and the spies had gone willingly to the amusement or repose they desired, we dragged the six heavy sacks of provisions one by one out of my room across the court to the dark yard by the main door. There was no moon. Tinned meat weighs incredibly heavy. We fell over a lot of loose stones and we imagined we made a good deal of noise. The peculiar form of an Arab dwelling, however, precludes the possibility of being overheard. We then dug stones and sand from the unfinished bit of the house and filled some most realistic looking dummy sacks which we artistically arranged in the place of real ones. At 11 P.M. we got one of those unexpected shocks that send cold shivers down one's back and desperate thoughts to one's brain. There was a sudden knock at the door. It was too soon for our fellow plotters in search of the luggage. "Min da?" asked Hassanein icily and I felt the tautened thrill in his voice. "Mabruk," answered the voice of the chief spy and then a long ramble about wanting to see the native garments already delivered, to make a pattern for the others his brother the tailor was making. As a matter of fact it was a perfectly genuine demand. We had asked the confidential wazir to hurry up the making of our clothes and he had done so to such good effect, by saying it was the Sayed's wish, that the unfortunate tailor proposed to work all night, but to our apprehensive ears it sounded very suspicious. I was glad that Hassanein had not got a revolver on him. He told me afterwards that his first impulse had been to shoot the man and bury him instantly! Instead of which he murmured that the "sitt" was in bed and the magical word which retards the progress of Islam. "Bokra!" (To-morrow.)

At 1 A.M. Hassanein, shrouded from head to foot in

a white jerd, was waiting just outside the main door.
A few minutes later there was the faintest scratch
on the heavy wood. Almost before he had pulled it
open seven dark figures, muffled up to the eyes, utterly
unrecognisable, slipped into the yard. Not a word was
uttered. Dexterously they shouldered the provision sacks
and stepped away into the night without a murmur. Of
course they simply revelled in the mystery and secrecy
of it, but we wondered how soon rumour would reach
the bazaar!

CHAPTER III

THE ESCAPE FROM JEDABIA

DECEMBER 7 dawned brilliantly fine. We rose from our camp beds feeling joyfully that thirty-six hours would elapse before we slept on them again. Our morning was enlivened by the visits of two or three friends from the neighbouring encampments. Sheikh Mohammed, the Haji, came in to tell us that we were welcome visitors to any Beduin camp. He drank three glasses of sweet tea in three gulps, asked in a mysterious whisper for a cigarette, hastily put the whole packet into his sleeve and demanded that I should repeat suras from the Koran to him. I did so to the best of my ability and he was much impressed. We meant to sleep in the afternoon, but the unsuspecting Sayed had most kindly ordered his slaves to perform a dance in our honour, so about 3 P.M. the sound of drums was heard outside our blind walls. Ali summoned us forth in great excitement. We sat on two chairs before our door and gradually the whole male population of Jedabia gathered round us, row upon row of shrouded white figures crouching on the sand. In an irregular circle round a couple of hide drums danced the black Sudanese slaves from Wadai, bought in the market at Kufara, presents from native potentates to the Senussi family, or children of slaves sent by the famous Ali Dinar, Sultan of Darfur. Slavery in the East is a kindly institution, quite unlike the horrors of "Uncle Tom's Cabin." The blacks are treated as part of the family.

They are proud of their masters and devoted to them. They are trusted and confidential. Thus Ali came to us one evening in honest grief. "That Mustapha is a bad man," he said. "He goes to the house of the doctor and says he has not had enough to eat here. It is not true. The Sayed is generous. There is everything here. It is not good for the Sayed's honour that such things should be said."

The blacks enjoyed the dance even more than we did, for we had just heard that through too much ardour on the part of our allies there was likely to be a hitch in the arrangements. The long-delayed camels for the caravan had arrived at last. The soldiers had come in from Zuetina. We had better all start together at midnight, said our confidant triumphantly. Anyone who knows the East will realise how difficult it is for even two or three people to slip away secretly. Everyone's business is known from A to Z. Projects are discussed in the bazaars while they are still formless in the brain of the plotter. The idea that a score of camels and a dozen soldiers, with luggage, tents, stores, guides, etc., could start secretly from Jedabia was ludicrous. Already there was a rumour in the suq that we were going to Kufara because of the unfortunate suggestion that we should accompany the caravan for a day or two! Therefore, even while we gazed at the gyrating circle of blacks, who flung themselves into extravagant postures, chanting their monotonous songs and clicking together short sticks, we had sent post haste to rearrange matters. News was brought us that the delightful cavalry officer from Zuetina had arrived, two days before he was expected.

"I think I will go and have tea at the doctor's," I said firmly to Hassanein. "I will stay with them there for two hours, which will give you plenty of time to get the caravan postponed."

The spies were as clinging as limpets that day. Mabruk leant over my shoulder as I spoke, pointing to the wildest dancer with a forced smile. However, I was determined to spoil his little effort and insisted that he and Mustapha should accompany me on my walk. "I don't like going through all these people alone," I said; and reluctantly they had to come with me.

Our last game of cross purposes will always remain in my mind, for, with one eye on the clock, I summoned every atom of intelligence to my aid. I allowed myself to be reluctantly persuaded to return by camion to Benghazi the following week. I asked reproachfully why no ekhwan could be found to accompany me on a little caravan tour. They assured me that none was willing to travel with a Christian, and that no one of that faith could journey beyond Jedabia. I took up and emphasised this point for some time, as it would eventually preclude their attempting to follow us. I allowed my bitter disappointment to be seen, was comforted and finally cheered up with a promise of visiting all the encampments on the way back. We parted the best of friends and I shall always retain a grateful memory of their kindness and care. So often we longed to confide all our plans to them. We were sure of their sympathy, but their very hospitality would have made it impossible for them to allow their erstwhile guest to venture her life on such a wild and dangerous journey.

Six months before I had talked to an Arabian Emir about my project. "Heya magnuna!" he exclaimed to his wakils. "She is mad. If she could get to Kufara, she could get to any place in heaven or earth!" Thus we knew from the beginning that we must hide our object from our generous Italian friends. If they hadn't thought that at least Hassanein had some political aim in coming to Jedabia, remorse would probably have added to our mental troubles, but, luckily, the fact that they were obviously watching us turned the affair into a game and justified us in having a few secrets also.

If my charming hosts in Cyrenaica read this book, I think they will forgive me for the part their own kindness and forethought forced me to play most unwillingly. They are all sportsmen. They, too, are travellers and lovers of the great desert. They laid the foundations of my journey by their long years of work in North Africa. They will reap the benefit when the friendship between European and Senussi is firmly cemented and the Beduins welcome the influx of commerce and exploration from over the sea.

I returned at 7 P.M. to our walled Arab house, but the fantasia was still continuing. The gift of our last packet of cigarettes had stimulated the performers to frenzy and they were prepared to spend the night in an orgy of dance and song. Ordinarily, I should have loved watching their barbaric vigour and I was exceedingly grateful to the ever-thoughtful Sayed for giving this festa in our honour, but we had still a good many preparations to make, so we regretfully thanked the performers and despatched them to their homes. After a hasty meal, Hassanein went off to make final preparations concerning changing our Italian notes into heavy silver mejidies, the cumbersome coin of the country, buying bread and eggs, collecting the native dress and a dozen other things that had to be done at the very last moment for fear of arousing suspicion. I wrote a note to our Italian interpreter, who had also proved guide, philosopher and friend, explaining that I was not to be entirely deprived of my desert journey after all, for at the last moment I was able to accompany an ekhwan who was travelling to an encampment a day or two away. I then made

relays of green tea in an inadequate kettle and filled
both our thermos flasks, also the water bottles.

It was then nearly 9 P.M., at which hour Hassanein
had said he would return, but the minutes dragged on
and there was no sign of his coming. At 10 I became
anxious. I couldn't lie still any more, and began walking up and down the big room by the light of one candle
guttering on the window ledge. Ali came to me to ask
if he and the servant, who was also a spy, could go home.
I said he must stay until Hassanein Bey returned, for I
did not want to give the boy an opportunity of inquiring
into my companion's designs, but each hour that went
by made our flight more and more difficult, for we could
not begin to pack beds, luggage, etc., till the house was
empty. At 11 I was nearly frantic. I don't think I have
ever spent a worse two hours. I began to wonder whether
the spies had discovered our plot and, deciding to
frustrate it at all costs, had arranged to have my ally
knocked senseless as he crossed the wide expanse of white
sandstone between our house and the scattered buildings
of Jedabia.

At 11.30, as I was preparing to set forth in search
and was actually winding myself into the intricacies of
a jerd so as to pass unnoticed in the dark, Hassanein
arrived, staggering beneath the mejidies, for a very
moderate sum in that coinage weighs intolerably. He
discharged eggs, bread and clothing in a heap and
explained that the usual Arab dilatoriness had delayed
him. The letters to sheikhs of zawias were not ready,
the eggs were not cooked, the clothes were not quite
finished. However, we didn't wait for much talk. We
sent off the servants with minute instructions about
to-morrow's work. An Arab spy is clever in some ways,
but he never looks ahead, so it is generally fairly easy
to lull his suspicions.

The instant the door shut behind them we literally flung ourselves on the luggage. We wrestled first with the beds and flea-bags, stuffing them into old sacks to look like native bundles. The tent had to be disposed of in the same way—its poles tied up in a red prayer-rug, its canvas disguised in native wrappings. Not one single bit of European luggage must be visible. My suit-case was already packed and it was but a minute's work to push it into a striped flour sack, but my heart sank when I saw Hassanein's room. It was still littered with what he called necessities. We packed and pushed and tugged at his bundles, getting frantically hot and tired, but always when we had, with superhuman effort, triumphantly strapped up a bulging roll, a minute later he would remember something he absolutely must put in and want the thing undone. When but half an hour was left before our departure was due, I became desperate and took matters into my own hands. I packed the food into one knapsack. The necessities I divided into two others. I shut his suit-case firmly on the most useful articles I could collect from the chaos. I stood over him equally firmly while he put mackintoshes with fleece linings, rugs and extra native dress into the bedding. I pulled the straps to a tighter hole myself before scurrying off to dress.

Let no one think it is easy to get into Beduin feminine attire for the first time. The tight white trousers presented difficulties over riding breeches. The red tobh was too tight at the neck. The barracan needed much adjustment. One end flaps loose over the head, which is already swathed in a tight black handkerchief hiding all the hair, while the other is wound twice round in the form of a skirt and comes up over the left shoulder to make the front bit of the bodice. It is all held in place by a thick red woollen "hezaam" at least twelve feet in length, which is wound round and round till one's waist resembles a mummy and is tied one side with dangling ends. Under this I wore my revolver belt, with two fully loaded Colts and a prismatic compass in a case.

Glancing round my room as I put on my huge yellow heel-less slippers, I decided it looked a very realistic picture of the abode left temporarily and in haste. My cherished blue tweed hung on one hook and a rose-red sweater on another. A few books and papers, with a hot-water bottle and some stockings, were scattered on convenient chairs. The cases and sacks of stones stood formally round the walls. A bottle of complexion lotion was prominent on a shelf and my European shoes were in their usual row! With a sigh of relief I dragged the sack containing my suit-case to join the disguised camp outfit by the main door and, blowing out the candle in my room, closed the door for the last time.

My cheerfulness rapily evaporated when I crossed the court to Hassanein's room. The litter was inconceivable. Everything that we had shut twenty minutes ago was open. He himself, with ruffled wild hair, was still in shirt and riding-breeches. To a casual observer he appeared to be playing a game of leap frog with the various bundles, in which the object seemed to be to upset as many things as possible. "You have exactly · six minutes in which to get ready," I said in an awful voice. A chair fell with a crash, breaking an eau de Cologne bottle and sending a mass of little tubes, bottles and boxes rolling to my feet. Thereafter followed ten minutes' best American hustle. In spite of feeling like a swathed Chinese infant in my cumbersome dress, I attacked that room with a personal venom that surely had effect even on inanimate things, for the suit-case shut almost unprotestingly on a huddled mass in which the

parcels of mejidies stuck out like Mount Everest. I
don't know what I said. I imagined at the time it was
quite unforgivable, but Hassanein is the most good-
tempered person in the world. He submitted to being
pushed and pulled into the white garments he had to
wear over his European riding-kit—voluminous white
pantaloons, long flowing shirt and woollen jerd. I
believe I banged a white kufiya on his head and flung
an agal at him before rushing from the room to take
up my position behind the main door with a tiny dark
lantern which revealed the piles of corpulent sacks.
When, a few minutes later, a stately white figure with
flowing lines unbroken save by the crossed revolver belts,
true son of a sheikh of the famous Azhar University,
joined me, I could hardly recognise in this solemn Arab
the wild individual who was playing at hay-making a
few minutes before.

Of course our fellow-plotters were late! We waited
nearly an hour crouched on the sacks, while the only
thing that broke the silence of a desert night was the
braying of a donkey near the suq. At about 1.45 we
heard the faint roar of protesting camels and our pulses
quickened. Some ten minutes later stealthy footsteps
approached. There was a light scratch on the door, and
the operation of the previous night was successfully
repeated, only this time we had another quarter of an
hour's suspense after the porters went forth with the
first sacks before they could return for the last. Our
confidant leant against the door, motionless and calm,
looking at the starlit sky. "Bahi!" he murmured, as
the mysterious figures reappeared, the only word he had
uttered the whole time. Shouldering knapsack, water-
bottle, thermos flask and kodak, I stumbled out of the
dark passage into the moonless night. A strong, cold
wind met me and I wondered, shivering, why a Beduin

woman does not freeze to death. I've never seen them
wear anything but a cotton barracan. Even while I
limped across the open white sands, for the camels were
hidden some three hundred yards away, near the rough
cemetery that surrounds the deserted morabit of Sidi
Hassan, I felt that I wanted an overcoat even more than
I wanted to go to Kufara!

Nevertheless, it was freedom at last and excitement
thrilled us. There was a moment's pause on the part of
our puzzled guide when absolute blackness on all sides
gave no hint of direction. Then a muffled roar told us
that a camel was on our left and the smothered sound of it
suggested that someone was probably sitting on its head.
A moment more and a dark mass loomed up beside a
broken wall. Thankfully I subsided on a heap of stones.
It is not the slightest use arguing with a camel-driver
about a load. It is waste of energy to try to hurry him.
He is used to weighing burdens minutely, to arranging
them slowly to his own satisfaction. So I was prepared
for an hour's wait while our retinue cut rope, made
"corners" to the sacks with stones, discussed loads, lost
camels, caught them again and were generally inefficient.
I was genuinely surprised, therefore, when in only twenty
minutes everything was noiselessly packed and the camels
ready to start. Yusuf el Hamri and Mohammed Quemish,
our two confidential servants, were introduced to me in
the dark and we exchanged a few florid sentences in
which the words "mabsut" and "mamnun" played a
large part.

Then I hoisted myself on to my camel, a huge, blond
beast, with no proper saddle. A spike stuck up in front
and behind and his hump was painfully evident between
the rolled straw of the baggage serg. On the top were
folded a couple of native mats and thereon I perched in
my uncomfortable, closely wound clothes, which made

mounting a matter of peril and difficulty. In spite of all
this, when my great beast rose to his stately height and
moved off into the night, exhilaration rushed over me.
I hadn't been on a camel for three months, and then on
the beautiful trotting "hajin" of the Sudan. This was
only a fine baggage "hamla," but he was in keeping
with the desert and the night and our wild, impossible
project. I was happy. Also, it was a wonderful start.
Sir Richard Burton wisely writes that the African
traveller must always be prepared for three starts—the
long one, the short one and the real one. Later we
realised how right he was, but for the moment, as our
little line of camels swayed off into the darkness beyond
the white morabit, we only felt that we had escaped.

"How amazing that they can find their way in
pitch darkness like this!" I exclaimed, and only when
Orion had appeared in four different directions did I
begin to wonder whether they could! We had started
just before three, striking a northerly course which surprised us, as we knew that Aujela lay to the south. We
comforted ourselves with the idea that our guides were
purposely avoiding the main track, and patiently we
bore the icy wind and constant change of direction.
When, after an hour, we turned completely round, we
decided it was necessary to expostulate. Yusuf, on being
shown a luminous compass, refused to believe that the
north was where the needle directed. We pointed out
the extraordinary movement of the stars and he remained
unconvinced. He looked pathetically at the heavens and
asked persistently for "Jedi," the star that had guided
him apparently in many wanderings over half Africa.
Unfortunately we could not find her for him, though we
pointed out most of the constellations from the Great
Bear to the Milky Way.

We continued our aimless progress for another hour.

THE AUTHOR AT JEDABIA

THE AUTHOR ON CAMEL-BACK

BEDUIN WOMAN AT JEDABIA

As we were merely describing irregular circles we were
not surprised when a little before five a chorus of dogs
barking proclaimed our nearness to Jedabia. "It is
an encampment," said Yusuf. "I know where we are
now!" and at that moment the donkey in the suq
brayed quite close to us! I couldn't help laughing. In
a few minutes our desperate midnight flight would land
us before the doors of the house from which we had
escaped so triumphantly three hours earlier. The distressed Yusuf, inexplicably bereft of his tame star, was
all for camping there and then to await the dawn, but, lest
the rising sun should reveal to the astonished eyes of the
early astir a dishevelled party asleep on the space before
the mosque, I firmly took command. By the compass
I marched them due south of the donkey's bray for half
an hour. At least we should be out of sight at dawn
and could then start off on the right track.

The wind seemed colder than ever as we "barraked"
our camels on the flat, sandy waste. We were frozen
and shelterless. Excitement, suspense and physical
labour had all combined to wear us out. My foot
was swollen and inflamed after its unusual exercise.
Hassanein had rheumatism in his back. There was an
hour to wait for the dawn. I doubt if a more miserable
couple existed than the two who rolled themselves into
the thin and dirty camel rugs and lay down on the hard
sand, their heads on tufts of spiky grass. I did not
sleep. It was too cold. The wind searched out every
corner of my aching body. I began to feel the strain
of our sleepless nights and days of suspense. Even my
sense of humour had gone. It was five weeks since we
had left England and we had got no farther than a
sand heap outside Jedabia! At six a flush of pale pink
appeared in the sky in a direction which amazed Yusuf.
Shivering, with chattering teeth, we rose to a windy

dawn! Mohammed was already murmuring, "Allahu Akhbar," devoutly turning towards the kibla at Mecca. We followed his example, abluting in the sand as is permissible when there is no water. Luckily it is only necessary to go through the "Fatha" and the requisite "Raqa-at." The kneeling position hurt my foot excruciatingly, and I could hardly get it into my huge yellow shoe again.

The men bestirred themselves to some purpose. Five minutes after the last "Salamu Aleikum wa Rahmat Allah" had saluted the angels who stand on either side to record a man's good and bad deeds, the camels were loaded and we were moving away from the white qubba of Sidi Hassan and the scattered mud houses which appeared but a stone's throw distant. There had been no time to eat. I tried to force a hard-boiled egg down my throat as I swayed along, but I could not manage it. Hassanein was doubled up with rheumatism and I tried every possible position to ease my foot. My hands were numb as I clutched the gaudy barracan, red, blue and orange, round me, and prayed for the sun to warm me.

Every few minutes we turned round to see if Jedabia had disappeared, but it must stand on a slight rise as the morabit was visible for three hours. Distance is illusive in the desert. Everything looks much nearer than it really is. One sees the palms of an oasis early in the morning, plans to arrive before midday, and is lucky if one reaches it by sunset. However, by 10.30 every sign of human habitation had disappeared and only a flat sandy plain, tufted with coarse grey brush a few inches to a foot high, lay all around us. Thankfully we halted, turned the camels to graze, spread the scarlet woven rugs in the sun, and prepared to eat.

Further troubles threatened when we discovered that our retinue, Yusuf, Mohammed and two coal-black

Sudanese soldiers, had brought no provisions of any sort. They had trusted either to us or to joining the south-bound caravan within a few hours. Consternation seized us. In order to travel light we had brought what we considered the least possible amount of food necessary for two people for a week—that is, one tin of meat per day, with a very small ration of flour, rice, dates and tea. How were we going to feed six people for perhaps a fortnight on it? At the moment we were too tired to think. We doled out to the retinue rice, tea and most of the hard-boiled eggs intended for ourselves and, after the frugal meal, insisted on immediate departure. There was a great deal of grumbling. They were all tired and they wanted to sleep there and then. The blacks were openly rebellious. "We are not your slaves," they said. "We will not over-tire ourselves." However, by force of sarcasm, encouragement and laughter, we got them to load the camels.

In Libya they do not girth the baggage saddles at all. They merely balance the bales evenly according to weight on either side of a straw pad round the hump. Thus, if the camel stumbles badly or is frightened and runs a few paces, the luggage over-balances and crashes to the ground, generally terrifying the beast into a mad gallop. I suppose ours were carelessly loaded, for the tent dropped off three times and tempers grew sulky.

About one we came to a small cluster of camel's-hair tents in the shelter of a slight rise and the retinue clamoured to stop there for the night. The Arab is greedy by nature, while the Sudanese is positively voracious. At one meal he will devour what would support a European family for a day. Having seen our meagre provisions, the retinue thought they would get a better dinner in these Beduin tents. They protested and argued violently, but we were ruthless. There was fear

of pursuit and of being recognised. Yusuf joined his
hands in prayer. "We will say you are the wife of an
ekhwan," he said, "and that we are taking you to
Jalo," but he pleaded in vain. We moved on and they
followed perforce, surly, bronzed Beduins in coarse
woolen jerds, rifles slung across their backs.

The impressions cherished since childhood are gradually disappearing from my mind. One hears so often
of the untiring endurance of the Beduin and of his
frugal fare. I used to believe that he could ride for days
without sleep and live on a few dates or locusts. He
may be able to do the latter if he is absolutely obliged
to, but normally his appetite is large and his amiability
depends on his food. With regard to his endurance, I
have met Tuaregs who had accomplished some amazingly
swift rides, but in the French Sahara, in Syria or in
Libya, as in the Sudan, I have never found an Arab
who did not want to camp several hours before I did.
South of Touggurt I once had a delightful guide called
Ali, a blue-eyed, ruddy-haired Tuareg, who must have
had Vandal blood in his veins and he used to get positively haggard after a nine hours' ride without a pause.

After 2.30 we could not urge our retinue farther.
It was obvious that they were very tired, but it is
doubtful if they were as exhausted as we were, for we
had worked very hard the preceding day and night,
while they were "fadhling" in the suq. However, Yusuf
seized my camel rein. "This is a good place. We
must rest," he said. It was no use exasperating them.
We had ridden for six hours. A camel does a regular
two and a half miles an hour, so we imagined ourselves
about 15 miles from Jedabia and safe from pursuit.

Almost before we had got the sacks off the camels
Mohammed had rolled himself in his jerd and was
actually asleep. Yusuf helped us half-heartedly while we

struggled to put up the tent, but we unrolled bedding, put down ground-sheet, doled out provisions, fitted the camp beds together ourselves. The Sudanese collected brushwood, yawning violently and infinitely wearily. We boiled tea and drank it sugarless, for the retinue had the usual Arab passion for sugar. I looked at myself once in a tiny hand-glass, and was thankful to put it down, for I hardly recognised the begrimed and haggard visage, yellow, sunburnt and lined, that peered out under the heavy black handkerchief between the folds of the barracan. A gale rose suddenly and nearly swept our tent away, but we did not mind. We slept fitfully, woke to cook rice on a brushwood fire and went to bed about 6 P.M. with a thankfulness too deep for words. Feather mattresses, frilled pillows, Chippendale or Louis XV beds all have their charms, but I have never been so grateful for any as I was that night for my flea-bag and my air cushion.

At 6 next morning Yusuf woke us with a cry of "El Fagr," and after the usual prayers we set to work to break camp. We informed the retinue that we intended to reach Wadi Farig and its well that day and therefore they must not count on a midday halt. Consequently they insisted on making a fire and cooking half our week's rations straight away! We started at 8 A.M. and continued a south-easterly-southerly course all day.

Wadi Farig is only 60 kilometres from Jedabia, but I imagine our first day we must have made a detour in order to avoid the main route, for it was not till 2 o'clock on the second day that a mirage on the horizon, a sheet of silver water bordered with purple mountains, proclaimed the position of the wadi. "It is bayid, bayid!" said Mohammed. "We cannot reach it before sunset. Let us rest now!" This time, however, we would not stop. We had shared our flasks of tea and our

dates evenly with him at noon and we felt that after
a good night's sleep, if we could ride nine hours on end,
they could too. It was an absolutely perfect day, cloud-
less and still, but the sun was very hot at noon. It
scorched through the thin folds of my barracan and
made one wonder why Europe and not Africa invented
parasols.

The character of the country remained unchanged.
Always the same sandy scrub stretched away as far as
the eye could see. Occasional jerboas or lizards scuttered
into their holes as we approached. Once a dozen gazelle
fled swiftly across our path. Mohammed tried a shot at
them, but he was too slow. Another time we passed a
large rabbit warren and a couple of white scuts disappeared into the labyrinth of holes. We struck a main
track about noon and I noticed a sage bush covered with
bits of different coloured threads. It appears that every
wayfarer adds a piece of cotton or wool from his attire
to show that this is a desert "road" and that caravans
pass that way. Yusuf contributed a white thread from
his girdle, and I a red one from my long hezaam.

All that day we met only two travellers. I discreetly
covered my face while they exchanged greetings with
our retinue. The desert telephone was at work again.
They brought news from Jalo which they exchanged
for tales of Jedabia. They were not interested in us.
Mrs. Forbes had disappeared into space, and in her place
was a Mohammedan woman called Khadija, travelling
with a kinsman, an Egyptian Bey, son of a Sheikh
el-Azhar. She wore Beduin clothes, followed their
customs, prayed to their God, lived their life. Her
language was certainly different, but the Arabic varies
so immensely between Baghdad and Marrakesh that my
faltering conversation was attributed to my being accustomed only to the classical language. Even Hassanein

could hardly understand the dialect used by the Libyan Beduins. It is not a case of accent or pronunciation. Nearly all the words are different.

I cannot imagine why Wadi Farig is marked on the map as a vivid green splash across the colourless desert. The slight depression running due east and west between the two faint ridges about 15 metres high varies in no respect from the surrounding country. No blade of grass or green thing decorates it. Nothing breaks the monotonous sand and grey brushwood except the one well of bitter brackish water. We arrived just as the sun was setting and had difficulty in getting the camels past the well in order to camp on the higher ground beyond. Hassanein was riding a nervous "naga" (female), who never kept her head in one direction for more than a minute or two. She now decided to race for the well while a playful companion kicked off a bale or two, upset the balance of the rest, caught her foot in a falling sack and tore wildly away, scattering her load to the winds. My stately beast was in an amorous mood, so, with guttural gurglings, he added himself to the general mêlée. I had to dismount and limp up to the rise, dragging him forcibly after me, while the men collected our belongings and reloaded them. It was a race with the sun, but we just won it. As the last crimson glow faded in the radiant west and the devout Mohammed lifted a sandy nose from his ablutions, the last tent peg was driven in. Brush fires gleamed on the rise opposite, for wherever there is a desert well there are a few scattered tents of the nomads whose homes move with the season and the pasture.

We made a flaming pyre and sat round it in a circle of pack-saddles. Yusuf had found his beloved Jedi and he pointed her out to me triumphantly—the Pole star! The silence of the desert encircled us and a faint scent

of thyme stole up from the cold sand. Farraj (both the
black Sudanese were called Farraj) began intoning verses
of the Koran—a melodious sound in the starlit night.
Then, surprised by his own song, he suddenly sprang to
his feet and chanted loudly, triumphantly, the muazzin's
call to prayer, "Allahu Akhbar. Allahu Akhbar. Ash
hadu illa Illaha illallah wa ash hadu inna Mohammedan
rasul Allah!" The Shehada rolled splendid, intolerant,
from his lips and his voice rose higher on the cry,
"Haya alla sala! Haya alla fellah!" till we all took
up the chorus of "Allahu Akhbar, Allahu Akhbar!"

As I undressed in the "harem" portion of the tent,
which had enormously impressed our retinue, I pondered
on the character of these men with whom we were to
live in familiar intercourse for months. Apart from
their fierce fanaticism, which made it a duty for them
to kill the infidel and the Nasrani as we kill dangerous
and pestilential vermin, they had the simplicity of
children. I felt that our blacks would steal all our food
one day if they happened to be hungry and defend us
most gallantly the next. They are utterly unable to
provide for the morrow. Their trust in Allah is of the
blind kind that does not try to help itself, yet the Koran
says, "Allah works with him who works." Again and
again we told them about the scarcity of food. We
showed them the pathetic limit of our provisions. They
said, "The caravan will come to-morrow! Inshallah!"

Knowing the dilatory habits of the East, I had very
little faith in the arrival of that caravan for at least a
week, but we agreed to their persistent request to camp
for two days at the wadi to give it a chance of joining
us. If it did not arrive on the evening of the 11th,
bringing with it all our provisions, we should have to
send back the two blacks, and continue post-haste to
Aujela with Yusuf and Mohammed. With that intent

we put into one sack the smallest quantity of food for
four people for five days—that is, a tin of meat or sardines
per person per day, with coffee and dates. When this
was done we were horrified at the little that remained.
The blacks wanted to bake great flat loaves of unleavened
bread morning and evening and we had so very little
flour. I began to realise that if the caravan did not
arrive we should die of exhaustion on the way to Aujela.
Let us once lose the way, let a storm delay us, let the
retinue prove unreliable and insist on eating more than
the day's meagre ration and we should be lost! Yet
we were determined on one thing only—not to go back.

"In any case we have the peace and quiet of the
desert," I thought, as I went to sleep and woke a few
hours later to pandemonium indescribable. I've heard
the roar of an uncaged lion in Rhodesia, but never before
had I heard such mad bellows of rage as made the night
hideous. "The camels have gone mad," I gasped, as
I flung myself out of the tent. Thunder of sound broke
from a heaving black mass only a few yards from our
canvas walls. Shouts came from Yusuf and Mohammed,
who seemed to be aimlessly dancing round the wildly
excited beasts. Then the mass crashed roaring to its feet
and two camels dashed madly past me, missing the tent
by a foot. I found Hassanein only half awake at my
elbow. "What are they doing?" he said blankly.
"In the spring the camels' fancy lightly turns to
thoughts of love!" "But it isn't the spring!" he
objected drowsily. "Never mind. God! They're
coming back!" We retreated hastily from the tent.
In Syria I had seen a maddened beast go right through
a tent in such a mood, and the vision of the crushed
poles and canvas, intricately mixed up with shattered
baggage and an absolutely flattened camp bed, flashed
across me. I took up a strategic position in the open

but the bellowing brutes staggered away again, their
roars mercifully fading in the distance. "Is this likely
to happen often?" I asked Yusuf. "Yes, when it is
cold," he answered indifferently. "Two things increase
in winter, the camels and the sea!"

We enjoyed the rare luxury of sleeping late next
morning and woke to another gorgeous day.   The
water from the well was almost undrinkable—it was so
salt and muddy—but we washed in it triumphantly.
Unfortunately, Hassanein was temped to wash his hair,
with the odd result that it thereafter stood up like a
tuft of coarse ostrich feathers. Everything dries appall-
ingly in the desert. One's skin is cracked and lined
after a few days. One's nails break. One's hair dries
and becomes brittle. Yet one does not mind. The
desert has a subtle and a cruel charm. She destroys
while she enthralls. She is the siren from whom there
is no escape. Cynthia Stockley, whom I met years ago
in Bulawayo, writes in one of her vivid stories of
African life that once the desert has stuck her claw into
a man, he must return to her, for only she can heal the
wound she has made.

The preceding night the wadi had been empty.
That morning it was crowded. Half-naked brown figures
hauled water for a great herd of camels who crushed
round the low mud walls of the well. A flock of sheep
waited their turn at a short distance. More camels
strayed slowly down the rise, grazing as they walked.
Some white figures came up to greet us, rifles slung across
their backs. They were the dwellers in the nuggas whose
fires we had seen the night before. The desert wires had
informed them of our imminent arrival before we had
left Jedabia! They sat round our brushwood fire and
drank tea sweetened with crushed dates, as the sugar
had run out. Hassanein and I left them to "fadhl" with

our retinue and went and sat on a sandhill and dreamed visions of the caravan, that would end all our troubles, coming over the rise opposite. Instead, we saw only Farraj go down the wadi to buy bitter camel's milk and date pulp, highly flavoured with sand, from the nugga men. When the sunset dyed the land to crimson glory we returned to our camp frantically hungry, for we had eaten nothing since 8 A.M., and then only rice and tinned vegetables, because the latter were disliked by our retinue. The two blacks were playing draughts on the sands with white shells and camel dung. "Fadhl!" urged Mohammed, smiling. "Fadhl!" "Do not live always alone," said Yusuf. "Mix with us a little. We shall not forget who is master." From this I knew that Hassanein had won another of his personal victories. He had a wonderful way of gaining the confidence and sympathy of Arabs, from the Sayeds down to the fanatical Beduin.

The mental atmosphere of our retinue had been most unpropitious during the first two days. We realised that our journey would be almost an impossibility unless it changed, but, wisely, Hassanein would not hurry matters. A word dropped here and there, swift rebuke or warm praise, hinted sympathy with the Senussi aims, tales of old friendship with the Sayeds, little councils of war in the outer tent, had all borne fruit. We felt the effect that night as we toasted ourselves before the fire, watching Farraj knead his heavy bread and cook it in the ashes. When it was baked, he pressed some upon us with a broad, toothless smile. It was hot, heavy and indigestible, but wholly delicious with our corned beef. Only the cocoa was a failure, as the water was terribly salt.

I settled myself into the double woollen flaps of my flea-bag that night with a great sense of peace. The thermometer had soared up at midday, but the nights were always chilly, and we were extremely grateful for our rainproof sleeping-sacks, sprinkled with insect powder, which, by the way, had no effect whatever on the fleas. The third morning in Jedabia I had spent a happy half-hour chasing agile insects round my bedding. Hassanein entered with breakfast at my most heated moment, when I thought I had cornered the largest. A sweet smile spread over his face. "There are dozens and dozens in my room," he said; "but it doesn't matter. At last I have found a use for my target pistol. Don't ever laugh at me again for useless baggage!" I thought of this as I heard a bed upset on the other side of the partition, but this time it was only a delicious little field mouse scurrying wildly round in search of her hole, which was probably somewhere under our ground-sheet.

A little later I heard the Koran intoned verse by verse and to its monotonous murmur I fell asleep wondering at the desert spell which had changed the Oxford "Blue" into a typical Beduin, devout as the fanatic whose prayers rose five times a day to Allah, aloof as the nomad whose wistful eyes are ever on a desert horizon, impenetrable as the jerd which muffled him from head to foot.

December 7 provided us with a "gibli," a strong south wind laden with sand, which nearly tore up our tent pegs and covered everything with a thick yellow coating. It was a most unpleasant day. Hair, eyes and skin were full of sand. Everything we ate was flavoured with it. The dust sheet was three inches deep in it. It oozed from the pillows and from every article of clothing. It penetrated every box and bag. The noise of flapping canvas and cracking pegs was a continual strain, and in the middle of it arrived a messenger from Jedabia, bearing a letter from Benghazi which our opponents had sent on with an amused message written on the back:

"Nous vous envoyons notre sincère admiration pour l'aptitude que vous avez pour des décisions très rapides, avec nos meilleurs souhaits d'un bon et très long voyage désertique!"

I think the French emanated from the cavalry officer with a sense of humour. From the beginning he may have suspected our whole project, but, a noted fencer, he was as clever with words as with the foils. However, we knew that a messenger who confessed that he had been told to follow us even unto Jalo would not be sent merely to bring us an unimportant letter. He was intended to find out our destination for certain, so we thought he had better wait with us until the caravan arrived or until we ourselves left for Jalo. Farraj amused us immensely, for, having got it into his head that the man was a spy, he wanted to shoot him at once. It took a good deal of persuasion on our part to prevent this bloodthirsty deed. "The Sayed told me to protect you. If I do not kill this man, the Sayed will surely kill me," he said morosely. We comforted him by telling him to watch that the man did not escape, but not to hurt him, yet when Hassanein was asleep that afternoon, and I heard the click of a rifle lock, I rushed frantically to see that the man was safe. He, too, had come without any food. The improvidence of the race had begun to anger me. Should manna fall from heaven, I believe they would eat their fill and pick up none for the morrow!

We broke the news to the retinue that we should have to leave the blacks at the nuggas to wait for the caravan and to hurry it up when it finally arrived, and ourselves go on to Aujela by forced marches. We told them we would start early and ride ten or eleven hours a day, pitch no tent to save labour, share our food evenly with them, but that they must expect to be very hungry for four or five days. There was a good deal of protest, because they looked with simple faith to the caravan and they could not realise that if we waited four days and it had not arrived, starvation would drive us back to Jedabia. The form of protest showed, however, how well things were going. They now looked upon us as their friends. The arrival of the spy had made a bond between us. "We knew that you were hurt by the coming of that man," they said, "but you are safe with us. It is our honour, too." We tried to explain the difficulty about food, and Mohammed suddenly showed the fine clay he was made of. "I have felt ashamed," he said, "that we have taken your food for three days, that we have asked you for sugar when you have none. I would have liked to share my food with you, as is our habit, but we were ordered to come with you at the last moment. We asked if we might visit our homes. 'No,' we were told. 'The caravan will follow with all things needful.' It is not our fault, but we feel it deeply that you are depriving yourselves for us."

This is the loyal spirit that lies at the heart of every Beduin. Greedy for food he may be and the stranger with gold is not safe with him, but once you are his friend he will never betray you. These men were beginning to realise our sympathy for their race, our love for their customs and country. They had eaten our bread and salt. We had shared all we had with them and we had taken them wholly into our confidence. We were guests of their lord, the holy one, the blessed of Allah. We were friends of their blood and religion. The Italians should not get us back. They swore to protect us as their own families. We had won another fight. "We will find food somehow in the nuggas!" said Yusuf. "No Arab

starves in the desert." We showed them a simple letter
of greeting from Sidi Idris. They almost prostrated
themselves to kiss the sacred writing. This was the same
ungrudging loyalty that we had witnessed among the
humble Auwaghir whose tents we had visited between
Soluk and Ghemines. Their lives belonged to the
Sayed. Therefore they were at our disposal. Their
courage and faith were undaunted because they were the
essence of simplicity.

Surely the glories of a race which can give its all so
ungrudgingly cannot be entirely in the past. The great
history of Omar, of Ibn Nebu Musa, of Harun-er-Rashid
and Saladin may yet be repeated. There are leaders who
understand the heart of their people, but perchance they
only know that they have power, without knowing how
they can use it. It has ever been the policy of European
nations to break up the Arab races, to create discord
among their princes, to induce their chiefs to oppose one
another. Is it not a short-sighted policy in view of the
widespread unrest in Europe to-day? Our Western
empires and kingdoms are large enough. Concentration
and not expansion should be our programme. In the
days of Mohammed Ben Ali a caravan under his protection could pass safely from Tripoli to Wadai. All the
great caravan routes were open for commerce and trade.
How many are open to-day? Strengthen the hand of
the native ruler with all the prestige of European support
and he will be responsible for the opening up of his
country for the safe conduct of travellers, for the friendly
intercourse that will allow grain and hides, dates and tea
to cross the age-old desert routes!

CHAPTER IV

ACROSS THE DESERT WITH SHE-IB

ALL that day we sat inside the tent amidst blinding sand. It was in vain that we shut every curtain and flap. The whirling dust penetrated as if by magic. We abstained from lunch in order to save food, and the only break in the monotony of removing continual layers of sand from faces and note-books was when a peg cracked under the strain and one side of the tent flew up with a scream of flapping canvas, tearing up half a dozen pegs with it. We used to go out half blinded by the force of the gibli and knock them in again and take the opportunity of scanning the distant rise for the prayed-for caravan. Once we counted eighteen camels coming over the brow, and hope rose high; but, alas! they were only grazing.

"Allah will send the solution to the problem," said Mohammed simply, and he was right, for, towards evening, when the wind had dropped considerably and we had gone down to the wadi to buy camel's milk, which I loved, but which Hassanein found too bitter, a small caravan of eight camels laden with luggage for Jalo, accompanied by half a dozen Mojabras returning to their homes after a shopping expedition in Jedabia, came down the rise. The situation changed at once. These men brought much news from the "belad" (village) we had left four days before. They knew all about our caravan. "Inshallah! It will arrive in a day or two. When we left, the men were buying their

NOMAD TENTS NEAR JEDABIA

OUR SOLDIER SLAVES AND THE GUIDE ABDULLAH

WELL AT JEDABIA

NOMAD ENCAMPMENTS ROUND JEDABIA

sugar and their jerds. But how is it you have come so far? Your people expect you to be waiting just outside Jedabia. They said to us, 'If you meet them, treat them well for our sakes, and the honour that you do them will be as if you had done it to us.'" We told them about the spy. "He is one of our tribe," they said sadly. "It is a shame that he has set one foot outside the belad on this errand. When we return to Jedabia we will surely spit upon him. Send him to us now that we may take him on to Jalo with us!" We thought, however, that the man would probably be safer with us!

It is a desert custom that when a caravan arrives at nightfall to find another encamped before it, the first arrivals give dinner to the late-comers. We were unable to do this because we had no food, so we could send only apologies and greetings. Just as we had finished our meagre supper of corned beef and rice, a messenger arrived from the hospitable Mojabras bearing two immense basins of barley grain cooked with native butter and pepper, with great cakes of hard sugar and actually a teapot. The joy with which we ate the savoury mess can hardly be described, and our retinue made relays of strong, bitter tea half-way into the night. There was much visiting between the encampment and a chorus of "Keif halak?" (How are you?) and "Taiyib" (Well) sounded constantly.

If two caravans meet coming from Jalo and Jedabia respectively, the former exchanges dates for the latter's tea and sugar. If any traveller reaches a camp at night he is freely given food and tea and a rug by the brushwood fire. Desert hospitality is amazing. Food and drink are always offered. We were never allowed to buy camel's milk. It was always given, for were we not nomads like the desert men themselves? One never

passes a fire with two or three white-robed figures clustered round it without being asked to sit down with
them by the one expressive word "Fadhl!" It is
customary to say "Keif halak?" at least half a dozen
times to each individual, though the reply is always the
same, "Taiyib."

That night, as we all sat round a fire with a cold
wind freezing our backs, yet feeling happily satiated
after our barley meal, the retinue became rhetorical in
its expressions of fidelity. The caravan had told them
that a motor had arrived from Zuetina the day after our
flight, and the town had instantly jumped to the conclusion that it was to take us back forcibly. We were
assured that the whole sympathy of Jedabia was with
us, that our opponents were very angry at our escape,
but could do nothing because they themselves had recom-
mended us to the Sayed. I very much doubted this latter
statement and we determined to move on the following
afternoon if the caravan did not arrive in the morning.
We thought that we could get sufficient food for our men
from the Mojabras and repay them at Jalo if they would
not take money. I felt sorry for the spy. He evidently
wished he had not meddled in the affair at all. Farraj
astonished us by suddenly rising to his feet and, with
hands held to heaven, calling Allah to witness that he
would protect us to the last drop of his blood. "Not even
a thorn shall enter your sides," he chanted solemnly, and
there was an awed hush after so mighty an oath.

Naturally our spy escaped in the night. Our retinue
were as unpractical as they were lazy. Therefore, when
December 12 dawned, they were extremely averse to
any talk of starting. We explained to them with infinite
patience that in twenty-four hours our whereabouts, our
plans, our intentions, our very thoughts would be known
in Jedabia. With the faith of children they said,

"The caravan will come to-day." The ever-kindly
Mojabras had sent over two more vast bowls of a floury
paste, somewhat like macaroni, cooked in the same rancid
butter, so, thoroughly gorged, the retinue were prepared
to await placidly the will of Allah! We had packed up
and hauled everything out of the tent by 7 A.M. At
11 there were still incessant councils round one or other
of the fires. The Mojabras were determined to come
with us. "You are the guests of Sidi Idris," they said.
Once more the holy letter was produced and kissed. We
had become used now to its magical effect. Apparently
it would produce anything but haste! The strangers
acknowledged, however, that they had not enough food
for all our men, meaning, of course, that they could not
hope to supply large quantities three times a day. We
could not hope to make them ration it out in small
portions, so we wanted to leave at least one of the blacks
to await the caravan and either hurry its progress or
send on a swift camel with provisions. There was instant
mutiny at the suggestion. The two Farraj refused to
leave us. "We have no authority over them," said Mohammed without surprise. "Their commandant would
whip them, but what can we do?"

Further discussion seemed useless, so we went down
to the wadi to buy dates from a caravan that had come
from Kufara. It was an amusing instance of how news
is carried in the Sahara. Before the question of dates
was raised at all we squatted solemnly in the sand
opposite the merchants from the far-off oasis, and
Mohammed submitted to a perfect inquisition on the state
of affairs in Jedabia. Afterwards he propounded his
list of questions—what was the price of silk, of wool, of
grain, etc., in Kufara? What was the price of dates?
"So much per ruba or so much per oka?" they quoted,
and for dates, "There is no price. They are plentiful."

"Who did you meet on the way?"   "What news of
such and such a family?"   "One of their slaves has
run away," or "he has married another wife," and so
on until all information was exhausted.

We actually left our low ridge above the wadi at
1.30, but we had ceased to worry.   The fatalism of the
East had begun to grip us.   We decided to put our
trust in Allah and join the caravan of She-ib and his
kinsman, Musa She-ib, merchants from Jalo who had
sometimes travelled to Wadai, a route that takes anything
from forty-five to sixty days, with bales of cotton stuffs,
to return with ostrich feathers, ivory, camels and hides
for the markets of Kufara.   We asked them how long it
would take to reach Jalo, and they replied, "There is
no time.   If you walk quickly you may arrive the fifth
day," but evidently they had no intention of hurrying
themselves.   They were a delightful party of six men,
with eight heavily laden camels and one or two foals
clumsily trotting alongside.

We made quite an imposing caravan as we struck the
track a little to the east and the camels began to march
together.   It was headed by old She-ib, sitting upright
on the top of great green boxes of merchandise, a rifle
on his back, a huge revolver slung beside him in a scarlet
holster, his ebony face half-covered, against the dust, in
the folds of his white kufiya.   Hassanein's brilliant kufiya
—orange, yellow and emerald—made a gorgeous flash of
colour on another camel and I followed, huddled under
the shrouding barracan, for I must not show my face to
the strange caravan.   Thus fate played a new card and
decided that we should wander slowly south with the
Mojabra merchants and learn yet another phase of
Beduin life.

Time forgetting and by time forgot, indifferent to
the caravan of stores that might or might not be follow-

ing, we drifted incredibly slowly along the vague track
marked by occasional cairns of stones. The aspect of
the country had slightly changed since we left the wadi.
It became undulating, with a series of slight waves
running from east to west, while the vegetation grew
scantier and scantier, till finally only a few tufts of coarse
grey bush a few inches high broke the wilderness of sand.
At 3 p.m. the undulating country lay behind us, and we
were on an absolutely flat plain. Two specks appeared
in the distance to materialise into a couple of travellers
on camels. They paused to ask our news and on hearing we were bound for Kufara they entrusted Yusuf with
a few mejidies to be paid to somebody at our destination.
If he did not get there himself, he was to hand the
money on to another traveller. This transaction was
evidently a usual one and roused no comment.

She-ib decided to camp shortly after 3, for he
observed a patch of slightly thicker grazing away to the
right of the track. Ten minutes after the last camel
had been barraked his men had made a wonderful
semicircular zariba of the boxes and sacks, with its
back to the wind, had spread rugs and blankets to form
a most comfortable shelter, and were busy making strong
Arab tea. It was done with infinite swiftness and deft-
ness, while we were still struggling with the tent in a
violent north wind. The previous day the gibli had
blown with a fairly high temperature at midday. This
morning the wind had been in the east, swinging round
to the north in the afternoon, yet the temperature at noon
had been nearly as high as on the previous day. Desert
weather seems to be quite illogical. The ground was so
hard that we could not drive in our tent pegs, so we
half buried the camel saddles in stones and tied the ropes
to them. Then we were called to try our skill at a shooting match with the Mojabras, who had set up a piece

of wood at fifty yards. My neat revolvers caused interest
and amusement when produced from under my huge
hezaam, but they were scarcely appropriate. Mohammed
won the match and was loudly cheered. We had begun
to feel some affection for this tall, lean, hard-featured
Beduin with his falcon's eyes and rare smile. We felt
that he might prove a loyal ally, whereas the plump
Yusuf, with his round face and sleepy, narrow eyes, loose
lips and glib tongue, only thought of getting home as
soon as possible.

Luckily for us the flight from Jedabia had been
interpreted to mean a political mission, and almost before
we were out of sight of the town the desert wireless
proclaimed that we travelled on the business of Sidi Idris.
After the first day it was painfully obvious to us that
only some extraordinary intervention of fate would
induce any one of our escort to brave the dangers of the
route from Jedabia to Kufara, so we encouraged the
belief in our mission by all means in our power. The
Arab dearly loves a secret. Mystery is the breath of
his nostrils. Our escape at midnight, the orders given
to Yusuf and Mohammed at the last moment, our
frantic desire for speed, the spy who brought a letter
from Jedabia in twenty-four hours, the large caravan
munificently fitted out by the lavish generosity of Sayed
Rida, all spoke to him of an important secret, to be
guarded with their lives and ours. We had ceased to
be the Sayed's travelling guests whose mad whim to visit
the sacred city should be discouraged at all costs. We
were rapidly becoming mysterious messengers bearing
sacred orders from their lord! Soon we should all
grumble together at the task that drove us forth in
winter on such a journey, but we should be suffering
for the work of Sidi Idris es-Senussi, and therefore for
the will of Allah!

December 13 we rose at 7.30 under the impression
that She-ib's caravan would take advantage of the cool
morning to travel, but three hours later we were still
drinking tea inside the comfortable semicircle of the
merchant's zariba. Beduin hospitality is always generous,
but these people overwhelmed us with kindness. That
morning they sent us a basket of nuts, followed by glasses
of bitter tea. Hassanein went across to their encampment to thank them and they insisted on his staying.
I joined them later, and the best red blanket was spread
for me beside She-ib. It is an erroneous impression in
Europe that the veiled women of the East are ill-treated
and over-worked. The Koran devotes half the third sura
to man's behaviour towards women. Ask the Syrian
woman if she would lose her veil, and she will reply,
"Not till the men are better educated," but the Beduin
woman only hides her face before strange men. With
her own tribe she mingles freely, and the work is evenly
shared. Often with the caravan I tried to hold a tent
pole or knock in a peg and I was promptly told, "This
is man's work. Do not tire yourself, Sitt Khadija."
Many times when old She-ib saw me resting at midday
he would say, "The Sitt Khadija is weary. Let us wait
a little longer." On the other hand, the Moslem woman
is expected to do all the work within the tent. She
should cook her menfolk's meal and wash the dishes
afterwards. Luckily, by this time our food was so reduced
that I lost no prestige by my inability to cook more than
damper bread, heavy and unleavened.

Tea-drinking is a ceremony which may last anything
from one hour to three. If one wishes to travel fast it
can only be allowed at night, but the Mojabras had no
desire to hurry, so we lingered over the glasses while
their two servants and our blacks cooked relays of tea
on hot ashes. They fill half the tea-pot with sugar,

another quarter with tea, and then pour the water on top. They taste the sweet, strong beverage half a dozen times, pouring it from one tea-pot to another, adding water or re-boiling it till it suits them. Then it is drunk with as much noise as possible to show appreciation. When the host thinks it is time to finish the party, he adds mint to the tea-pot, and the guests take the last sweet-scented cup as a sign of departure. Meanwhile they have exchanged every form of gossip and told long, rambling tales with a flavour of the Arabian Nights. Their courtesy to one another is amazing, and it is an honest courtesy that expresses itself in deeds as well as words. While Yusuf and Mohammed rarely addressed each other without the respectful prefix of "Sidi" (my lord), they also warmly urged each other to ride the only available camel at midday heat. Once Mohammed was riding it, and he noticed Musa She-ib looked tired. "We share alike," he said. "What is ours is yours," and scrambling down he insisted on the Mojabra mounting.

It was a very friendly caravan that crawled south by short stages. Our only troubles really were Yusuf's laziness and the grumblings of the blacks, who shirked even the lightest work. On the 13th we started at 9.30 and camped at 3.30, while the sun was yet hot, for we happened to have arrived at a patch of coarse, odourless grass for the camels. At noon the men had slipped away from the caravan one by one to prostrate themselves with a murmured, "Bismillah arahman arahim." Generally two of them marched a couple of hundred yards ahead with their rifles ready, but we saw nothing more exciting than a few distant gazelle. As soon as we had unloaded the camels we all said our evening prayers, the "Fagr" or fourth of the series. It still gave me much pain getting in and out of my yellow shoe, but the fanaticism of the Senussi was a very strong spur to the observance of every Moslem duty.

She-ib and his relations always insisted on helping us to put up the tent. There used to be a regular little fight as to who should hammer in the pegs, much to the delight of the lazy blacks. I remember that night was the most perfect we had yet spent in the desert, windless and calm, with a crescent moon and the strange translucent blue that you sometimes get in the Sahara. Mournful, monotonous chants came from the friendly encampment beside us and the wide, white desert, unbroken by ridge or dune, spread all round us.

We had mounted slowly and imperceptibly from the Wadi Farig (empty valley) to a low tableland with occasional ripples running east and west and a few scattered sandhills with square tops. Just before we reached Bir Rassam, the following day, the ripples became accentuated into ridges and the country looked almost volcanic, for a series of high, square hillocks appeared on our right with some sort of rock formation on top.

We could easily have reached the wells on the evening of the 13th, but our friends had their own settled ideas about camping and nothing would change them. They wanted to spend the heat of the day at Rassam and water at their leisure, so we were wakened at 5 A.M. on the 14th, and were actually away by 6.15. It was a glorious morning, but, as usual, chilly. Hassanein walked with old She-ib, who promptly quoted the Arab proverb, "A man should not sleep on silk till he has walked on sand," but I rolled myself in every available blanket on the back of my jealous camel, who divided his time between biting the rival males and amorous assaults on the females!

Besides being cold, one had begun to feel extremely

have with you. What more do you want?" said She-ib.
"Even now you are wearing the Sitt's coat." Our
retinue had complained bitterly of cold one night at
Wadi Farig, so we had lent them two fleece-lined
waterproofs which we had hidden in our bedding and
they wore them day and night, even in the fierce
noon sun!

We departed leisurely at 3.30 P.M. and trekked
through blinding, white sand, soft and deep, till 8.30
P.M., but the last hour we went very slow, as the
grey brush appeared again and the camels grazed as they
walked. We passed a herd grazing and She-ib went to
greet the owners, encamped in a zariba of piled luggage,
and to drink strong tea. We camped under some huge
grey bushes with a wonderfully sweet scent and ate the
rest of Mighrib's black damper, with camel's milk and a
half-ration of meat, while another marvellous sunset
painted feathers of flame and rose below the silver sickle
moon.

We used to shut the tent flaps after our evening meal
to write our diaries and make our simple route maps,
for if we pulled out note-books and pencil in the daytime
it caused great suspicion. We had made plans in
England, while lunching in the oriental splendour of
Claridge's, to do a little survey work in Libya, but we
had not counted with the fanaticism of the Senussi. It
seems to me now that we were mad to imagine that a
Christian could show his or her face beyond Jedabia,
in a land where it is every man's sacred duty to kill the
Nasrani. True, the mental atmosphere had changed since
the first day out, when, if we carelessly asked the name
of any tribe or district, we were looked upon as spies.
At our first camp I told one of the blacks to fetch me a
camel, whereupon he turned to his fellow-soldier exclaiming, "Are we to be ordered about by a cursed Christian

woman? One bullet and we will send her back to her Christian country!"

After that their attitude had changed. "The ways of Allah are strange," they said, "for she is in truth a Moslem." Still, the general friendliness did not extend to instruments or diaries. "Why do you need a compass?" asked Yusuf. "We know the road as we know our own hearts." We took the hint and hid our compasses under the voluminous folds of our native dress, studying them only in secret. The barometer amused them because it showed what the weather was like, so the actual retinue did not mind its occasional presence outside our tent, but it had to be concealed from all visitors. A theodolite would have been an absolute impossibility. Anything that suggested map-making was abhorrent to our guides. "We carry the road in our heads," they said. I dared not even write an ordinary diary in public unless I could pretend it was a letter!

Gradually we drew them on to talk about routes and places with rather less suspicion, but for a long time it was a dangerous subject and, even when we had more or less won their confidence, we had to treat their replies concerning names and positions exceedingly casually. To have made an instant note of a name would have roused sharp suspicion. Before we could get real information from them we had to destroy their original idea that we were travelling for our own pleasure and laboriously build up, word by word, deed by deed, a wholly new situation—that we had been sent, much against our will, by Sayed Idris on a mission so secret and important that it justified our midnight flight and the hardships of an almost intolerable journey.

December 15 saw us on our way by 7.30 A.M. after a troubled packing in the teeth of a sharp gale. The

camels ran round in circles and upset their loads and a
little of our precious water dribbled out of the fanatis.
Bir Rassam is the last good well on the way to Aujela.
Three long waterless days lay before us and the blacks
were horribly careless. We ourselves used only a quart
of water each per day. Since we left Wadi Farig our
daily ablution consisted merely of washing hands and face
every evening in an inch of muddy water! After a week
one got used to never washing, and by the time we
reached Aujela we had forgotten even to feel dirty! It
became a competition who could use least water and so
prepare for the deadly Kufara route with its one well in
twelve hard days.

December 15 provided us with few incidents. We
did a dreary seven hours' riding with a cold south wind
blowing straight in our faces. We wrapped our jerds
and blankets round us and tried to pretend we were not
hungry after a lunch of five malted milk tablets. We
passed a camp of Mojabras who were resting for an hour
at midday while their camels grazed and, as I hid my
face in my barracan and urged on my camel, Hassanein
went with She-ib and Mohammed to greet them. When
he rejoined me twenty minutes later I asked him with
primitive fierceness, "Did they give you tea?" before
I realised to what ridiculous depths hunger drives one!
He looked at me with wan blankness. "No luck," he
said grimly; "but they asked us to wait for them at
sunset."

The one cheerful moment was when, about 2 P.M., I
produced a thermos flask and offered each of She-ib's
caravan a mouthful of hot tea. "There is no fire," said
the old man. "We cannot stop to make one." It was
Hassanein's greatest triumph. I had fought against
bringing that huge flash. It was bulky, heavy and, of
course, it had no case or strap. It was his pet possession,

however, and though I firmly discarded it half a dozen
times, it always reappeared. Now Musa She-ib drank
from it, amazed. "But where is the fire?" he asked;
and, lest we should be shot as magicians, we instantly
entered into intricate explanations as to the making of
a thermos.

We met but one traveller on that cold, dusty day.
"Now for our newspaper," said Hassanein. "It is
rather a late edition." But the man was devoid of news
save that a caravan might possibly be starting from
Jalo for Wadai within a week or two. As for our own
caravan, the Mojabras, who proposed to join us that
night, had made a quick journey from Jedabia, leaving
on the morning of the 12th, three days after She-ib.
They told us our men were still buying "necessities," but
proposed to start next day. From that moment I think
we mutually decided against putting any faith in their
arrival. The behaviour of the two blacks had made us
realise the danger of being at the mercy of a dozen such
creatures for thirteen days, beyond reach of any human
aid. If the water ran short they would certainly steal
ours. In order to be able to over-eat they would probably
overload the camels. They would refuse to start early
or ride hard. Consequently the perils of the waterless
seven days, after which time the camels begin to get
tired, would become insuperable. We began planning
to leave Jalo before them, taking only Mohammed and
Yusuf and a couple of reliable guides.

The last hour of the day's march is generally the
most cheerful, for everybody is in a hurry to reach camp,
and it is a curious fact that camels walk more quickly
and straighter to the sound of singing. Therefore the
blacks and She-ib's drivers used to chant wild melodies
of love and prowess till even my great blond beast forgot
his amorous gurglings and kept his nose in a bee-line for

the horizon. That particular day we had ridden due south across rolling sandy country without much vegetation except where the sudden square hills and mounds appeared on our left at Bir Mareg, some 18 kilometres from Rassam. The well holds only salt, undrinkable water, but around it there is about a mile of rough scrub with large bushes of the scented furze which had perfumed our sleep the preceding night. On the only maps I have seen a green wadi is marked running the whole way from Rassam to Aujela, but it exists only in the imagination of the chart-maker. In reality there is no trace of valley or of verdure.

Across rolling white sand we rode till 3 P.M., under a sandy rock a few hundred yards from a square hill called Arida. We camped by the last patch of rare fuel. The south wind rose in the night and added more sand to ourselves and our surroundings. The tent pegs on one side blew up and we crawled out in murky darkness to knock them in again.

December 16 saw us started by 7.30, for the Farraj had succeeded in upsetting one of the fanatis and old She-ib was wisely frightened about our water supply. Feeling that a certain amount of sympathy now existed between ourselves and our retinue, we tried the passometer for the first time that day. The nervous "naga" ridden by Hassanein objected strongly and, as she always progressed in circles, she was not of much use. My stately beast never altered his step except to bite one of the other animals and after a few furious stamps he submitted to the strap across his knee, but the labour of keeping him absolutely straight for eight hours on end was very trying. However, the instrument measured fairly accurately, and after an eight hours' march it gave us 36 kilometres.

There is no one track from Jedabia to Aujela. The

SAYED RIDA ES SENUSSI

THE AUTHOR IN BEDUIN DRESS

distance as the crow flies is about 220 kilometres. There
is a main route as far as Wadi Farig. Thereafter one
may wander south anywhere on a stretch some ten miles
broad. We travelled on the route which our friends considered provided the best fuel and grass, but it was the
least frequented and, therefore, the most dangerous.
"No one comes by this track without fear of a battle,"
said the delightful Mighrib, and hardly half an hour later
a party of eight men, without camels, six blacks and two
Arabs, appeared from the sand mounds. "Dersalaam!
We are going to be attacked," said She-ib with calm
interest. Any party of men without camels is looked
upon with suspicion in the desert. Thus travel the robber
bands in order to be able to scatter quickly. "Some of
them will come up and talk to us. Their friends will
be hidden behind those mounds. They will fire into the
air to attract our attention and then the people who are
talking to us will attack us. If they kill us they will
take the caravan." The blacks cheered up at once. The
prospect of a fight always stimulated them. Everybody
pulled out a rifle, but evidently the display of force or
the Sudanese intimidated the mysterious party, for they
suddenly sheered off without any salutation and vanished
as suddenly as they had appeared.

It is curious the fear with which the Beduins regard
the black slaves who are sent from the Sudan as boys
of eight or ten and who are trained as soldiers by the
Senussi family. They are more brutes than men. I
have seen sheer murder in the eyes of the toothless
Farraj when I refused him extra sugar, yet they are
courageous and faithful to their masters. A good black
slave like Ali, our beloved cook at Jedabia, is worth his
weight in gold. There was much difference of character
between the Farrajes. One had a square, bestial face with
a few broken yellow teeth. He was a grumbler and

infinitely lazy, shirking all work, stealing everything he
could lay his hands on. The other was big, brutal and
stupid with something of the nature of a kindly bulldog.
He would occasionally return us dates or flour, saying,
"We have enough. Why do you not eat yourselves?"
We thought he might be turned into a good servant
eventually, for he did not mind cooking and washing up.
The point of view of both was that they were soldiers and
not servants. They were prepared to fight, but not to
work. As a matter of fact a caravan guarded by blacks
is rarely attacked, as the Beduins know it will generally
be defended to the last inch.

When first the rumour spread through Jedabia that
a rich woman was travelling into the interior and a guard
of sorts became necessary, Sayed Rida instantly offered
some of his soldier slaves. Not till after we left the little
mud belad on the edge of the world did we grasp all the
threads of the situation we left behind. It had been a
cunning woof of plot and counter-plot from the moment
when the aged ekhwan, Haji Fetater, had vowed on the
"Fatha" to take the Englishwoman safely to the Holy
Oasis, to the night of our desperate flight without other
guard than Mohammed and Yusuf. From the very day
we first spoke tentatively of our journey among the
Ulema of Jedabia, one ekhwan, fanatical and terror-
stricken, had been strongly opposed to it. He successfully dissuaded Haji Fetater from accompanying us.
"You are too old," he said. "You will die on the road.
Where is your dignity? Is this travelling with a Nasrani
to be your last action on earth? Heaven forbid!" As
the ancient man was over eighty we were not sorry to
hear of his change of front.

Another ekhwan was suggested, but as he asked for
forty men to protect us, among whom only ten were to
be blacks, our suspicions were aroused and we refused his

company. We learned afterwards that, believing the bazaar rumour about our wealth, he had planned to kill us in the desert, seize our money and return sorrowfully, saying that a vast force of Tebu spearmen had attacked us, that he had defended us gallantly, but that we and all the blacks had been killed. This because he *knew* that the Sudanese would fulfil the orders given by their master the Sayed and protect us to the last. There is always faint friction between these black warrior slaves and the Arabs. They could never combine. For this reason the crafty ekhwan decided that his force must be large enough to murder the soldiers as well as us. The proportion of Beduin to Sudanese shows his high opinion of the latter's value. Their ruthlessness is encouraged by every means, even by brutal punishment. If a soldier disobeys an order he is flogged or his hand is cut off!

December 16 was enlivened by Mohammed's marriage prospects. One Omar, owner of two or three camels, a one-eyed creature of hideous and ferocious aspect, was travelling with She-ib's caravan. He was reputed to have a very beautiful sister. Mohammed was thrilled. He made discreet inquiries and finally offered to marry the girl on his return journey. Mohammed was a big man in the eyes of the Beduin. He enjoyed the confidence of the Sayed and, moreover, he was tall and straight and clean of limb, a fine lean Arab with pride of race and tradition written all over him. Omar accepted the suitor at once and three camels were agreed upon as the dowry to be paid by the bridegroom to the bride's father. Thereafter everyone made plans for marrying, mostly for the third and fourth time. Hassanein heard there were slaves to be bought at Kufara and he instantly decided to add a beautiful one to his possessions when we reached our far-off goal.

There was one member of the caravan who took no

part in the plans. For five days he had plodded along
with the party, singing and talking cheerfully, doing his
share of the work, and we never guessed that he was
different from the rest till Mohammed, in his excess of
matrimonial enthusiasm, let go the camel he was leading
and called out, "Ya Amma! Imsikhu!" (Thou blind
one! Catch him!) Unfalteringly the sightless boy
caught the beast. It was most extraordinary. Thereafter I watched him carefully. I saw him driving camels
in the right direction. He measured distance much
better than the others. He was more accurate in his
judgment of time. He reminded me of the famous
mediæval Arabian Bashar, the blind poet of Aleppo, who,
arriving in a certain city, was told to bend his head in
one of the streets as a beam was stretched across it from
one house to another. Ten years later he rode into the
same town, and his companions were surprised because
he bowed low in the middle of an empty road. "Is the
beam still here?" he asked.

The Beduins have no idea of distance. "How many
hours is it to Aujela?" one asked. "There are no
hours in the desert," they replied. "We do not know
them." "Are there days in the desert?" "Yes, there
are days. If you walk quickly it is one thing. If you
do not let yourself out, it is another thing." The
difficulty in measuring by day is that, except on the
big caravan routes, each man's estimate of distance varies
according to his energy. The whole life of a Beduin is
reduced to the simplest possible effect. He uses very
few words. The same verb has a dozen meanings. For
instance, "Shil" means anything from "take away,
pick up, carry, put on, throw away, to pack, unpack,
drop, lose," etc. "Akkal" should mean to eat food, but
when two camels fought hideously Mohammed said,
"They are eating each other." Desert Arabs have no

names for plants or flowers that they see each day. I asked about a huge, feathery tree something like a coromandel which first made its appearance at Sawami and I was told, "It has no name. It is for making houses and firewood."

At 3.30 P.M. we were still more than a day's march from Aujela and our water was running out owing to the carelessness of the blacks. Grave colloquy followed. We were relieved to see that even the lazy Yusuf grasped the seriousness of the situation. We had two single-ration tins left and about two pounds of flour and one pound of macaroni. It was decided that we should camp for a couple of hours, in order to rest after our three hours' riding, and then push on by starlight. We gave half the food to our retinue with the last morsels of sugar and made ourselves coffee on a tiny fire in a hole scooped in the ground. Earlier in the day we had collected wood from the last patch of scrub that we passed and loaded it on one of the camels. We hated opening the last tin, but we knew that we must keep the cereals for the men's breakfast next day. We had had nothing to eat all day except a few dates and a small bowl of camel's milk which the adorable She-ib gave me at sunrise. I shall always remember the dear old man's twisted smile. "When you are happy I am happy," he said. "For the honour of the Sayed we would carry you on our heads!" Luckily it was a glorious night. At 5 P.M. we said our sunset prayers and to the usual formalities I added a very passionate supplication that we might reach Aujela on the morrow. I should never have believed it possible for our indolent retinue to have collected so much energy. As the evening star rose red above the horizon the camels were loaded and at 5.30 we set off under a crescent moon in a vivid starry sky. A caravan always marches better at night. The camels cannot see

to graze. It is cold and the men step out briskly, singing
continual wild songs and urging on their beasts by strange
shouts and yells. "Thou beautiful one, walk on!"
"Let yourself out, for soon you will have rest!" "Be
patient, thou strong heart, do not stumble!" or else
a monotonous, repetitive chorus, "Shey latif! Shey
latif!" (A pleasant thing), "Ma salaam!" If one
person fall silent for more than a minute he is urged
by name to let his voice be heard. So in ever-increasing
cold, to the accompaniment of chants and shouts, we
marched for three and a half hours, by which time She-ib
considered it was safe to camp, for we were within a day's
journey of Aujela.

A few sandy mounds broke the surface of the vast
plain. In a white starlight, clear and cold, with the
rising south wind that is the bane of the desert, we laid
our flea-bags on the lee side of the largest hillock and
crept into them without undressing. We tried to put
the flaps over our heads, but the sand, as usual, covered
everything and we ate grit mingled with dates for
breakfast. We meant to start before the dawn, but the
camels had strayed far in search of scarce grass. When
collected, they displayed a fiendish ingenuity in throwing
their loads and tangling themselves up in every possible
strap. The wind was bitterly cold and my barracan was
in its most irritating mood when it wrapped itself round
everything but me! The Farrajes would not walk
because they were cold. The gibli blinded the camels
and they swung round in circles. Even Hassanein was
not feeling energetic on six tablets of malted milk. In
the middle of the frozen muddle I suddenly lost my
temper, saying, "I will show you how to walk." I
dropped from my camel and, throwing my barracan over
my arm, set off with great strides in a southern direction.
The action may have stimulated the caravan into move-

ment, but it certainly undid nearly a week's work. For twenty minutes, as they followed my racing steps, Omar and Mighrib discussed Christians and their ways. "These Feranji women walk well until they get fat and they cannot move," they said. Hassanein changed the conversation two or three times, but it always came back to the difference between the Nasrani and the Moslem.

Old She-ib had walked on and I found him waiting on the top of a slight rise from where the beginning of the longed-for oasis showed a faint blur of green surrounded by a mist of mirage. "There is Bir Msus," he said. "You will have eggs and bread and milk to-night." "I think I want a tailor even more," I said ruefully, regarding my torn white trousers, rent at ankle and knee. "These must be mended." "I think new ones would be better!" said She-ib diffidently. At 10 A.M. we saw the dark line of Msus in the distance, but not till midday did we draw level with it, trekking steadily south over a flat, sandy plain with no sign of wadi. As there is only a well as Msus and no village, we left it to the east and went straight on towards Aujela, which lies at the south-west end of an S-like wadi, whose other extremity is represented by Msus. At 12.30 we breasted a slight swell, and below us lay the wide green wadi full of coarse grey shrub with a mass of palms on the farther side. "Hamdulillah!" exclaimed the devout Mohammed, and slipped off his camel for the noon-day prayers.

CHAPTER V

WE crossed the wadi at 12.30, our faces stinging and burning in the cruel wind. The air was full of sand and the heat was excessive. The body of the long winding oasis is composed merely of palm gardens, each with its separate well or wells, known as Sawani, but the village of Aujela lies in the farthest western curl. In Sawani there are only a few broken-down buildings with crumbling walls, where perhaps a tattered blue tobh shows for an instant beside huge feathery foliaged trees with coarse-grained bark, something between a spruce and a mimosa, but, of course, nameless.

For three hours we plodded south-west along the line of Sawani's palms. An ancient square tower appeared on a sand-hill to our left—the morabit of Sidi Saleh—but we left it behind us before the top of another long swelling rise brought the longed-for Aujela into view. The sun was blurred behind the flying sand, but we gazed eagerly at the mass of palms broken only by the low white dunes which stretched south for nearly a mile. At the farther end lay the clustered mud houses, all heaped together under the shadow of the palms, with here and there a square of small clay cupolas' on the roof of a mosque. It was very different from the isolated houses of Jedabia, widely scattered over a white sandstone plain. Aujela gives a first impression of a ruined town, because of its small roofless mud courts, its irregular doorways and unfinished walls; but it is exceedingly picturesque seen against a red setting sun.

We camped just before four in a hollow beyond the last fence made of plaited palm leaves. We were so hungry that we could hardly wait to put up our tent. Visions of milk and eggs and fresh crisp "hubz" danced before our eyes. We sent the fat Yusuf to inquire. Meanwhile, Omar had departed to his home in the town, to return a little later with a basket of fine dates. It was a resplendent being who found us flat on our camp beds, too tired to care any more about food. We had discovered a small stick of chocolate in a knapsack. Hassanein wanted me to eat the whole of it, but the desert teaches only two laws. The European code of morals disappears altogether. One becomes a simple savage being who may commit most crimes with impunity. In opposition, how- ever, one gradually realises that two or three actions, considered natural and justifiable in London, are unfor- givable sins in the Sahara. The laws all true wanderers obey are these: "Thou shalt not eat nor drink more than thy share," "Thou shalt not lie about the places thou hast visited or the distances thou hast traversed."

Omar had changed his dirty, torn white chemise, with his ragged jerd, for a blue, braided jubba and a new striped jerd. We thanked him earnestly for the dates and listened indifferently to the stern fact that absolutely nothing could be bought in Aujela. Doubtless, as we were the Sayed's guests, he said, the important people of the town would send us gifts of food on the morrow, but for the moment, short of begging, nothing could be done. It was beneath our dignity as important Egyptians travelling on the Sayed's business to explain the state of our commissariat, so we made up our minds to a supper of milk tablets and dates. At the last moment, however, one of our guardian angels, Musa

She-ib, appeared smiling, with his scarlet mandil full of fresh eggs! Our joy was unspeakable. I don't know how many we ate. I remember kneeling in the sand for ages under a calm, starlit sky, half blinded by the smoke of a brushwood fire, poaching those blessed eggs one by one. "I like your particular sauce," said Hassanein. "I shall miss the taste of sand in Cairo!"

We managed to wash a little afterwards, the joy of which was diluted by the fact that we were suffering from a violent rash all over us. We politely called it heat, but I think it was dirt! Just as we had finished our eggs, Mohammed came with excitement to tell us that the sheikh of the zawia, Abdul Kasim, with the ekhwan and the important people of the belad, were coming to visit us, as they had heard we had letters from Sayed Rida. We had no clothes to wear. We could not even offer them the usual sweet tea. She-ib came to the rescue, as usual, and it was agreed that the meeting should take place in his tent. Hassanein was hurriedly rigged up in my beautiful silk jerd, with an hereditary brocaded white kufiya which he had brought from Egypt on his head, the gorgeous one the generous Sayed had given me wound gracefully round his neck. The meeting was most impressive. The dignified sheikhs sat round the narrow tent on dyed camel's-hair rugs, their rifles stacked against the centre pole. With the utmost solemnity the letters of Sayed Idris and Sayed Rida were read. With one voice the ekhwan murmured: "The orders of the Sayed are upon our heads."

Then details were discussed. The matter of distance was again very difficult. "As far as a man may go on one girba," is a favourite expression. A "girba" is a dried goat-skin used for carrying water. It holds from four to seven gallons. The Beduins say a man may travel on a small one for five or six days in winter and for

three in summer. After much argument we were told
that it was actually thirteen days from Jalo to Kufara
by the direct caravan route which goes on to Wadai.
There are two wells, one at Buttafal, a day's march from
Jalo, and another at Zieghen, seven days farther on.
This well, which stands alone in the desert, is wrongly
marked as an oasis, Sirhen, on the map. There is
another so-called route from Jalo to Kufara, that chosen
by Rohlfs. It runs in a more westerly direction to the
oasis of Taiserbo, erroneously supposed to be one of the
Kufara group. This oasis contains several villages, the
biggest being Kseba, Mabus, el Kasr and el Wadi,
inhabited by Zouias and Tebus, the latter being the
original dwellers in Kufara, from which they have been
gradually driven by the conquering Senussi. Beyond
Taiserbo there are various savage tribal bands, who
delight in sacking caravans and murdering their escorts.
They are sworn foes to the merchant and Zieghen is,
occasionally, a dangerous halting place, because the Tebus
sweep east from their Ribiana stronghold, or the lawless
Zouias from Buseima fall upon the caravan and have
vanished into the desert before the news has reached
Kufara. From Taiserbo a six or seven days' route runs
via Buseima to Kufara, but, besides the fear of attack,
it is dangerous owing to sand dunes.

It is also possible to go direct from Jalo to Buseima,
a route unmarked on our map. One passes through the
"hatia" between Zieghen and Taiserbo, in the bed of
which there is water, and sees the dark strange mountain
two days before one reaches the oasis in its shadow.
Buseima always appealed to me fatally because of its
lovely black mountain and its lake! A lake in a Libyan
desert! Surely that is sufficient to make up for any
number of robbers! I tried hard to persuade Abdullah
to ignore Taiserbo, apparently much akin to any other

flat desert oasis, and go straight to the country of dark
mountains, but about this he was adamant. He would
not risk this dangerous route and so we each *privately*
made up our minds to outwit the other. He would take
me to Taiserbo with the secret intention of then going
to Zieghen and by the main caravan route to Kufara. I
agreed to the Taiserbo route, but with the equally firm
determination of continuing to our goal by way of
Buseima.

Two other possible ways to the sacred city were
mentioned. One due south from Jaghabub, and one
west from Farafra in Egypt, but both necessitated twelve
or thirteen days without water. Nobody seemed to know
much about the latter, but the casualties on the former
had been appalling. The last Arab who attempted it
had died on the way because his water went bad. Sayed
Ahmed, traversing it with an army, had been forced to
leave his luggage, stores and horses behind. Another
party had lost their way and, after half their number
had died, the remainder arrived at Siwa by mistake.
"The guides lost their heads," said Abdul Kasim.
"One mistake is sufficient and you must die!" We
were very anxious to return by this route, but they all
dissuaded us. "Return to Jalo," they said. "It is only
seven days from there to Jaghabub, but it is all without
water. The wells were closed in the War."

We asked more definitely about the position of
Kufara. Five days from Zieghen and seven from Taiserbo, the oasis generally called Kebabo is really Kufara.
It is not one of a group. It lies entirely alone, and it
contains five villages.

All this was told by grey-bearded sheikhs by the
light of two guttering candles in She-ib's humble tent.
The atmosphere was very friendly. They sympathised
and wanted to help. "Only good can come out of your

journey," they said. "You have the Sayed's blessing.
Therefore, your coming is an honour to us. Stay with
us a day and let us see you again." The air was full of
warm enthusiasm and we felt we were among friends.

In the morning, of course, it had all changed. It
is difficult in Europe to understand the mentality of these
children of nature. They are simple and emotional.
Such a little way below their impulsive kindness and
generosity lies the almost maniacal fanaticism of their
tradition. We were playing a difficult part and the
threads were apt to get complicated. We had to pretend
to be poor for fear of attack by robber bands, yet we
had to be able to bribe when necessary. I had to be a
Moslem woman, yet I had to talk to ekhwan and sheikhs.
We had to be important Egyptians to be worth protect-
ing, yet we had no clothes or stores. We were travelling
on a secret mission for the Sayed, yet we wanted to go
to places where there could be no chance of work. It
was no wonder that suspicion constantly followed us.
Tales of a Christian woman and her secretary came from
Jedabia. It was possible that they would cling to us
all the way.

Apparently a morose Beduin had come to She-ib's
tent the previous night and protested violently against
the arrival of these strangers from Egypt. "They are
not of us," he said. "We must put them through the
usual searching questions. Then we shall know who they
are and what is their business." "They have letters
from the Sayed. Is that not enough for you?" said our
friend. "They must learn that it is difficult to travel
in this country," insisted the Beduin. "No strangers
may come here." Apparently one of the important
people of the town was of like opinion, for next day the
ekhwan were divided into two camps. One party was
for literally obeying the gracious letter of Sayed Rida

and giving a feast in our honour.   The other, led by an
unruly Arab, head of a section of the Zouia tribe, who
always made a habit of opposing the Sayed's wishes,
wanted to ignore us.   The result was a compromise.
They showed us no hospitality, but they met in the zawia
in the afternoon and received us with friendliness.   They
signed their names to a curious document stating that,
in accordance with the Sayed's order, they had hospitably
received Hassanein Bey and the Sitt Khadija, and I think
they were ashamed as they did so, for one, Ahmed
Effendi, who came from Jalo to collect the Government
taxes, said boldly, "I will sign that when I meet you
in my town in a few days."   We learned afterwards that
he had made a loyal speech in the morning, saying that
they must all do honour to the Sayed's guests, and the
formal reception in the zawia was probably due to him.

There are between thirty and forty ekhwan in
Aujela.   The sheikh of the zawia is Abdul Kasim.   The
zawia stands on a low rise in the centre of the town.
It is a square mud building with heavily barred windows,
looking more like a fortress than a college.   Below are
gardens of bisset and onions with a few pumpkins.
Barley is grown under the belad's broken walls, and in
broad shallow depressions one sees rows of sand bricks
baking in the sun.   In the morning we wandered through
the town, followed by a crowd of amazed children who
had probably never seen a stranger before.   Women
peeped at us from low doorways.   They were muffled
in folds of long indigo tobhs which were delightful in
the brilliant sunshine.   Occasionally one made a vivid
splash of colour in orange or scarlet.   They wore gold
ear-rings and all had tattoo marks on forehead and chin.
Most of the people of Aujela speak a dialect similar to
that of the Tuaregs and of some of the Siwa people, but
it is not understood in Jalo.

We went through the narrow winding paths bordered by high mud walls, with here and there a palm drooping over a grey feathery bush, till we came to the biggest mosque, with its square roof covered with clay cupolas. Here we met some of the ekhwan, who greeted us kindly and took us to the zawia to see the qubba of Abdullahi Sahabi, the supposed clerk of Mohammed, who is buried there. By a narrow passage one passes into a square sandy court, with a narrow roof running along three sides, under which the ekhwan sit on mats. A door leads into a further smaller court, and from there one passes through a carpeted antechamber into the mosque. The tomb stands in the centre, covered with gaudy cotton stuff, and the walls are hung with cheap mirrors and ostrich eggs, the latter the gift of pilgrims from Wadai. We walked round the tomb, chanting the Koran, after which we kissed it and solemnly repeated the "Fatha." The ekhwan spend whole days reading and studying the Koran round this tomb.

We asked them about Rohlfs' caravan, but they knew nothing except that Mannismann had been there before he started on his doomed journey west, having already signed his death-warrant by writing that he did so at his own risk. They told us the zawia had been founded by Mohammed el Mahdi in 1872. Near by is the old Turkish Kasr, residence of the Ottoman "kaimakaan," now used as an office by the clerks of the Senussi Government.

We had just finished a mighty lunch suddenly provided by the generous Omar, masses of hot flat "hubz," eggs and a chicken cooked in a bowl of savoury juice and red pepper, and were trying to cool our smarting mouths and watering eyes after burning "fil-fil," when the great event of many days happened simply and unexpectedly. We had searched the far horizon for so many weary hours. We had magnified so many grazing herds into our longed-for caravan that when Yusuf, standing on the rise above us, said, "There is a caravan coming," we took no notice. We had eaten our first good meal for eleven days. Our souls were full of gratitude to Omar and our only worry was how we could reward him for his generosity. (In parenthesis it may be said that the only thing he coveted was some imaginary scent he had smelled on me. We traced it eventually to some Coti face powder which I was carefully treasuring against my arrival in Cairo and he departed happily with a quarter of the box.) When, however, Yusuf raced down the hill screaming, "Our caravan, Hamdulillah! Our caravan at last!" lethargy departed and we all rushed up the rise with more speed than dignity.

It was quite true. Twelve camels and a dozen men were within a hundred yards of us. First came a stately figure in white burnus, Abdullah, a famous guide, who knew all the Libyan routes, of whom the Beduins said, "He has a great heart," and next the neat, brisk little commandant, with his thin, humorous face and quiet, dry manner, the ebony Abdul Rahim. He was followed by a sergeant, Moraja, whose home was in Kufara, and six men. Somewhere in the background lurked a cook, but we did not see him that evening, for he was immediately sent to prepare a banquet for our friends the She-ibs. After the first rush of joy, in which everyone shook everyone else's hand a score of times, and "Mabsut" and "Taiyib" and "Hamdulillah!" filled the air, we watched the barraking of the camels with blank amazement. Used to the indolence of the two Farrajes, we could hardly believe our eyes when, literally in five minutes, under the shrewd eyes of Abdul Rahim, the camels were freed, the luggage and rifles stacked, and the men rapidly putting up the tents. We could only rub our eyes and gasp, while my eyes wandered

UNLOADING ON THE SECOND DAY FROM JEDABIA

WADI FARIG: CAMELS AT THE WELL

A HALT FOR THE NIGHT

CAMP OF MOJABRA MERCHANTS AT BIR RASSAM

over the baggage in search of the sacks which had been mysteriously taken from our Jedabia dwelling at dead of night. I recognised them one by one and peace visited my soul, even though, when I looked down, I saw the striped legs of my pyjama trousers appearing beneath my red tobh, for the ill-used cotton pantaloons had given way altogether the previous evening.

We asked for news of Jedabia. "They say in the suq that you escaped in an aeroplane sent by Allah," said Abdullah gravely, but Abdul Rahim smiled his wise little smile. "They asked me where I was going with my big caravan," he said, "and I told them I was travelling to punish some Beduins who had not paid their taxes to the Sayed." We learned through a letter from our ebony confidant that it was the second messenger who had discovered us by the Wadi Farig. The first had searched in vain and returned without news. The ekhwan and the party who had opposed our going were furious at our escape, which had been quite unsuspected. So apparently were certain robber bands upon the road, for near Bir Rassam the caravan, marching day and night to overtake us (it had done the 220 kilometres in four and a half days), were accosted by some armed Beduins who asked where they were going, while two or three others who gathered in the vicinity said, "Where is the rich Nasrani woman who is going to travel south with large stores of food?" "I know nothing about her," said Abdul Rahim. "There is no woman with us, but if you want to fight us we shall be delighted!" The disappointed Arabs retired hastily.

We did not go to bed without further evidence of the Sayed's generosity. A huge sack of dates was brought to my tent. "From Sayed Rida's gardens. We received a message to give them to you."

There was much "fadhling" in the various tents that

night, exchanging congratulations and good wishes. The
She-ibs and our Beduins were feasting in one and the
soldiers in a second. Several little fires burned merrily.
We went from one to another, making coffee from our
newly arrived stores in true Arab fashion, tasting it and
pouring it back into the pot if it were not sweet enough.
Then we went up on to the rise above the sleeping town,
and talked about all that we had done, which was so little
in comparison with what remained to be done. Yet we
had won the first trick in the game and we felt we now
had a fighting chance of success! But even while peace
enveloped us and the calm of the desert might impregnate
our souls, the first seed of a strife that was very nearly to
wreck all our plans was being sown in the camp below.
The blacks had got the idea firmly fixed in their heads
that they were to guard us. They posted a sentinel.
Musa She-ib, returning late, was challenged as he stood
beside his bales. "I am the owner of the tent," he
replied. "Then go inside or go away altogether!" came
the order. Both ruffled plumages had to be smoothed
down in the morning. The soldier was only doing his
duty, but the She-ib's caravan had rescued us from defeat
or starvation!

We started at 9.30 A.M. on December 19 for the six
hours' ride to Jalo over a flat country of fine gravel,
brownish-yellow, without a speck of vegetation, but it was
a divided party. The blacks, always lazy when there was
no necessity for a spurt, rode the camels, perching pre-
cariously above sacks and bales. Yusuf was furious,
chiefly because he wanted to ride himself. "The camels
will never reach Kufara if they are ridden," he said. "We
shall all die on the way. There will be a fight and we
will kill these black slaves." He went away to join
Mohammed, and the two kept away from the caravan
the whole day. Abdullah, the most famous tracker in

Libya, who had recovered four of She-ib's camels which
had strayed the previous night, following their footprints
among many thousands on the soft sand, led the caravan.
I kept the compass on him for an hour and he did not
vary his direction by one point. We made an absolutely
straight line between the two oases. At 11.30 A.M. we
saw a blot of palms on the horizon—Sharruf, the northern
end of the big oasis. Two hours later we entered the
wide semicircle, stretching south-south-east. The palms
were thickly clustered at the Sharruf end. A thinner belt
swept round to another cluster at Manshia.

She-ib got off his camel and started walking briskly.
Mighrib smiled. "The feisha," he said. "It is the
feisha." When a man goes on a journey his wife sometimes places a hollow gourd or pot in a certain position
on the house-top so that it catches the wind. As long
as it thrums with the sound of the breeze her husband's
heart will throb for her and he will return to her as
quickly as possible.

At 2.30 we entered the thin belt in the middle. Here
the palms were dotted over thick white sand rolling up
to low dunes. There was no sign of a belad, though a
thousand camel tracks went in the same direction. A
chill wind had risen, so I tried to go to sleep behind my
shrouding barracan. When I looked out an hour later
the scattered palms had grown rarer and we had swung
round a broad dune, so that we faced another rise on
which stood a formidable row of walled buildings. The
desert cities of Libya each have their own special
character.

There are two separate villages at Jalo—El Erg and
Lebba. The former looks like a fortress at first sight.
Its long, solid mud houses with their strong-walled courts
line the brow of the rise. Behind are the quaint curly
streets, the mysterious low arches, the huddled dwellings

of sun-baked bricks; but as we drove our camels upwards
we saw only the bigger houses, with scattered groups of
women and children wrapped in black and indigo robes.
To the left of the buildings stretched what appeared to
be a long, low, white wall, solid and even, which continued indefinitely. Mohammed, seeing it, rushed forward excitedly. "It is a royal reception in your honour,"
he shouted. "En nahs tayibin hena. Ana Mabsut! Oh,
they are good people here! I am happy! They love
the Sayed! They wish to honour him and his guests!"

Bewildered, I looked again at the long, white wall.
It was a solid mass of white-clad Arabs. Line upon line
of Beduins stretched in rigid order from the corner of
the last house along the whole length of the rise, at the
end of which the splendid wall of humanity dwindled
away into groups of women and children. Thrills of emo-
tion warmed us all. It was so spontaneously generous
and kindly. I could have cried from sheer gratitude and
Mohammed's dazzling smile was reflected on all our faces.
The camels were driven with shouts into more regular
order. Abdul Rahim ordered his men into line. Mighrib,
wild with excitement, seized my camel and almost dragged
me off it. "Are you happy? Are you happy?" he
kept asking. Yusuf was dancing with delight. We tried
to collect our scattered wits and march up the rise in
dignified fashion. The Sudanese achieved it, led by their
sergeant, but now that my foot was less swollen both my
great yellow shoes fell off at every second step, while
Hassanein's jerd described odd, wind-blown antics on its
own.

I shall never forget the mass of tall, grave figures in
snowy jerd and burnus, drawn up in military formation.
The setting sun blazed red behind them, and from below
came the wild "Ullula-een!" of the women. We came
as strangers, as pilgrims to the land of the Senussi. We

had no claim on their hospitality. We had no right to enter the most closely guarded country in the world. Beggar or prince, Beduin or sheikh, must prove good reason ere he is made free of the south-bound tracks to the sacred city. Our only passport was our love of the Arab race, our sympathy with their customs and their Faith. We dared offer no other plea. We asked but the right of the nomad to travel with his camels wherever the desert called him. Sidi Idris, with a mystic's vision, responded to our desire. "The Beduins sense those who love them, and they answer to the bond," he said. "You will go unharmed." We had received a blessing and we might wander south by desert city and guarded well to the mysterious, secret oasis. Little did we realise that we had been marked as the honoured guests for whom no generosity was too great! "The hospitality that you show them will be as if you had shown it to us," had written Sayed Rida and, by his will, we shared his lordship of the desert.

As we approached the white ranks bowed with dignity, and a chorus of grave "Aselamu aleikum, Marhaba, Marhaba!" "Bisilama" welcomed us, but the lines never wavered. We shook hands with the kaimakaan, Hameida Bey Zeitun, with the sheikh of the zawia, Sidi Mohammed es Senussi, and with many ekhwan, following their example by afterwards kissing our hands and touching our foreheads. We murmured gratitude unbounded for the honour they did us. "All that we have is yours," they said. "We belong to the Sayed." A house had already been prepared for us. The white mass parted to let us through. Surrounded by the dignitaries of the town, amidst a swelling murmur of welcome and blessing, we followed the hospitable kaimakaan into the narrow sand streets.

It was a strange, muddled phantasy seen through a

gap in the folds of the barracan—dark-robed women peeping from low doorways, shouts of flying children as the thonged whip of the commissaire swept them from our path, thick sand, pale walls and the white crowd of kindly smiling elders pressing round us. We stumbled through an arched door into a dark anteroom, on by odd little yards and passages, into a small court. "This house is all yours," said the kaimakaan, "and the government is at your service. Food will be brought you and all that you ask for we will gladly give."

The last scene remains in my mind. We stood in the doorway of the largest room, a mud-walled chamber twelve feet square, with a central pine trunk holding up the flat roof made of plaited leaves, the floor of the desert's own sand, thick and unmatted. The most reverend ekhwan gathered in the court, and the Sayed's letters were formally read. "Good! Very good!" came a contented murmur, and then the kisses and the formula, "The Sayed's orders are on our heads," as they touched turban and jerd and ma-araka!

By this time it was 5 P.M. and dark, so we thought it was time for the day's second meal. The first had been eaten at 7 A.M. at Aujela. Mohammed would not hear of it. "They will come back. They will bring everything. We must make ready." From somewhere he produced mats and a carpet, his own I believe, which he spread on the sand. It is difficult to arrange bulging sacks of tinned food and cereals artistically, but he did his best, while I made a royal illumination by sticking a lighted candle on the top of every sack. Just as we finished the ekhwan trooped back, all bearing gifts—one brought dates, another bitter native butter, a third great bowls of camel's or goat's milk. A white fluttering hen was pressed into my hands, and a huge horned sheep dragged to our feet. Bread enough for a regiment was

piled in a plaited basket. Eggs and tea and sugar
followed. We stumbled over our thanks in sheer amazement at their hospitality. "At least not the sheep," I
said frantically, probably in English, as no notice was
taken.

When the clamour had died away and the rejoicing
Mohammed had piled our rich gifts in every available
corner, a small council of war gathered, sitting cross-
legged on the largest mat. I was offered the place of
honour, but I felt that refreshment was needed, so Farraj
and I made a tiny brush fire in a corner of the court and
laboured to make strong sweet coffee. Our baggage was
wildly mixed, but the black rose to the occasion. He
produced a tin of coffee from somewhere and I broke one
of the great square slabs of sugar with a stone. We
puffed and blew at the wavering fire till our faces scorched
and the water boiled. Mohammed jumped excitedly
round, upsetting things and offering impossible suggestions, but the coffee, bought at my pet London grocer's,
was good, and though there was a deficit of glasses, the
guests appreciated it warmly. As I brought in a second
relay of cups on a tin plate they formed a favourable
impression of the Sitt Khadija and decided that perhaps
her mixture of blood was a pity but not a crime!

The grave Abdullah joined us, his keen, pointed face
with small dark beard, lean and weather-beaten, burnt
almost black in contrast to his thick white burnus. We
talked of routes. The fat Yusuf naturally wanted to go
straight to Kufara by the Wadai caravan route and
return the same way. The kaimakaan and two sheikhs,
Ibrahim Bishari and Mohammed Maghruf, wished to
uphold the honour of the Senussi. Therefore, they
assured us that all routes were safe. Abdullah was anxious
not to go to Buseima. He said, entirely incorrectly,
that a band of Tuaregs dwelt in Ribiana and their whole

business in life consisted in robbing any chance travellers between Buseima and Kufara. He said that caravans cannot cross the steep dunes. The camels slip and cast their loads or break their legs. "Our camels are not strong," he urged, "and they are not used to deep sand. While we are labouring in the dunes, the Tuaregs will attack us and take the caravan." "Is there no way of avoiding them?" I asked, determined to see Buseima. "None. They will know where we are passing, and they will lie in wait to surprise us. One man might escape them, but how can a caravan pass unseen?" He told a gruesome story of a caravan passing that way from Wadai a few weeks ago and of a successful Tuareg attack which seized the camels and put to flight those of the escort whom they did not kill. I could believe it, because in the French Sahara I had known the masked Tuaregs, and their swift-trotting camels, date-fed. They never remove the cloths which hide their mouths, but they are the salt of the Beduin race—tireless, fearless and cruel!

Ibrahim Bishari proffered the fact that there was a route between Taiserbo and Zieghen, one day's journey or a day and a half at most, so if, after reaching Taiserbo, we did not wish to face the dunes or the Tuaregs, we could go to the lonely well on the caravan route, and thence in five days to Kufara. Only Yusuf protested. "In Buseima are enemies of the Arabs," he said. "There is always danger there." But I sternly insisted. "The honour of the Sayed is in your hands. You must prove to the Ferangi that his influence is strong enough to protect his people anywhere." This phrase spiked his guns for the moment. It was enthusiastically received by the others. After deciding that we would stay in Jalo for two or three days to procure girbas to carry sufficient water for our large party, food for the men, information about the route and generally to reorganise the caravan, and that we would then go to Taiserbo, the party broke up with many "Aselamu akeikum's" and "Rahmat Allah!"

At last we could devote our whole attention to food! First, however, I was taken by Moraja to see the sheep, which had already been slaughtered, skinned, and cut up into bits. "Choose which piece you want, and we will eat the rest," said the sergeant. I picked out a leg and departed hastily, but the blacks were amazed at my frugality. Two rushed after me with strange-looking fragments, which I had never seen on a dinner-table, and pressed them upon me. "They are very good," they said. "You will be happy."

December 20 and 21 we passed in the little sand house with the maze of odd courts and antechambers. After forty-eight hours within its hospitable walls I still lost my way coming from the main door to my room, so intricate were the twists and turns. It does not sound a very lengthy affair to procure and issue food and girbas sufficient for seventeen people for a fortnight or three weeks, when the Government's stores are at one's disposal and the kaimakaan is as capable and energetic as Hameida Bey Zeitun. Yet we worked about eighteen hours out of each twenty-four. Flour rations for the caravan! Yes, the grain is in the village, but it must be ground, and for this purpose a little must be doled out to each house in Jalo, for no family possesses more than one primitive handmill worked by two blue-robed women, who slowly turn the great stones one above the other. Sixteen girbas for water! Yes, but some of them leak, and there is no tar to repair them.

So it is with everything. The soldiers would not travel without a large supply of "zeit" (oil) in which to cook their cereals. Mohammed wanted to have a change of

raiment made and was only comforted by hearing that
the prices were much cheaper in Kufara. The dark
Abdullah would not move an inch without being satisfied
that the caravan carried sufficient water. The full army
allowance for washing, cooking and drinking is a gallon
per day per man. There were seventeen people in our
party, so for seven days we should have had to carry
133 gallons. The largest girbas hold seven gallons, and
a camel carries four of them. Therefore, five loads
would have had to be devoted to water only. This was
impossible, as we had also to carry dates for our animals
at an allowance of one sack per head per day, and we
had only eight camels.

Every moment that was not devoted to the considera-
tion of these practical details or to settling the grievances
of the men—Yusuf had several new ones each day, and
even Hassanein was aggrieved because the solemn tailor
did not finish his new white chemise and trousers in
time—we spent in the delightful practice of "fadhling."
It is not an easy thing to gain information among the
Senussi. The simplest question generates suspicion. A
remark about the price of cotton stuff or the position
of a well arouses the darkest forebodings. The sight of
pencil and note-book seals their lips. One needs infinite
patience and understanding before one can penetrate
their reserve. They are a silent race with rare bursts of
loquaciousness. At an Arab gathering it is not necessary
to talk. After the oft-repeated "Keif halak" and
"Taiyib," the men sit gravely silent, staring into space
and sipping their strong green tea. The desert breeds
reserve. If a man travels alone for many days or weeks
without sight of a human being, without exchanging a
word, he learns to commune with himself and his god,
and he shuts his heart away in a sealed chamber.

The Senussi are particularly difficult of approach, as

they are a closely knitted religious fraternity imbued with a distrust of strangers that almost amounts to hatred! Not only does the Nasrani not cross their border, but practically no Arab outside their brotherhood travels by their routes. Hence the advent of any stranger, even protected by the "Sayeds," gives birth to a storm of conjecture, criticism and suspicion. When this is satisfied and allayed, their loyal friendliness appears, and they welcome one literally as one of themselves. "All that we have is yours," is not a form of speech in Libya. It is true so long as the friendly atmosphere exists, but one may have worked for hours or days to create the right impression, and a chance word may destroy it. I think utter simplicity and little speech are the best methods of approach. Flowery words impress them, and they say, "Thy conversation is like honey. Allow me to return that I may drink of it." But to themselves they murmur, "He is a juggler of words. Let us be careful lest he bemuse us!"

They always suspect an ulterior motive and it is best, therefore, to satisfy their love of mystery and let them gradually decipher a suitable one. The basis of their life is their faith and, like every ascetic sect, their strict practice isolates them from the rest of humanity. Outside the distrust engendered by their lives, aloof and remote from any code but their own, they are as simple as the shepherd patriarchs of old. The mentality of Abraham exists to-day in Libya. Also they are as easily impressed, offended or hurt as children. The poorer people show the amused, expectant curiosity of children, with the same eagerness to question and to learn. Once they have admitted one to their friendship, the sheikhs ask intelligently about politics in the Middle East, and for hours one may discuss the Ottoman Empire, the Hejaz and Egypt. Before, however, one can even attempt to joke, much time must have been spent "fadhling."

One by one the important merchants and sheikhs came to visit us. Gradually the circle seated upon our one carpet under the palm leaf roof widened. Grave, bearded faces peered from the hoods of dark blue burnuses, braided, lined with red. Sunburnt hands flicked away the myriad flies with whisks of palm fronds. There was the plump kaimakaan, with pallid, intelligent face and stubble of black beard round thick, smiling lips, and Garboah Effendi, with humorous expression on a face which might hail from Europe—firm lips, square jaw, pale skin, wide, quizzical smile. I think stray Vandal blood must run in his veins. His mother lived in Benghazi, and he was interested in the ways of Europe. There was the white-faced sheikh el zawia, Mohammed es Senussi, with dreamy eyes and dropping jaw, and dear, fat, old Sheikh Mohammed Maghruf, with round, lineless face as brown as a nut, a succession of circles from his little pursed mouth to his round brown eyes, and Sheikh Ibrahim Bishari, the traveller, who had taken his laden caravan from Wadai to Egypt, from Kufara to Lake Chad.

We discovered, after much sweet tea had been drunk with loud sucking noises and our best coffee was perfuming the air, that Jalo is a community of merchants. The date palms are a minor thing. The village lives by its trade, for it is on the main caravan route between the Sudan and the Cyrenaican ports. Sidi Mohammed, the Mahdi, founded this great desert highway through Kufara. Before his day all caravans passed by way of Tripoli and the Fezzan. We learned that ivory was bought at Wadai for five or ten francs the pound and that when the expenses of the long journey were deducted, the Beduins counted on making a profit of fifty per cent.

in Benghazi. Southbound caravans took needles, soap, scent, sandal, cotton stuffs, sugar and tea. They returned with ivory, feathers and smuggled slave boys and girls of eight to ten years. Some of these latter were adorable —solemn little beings, with chubby black faces peering out of the pointed hood of minute camel's-hair burnuses. They were sent by their masters to bring us gifts of eggs and milk and they regarded us with aloof scorn till we propitiated them with handfuls of dates.

The friendly circles discussed every Sahara route, marked or unmarked, upon the maps. We learned the position of every well and the taste of the water therein. We also learned that in winter a camel may actually go fifteen days without water, if lightly loaded and carefully driven. Therefore, Siwa, Jaghabub and Farafra are all possible outlets from Kufara, though a single mistake or mishap means destruction. As the hours lengthened and the coffee grew sweeter, we passed from business to politics. The eyes of all were turned to Egypt's struggle for freedom as an earnest of the future of Libya. To my surprise, Britain was regarded with respect and affection. The destruction of the Senussi zawias in Egypt was put down to the result of Sayed Ahmed's mistaken policy. Apparently the whole country had realised Britain's disinterestedness with regard to Libya and, therefore, had entered but half-heartedly into the projects of Mannismann and Nouri. Sayed Ahmed is regarded with respect and reverence as a devout Moslem, but his politics are regretted. Sayed Idris is looked upon as the saviour of his country. He came forward at a moment when the Senussi saw a prospect of the whole land slipping into European hands. By his tactful policy he preserved the power of his people, who respect him for his friendship with Britain and for his intelligent and amicable attitude towards Italy. They look to him to preserve Libya for the Senussi, while realising that Italy will always have a hold in Cyrenaica. It is too early yet for the new constitution to be appreciated in Libya. The terms of the accord at Regima have not yet been transmitted to the desert oases. Therefore, there was still much doubt in the minds of our visitors as to the future of their country.

When the broadminded policy of Italy is fully known, there should be an excellent understanding between the Senussi and their Latin allies. The whole prosperity of the country will depend upon that good understanding. Two men are responsible for its initiation. The Beduins owe their present peace entirely to the straightforward, progressive spirit of Sidi Idris. Italy owes hers to the Governor of Cyrenaica, Senator de Martino, who appears to be the first European statesman of this era to realise that in dealing with Arab races it pays to keep one's pledged word. *"C'est une mauvaise politique de promettre et de ne pas tenir bon,"* His Excellency said to me while I was staying with him at Benghazi. *"C'est l'erreur qu'a fait l'Angleterre. Ici on à confiance en moi parcequ'on sait que je tiendrai ma parole!"*

When the candles were lit and mint leaves put in the tea our guests grew confidential. They told us of their love of freedom and of their desire for a quiet life without political intrigue. The war had done them much harm, for it had raised prices and closed routes. The trade of the country was almost at a standstill. The export of hides had stopped altogether.

Bitter feeling had to a large extent died down, but it could be rekindled by any act of aggression. The Arabs hoped at the moment that Italy would come no farther inland, but I imagine that their merchants will be anxious to avail themselves of the increased facilities for trade which Italian protection will give to Cyrenaica. Sheikh Ibrahim asked about the Hejaz kingdom. There is a famous Senussi zawia near Mecca and the bonds between Libya and the Hejaz must always be close because of the pilgrimage to the "Beit Ullah!" It is to the interests of every devout Moslem, especially to these ascetic fanatics, that there should be peace in the territory of King Hussein. All were interested in the career of the Emir Faisul and they asked when he would return to Damascus. To this embarrassing question we were obliged to give evasive replies, but the point was pressed with more decision than usual. "Is not England going to help him?" asked the kaimakaan indignantly. We tried to explain the complicated policy of my country, but the oldest sheikh shook his head impatiently. "Are not the English strong enough to protect their allies?" he said. "We were sorry when Sayed Ahmed made war upon England, because we thought she was strong and powerful. Has she become weak now?" We changed the conversation lightly, but the little sting rankled.

Once more it was brought home to us how British prestige among the Arabs had dwindled during the last years. We have won the war, but we have lost the peace! Maybe we have lost an even greater thing! As I listened to the words of censure of our Beduin guests I remembered the last speech I had heard on the subject. It came from the lips of a great statesman at an Asiatic Society dinner in London and, delineating Britain's future policy in the Middle East, it left its hearers bewildered by rhetoric but ignorant of fact!

CHAPTER VI

CHRISTMAS IN THE DESERT

THE oasis of Jalo contains two villages a few hundred yards apart. El Erg is the seat of the Government and contains the Kasr, or Government Office, the kaimakaan's house and a new zawia with some forty ekhwan. The belad rambles by circuitous narrow lanes, bordered by windowless walls, pierced by low doorways, over a rise and down the farther side to the foot of a large dune, from the top of which one sees mile after mile of scattered palms, with here and there a well, its mouth strengthened by palm trunks. Generally a group of picturesque figures surrounds it and gossips while the day's water supply is drawn. An effective contrast to the glaring white sands are the indigo and royal blue tobhs with which the black slave-women mingle the orange and reds of their more barbaric taste. At the door of every mosque one finds a group of swathed white figures, sunk in contemplation or in sleep, yet mechanically flicking away the ever-attentive flies.

I rode across the hollow to Lebba on a big white donkey lent by Homeida Bey Zeitun. It is a twin village except that the streets are broader and straighter, and the whole place is dominated by the square tower of Sayed Hilal's house. As I passed below its latticed windows a very pretty face, framed in its sapphire veil, peeped out. It was olive-skinned and round, with dark kohl blurred round darker eyes, long-lashed and misty.

The blue tattoo marks on chin and lips but served to
throw up the gleam of pearl-white teeth, and great silver
ear-rings, red-studded, swung against plait after plait of
midnight hair.

Lebba possesses a very old zawia, founded by Sidi
Mohammed ben Ali. I went through its palm-filled yard
to the court of the mosque, where I was warmly greeted
by Sheikh Omar, who told me he was happy to meet
anyone with English blood. He introduced me to all his
teachers and his most intelligent pupils, who wanted to
show me there and then how well they could write.
"You are cleverer than I, for I cannot write Arabic,"
I said, and a murmur of surprise and scorn ran through
the group. "She cannot write and she is big, so big!
I believe she is older than Fatima, or Ayisha!" or any
other female relative of advanced years! There are a
hundred and fifty boy students at the Lebba zawia and
about eighty ekhwan. The long, low mosque is very
small, clean and white, with its sand arches and palm
walls—a few palm mats on the floor and a little painted
"mihrab," fragile and bent. "It cost two hundred
mejidies to build," said the sheikh proudly; and again,
as I left, he spoke kind words about my country,
which were balm after the censure of the previous
evening.

On our last afternoon we had a council in the house
of the kaimakaan. We left our shoes outside his door
and sat cross-legged round the walls of a room, empty
save for a packing-case which carried little-used writing
materials. "Now is everything ready to start to-morrow
at dawn?" I asked briskly. A most dubious "Inshallah " came from Yusuf. I have always thought it rather
hard that the Deity should be made responsible for the
whole doubt of the East! The question repeated, each
produced a pet difficulty. "The oil has not come," said

the portly sergeant, Moraja. "Take two soldiers and get it," ruthlessly replied Hassanein. The man relapsed into prompt silence lest he should really be obliged to leave before the arrival of delicious hot sweet milk flavoured with cinnamon. Mohammed wanted to write letters for Jedabia. Abdullah pointed out that some of the girbas were new and smeared with oil instead of tar, which would melt in hot weather and make the water nauseous. Yusuf frankly wanted to stay under a roof where he could eat and sleep all day. His fat face had assumed an expression of habitual discontent, and through much yawning his eyes had almost disappeared in two narrow slits. All the retinue had donned their best clothes in Jalo. Abdullah retained his snowy woollen jerd and burnus, with scarlet belt supporting his huge old-fashioned wooden pistol inlaid with much silver, but Mohammed and Yusuf wore short embroidered jackets of green and blue and striped silk jerds crossed with gay agals worn like aiglets.

We alone could not change and I wondered how long I should have to appear in the same unwashed red tobh and chequered barracan. There is no good water at Jalo, so the washing is always sent a day's journey to Buttafal. This is the last well on the route to Kufara and Taiserbo. Therefore, we decided to depart thither on the morrow and camp for a day beside its sweet waters before starting on our stern journey south. When they saw that we meant to insist, the retinue became almost brisk and to my great surprise even the lazy Yusuf was up the next morning at 4 o'clock busy with preparations. Nothing ever arrives till the last moment in the East, but one must always be prepared for it to come just when one has made up one's mind to do without it. Thus, when everything was packed, the hard-boiled eggs and bread, ordered twenty-four hours before,

made their appearance and had to be dumped into the
first available sack.

It is no easy matter loading a caravan that has got
to travel two hundred and fifty miles with a seven days'
waterless stretch. I looked at our eighteen camels with
much anxiety. Some of them were small and weak.
One of them was a living picture of all that a camel
should *not* be. He might have been used successfully
by the Khartoum Camel Corps as an example to enthusiastic young officers of what *not* to buy. His feet were
worn, his hump was soft, his elbows rubbed together as
he walked, his chest pad was insufficient, and he had
sores under his shoulders. Besides this, many of the
nagas were in foal. However, it was no use worrying
in advance. Long ago I had realised that we should get
to Kufara only if Allah so willed, and the farther we
moved into the desert the more I felt impelled by some
ulterior force. I was never surprised when difficulties
piled themselves up and then vanished without reason at
the last moment. I began to feel a fatalistic trust in
the destiny that had dragged me from hunting and hunt
balls and sent me out into the white Sahara to find the
Holy place which had been a secret for so long. The
feeling of Kismet was so strong that it prevented my
troubling excessively over our weak camels, even though
I felt that they were dangerously overloaded. Our party
had increased to nineteen by two black slave girls in
vivid barracans and little else, property of one of the
Sayeds, who wished them sent to Kufara.

In spite of the utmost exertions the caravan was not
ready to start till 11.30, when, amidst a chorus of kindly
wishes, regrets and blessings, we plodded slowly out of
the hospitable town into a raging north-westerly wind.
We meant to march on into the night and reach Buttafal
about 10 P.M., but fate decided otherwise, for almost

before the walls of Jalo had disappeared the wind strengthened into the worst gibli I have ever encountered. It was behind us, for we were heading south-east, yet the camels staggered and swung round, huddling against each other for shelter. I was nearly swept off the back of my blond beast. Every loose mat and blanket flapped in wide circles and loads began to sway dangerously. On all sides palms were bending and cracking in the sudden gale, while great leaves were torn off and whirled whistling above our heads. The air became a thick sheet of sand. Sun and direction were blotted out. Screaming gusts stung our faces and blinded us. It was the most extraordinary sight, for one minute camels and figures would be blotted out in a whirling white fog; then a head or a wildly gyrating blanket or a portion of a labouring camel would appear for an instant through the shroud and vanish again in the smarting dusk. We stumbled and choked and fell through the storm till even Abdullah saw it was useless. In an instant's lull a palm tree fence appeared to our left, with a small boy crouching beside a garden plot of onions, radishes and pumpkins. We turned our camels towards the low shelter and they sank heavily to their knees beside a clump of the grey, nameless trees. The boy gave our guide some radishes as he passed, and in spite of the agony of flying sand the Beduin turned to me with a smile. "It is a blessed journey," he said. "Look at the green which has been given us!" It is proof of how far one had wandered from the mentality of London and Paris that his words gave me great comfort.

I gathered the thickest blanket round me and dug myself into the sand, while a hail of dust and grit beat upon me. Through a narrow slit I saw the blacks, with kufiyas tied across their mouths and noses, staggering about with sacks and boxes. They appeared like phan-

tasmic figures on a lantern screen, to vanish in the next
strong gust of wind. It was impossible to put up a tent.
The camels were barraked in a semicircle, where they
lay groaning but not attempting to move. The baggage
was piled to form zaribas, and in the lee of these we
crouched for four or five hours, blankets covering our
faces, handkerchiefs wound over our mouths. I thought
the retinue would look upon the storm as a bad omen,
but Mohammed only smiled with dust-parched lips.
"This will be a successful journey. We shall have good
luck," he said, "for when the Sayed travels there is
nearly always a gibli thus!"

Once when I tried to change my cramped position I
felt something soft huddled against me. I peered out
of my wrappings cautiously and found the black face of
Zeinab, the prettiest slave girl, almost on my shoulder.
She seized my hand and kissed it devoutly, while her companion, Hauwa, drew closer. Their thin, gaudy barracans
were no protection against the madness of the sand, so I
offered them a share in my blanket and we made friends
under the sheltering thickness. Zeinab was young, about
sixteen, and round-faced, with curved full lips and big
velvet eyes modestly downcast. Hauwa looked ancient
with her wrinkled skin and yellow, uneven teeth, but her
years were only twenty-four. The Sudanese marry, if
the parents have money, when the girl is nine and the
boy thirteen. Therefore these ebony slaves may be grand-
mothers at the age when an English girl is wondering
whether she is old enough to wed! My little companions
were full of questions and comment, mixed with praise
of Sayed Rida. They wanted to give me the eggs they
had brought for themselves, and it is almost impossible
to refuse a gift in the East. It is accepted as a matter
of course without expression of thanks. It used to surprise me at first that if one gave a man a watch or revolver

he took it without comment, but gradually I realised that they give and they receive with the same simplicity.

Zeinab wore huge silver ear-rings and bracelets and an embroidered leather belt carrying a dozen gay little pouches for her toilet necessities, while Hauwa had tied her barracan into a sort of hood, with a strip of crimson leather bearing some "hejabs" (charms) in tiny wallets. Both had broad sticks of scarlet coral stuck through holes in their nostrils. When the storm abated, about 5.30 P.M., they emerged from the blanket and busied themselves, briskly preparing the Beduin evening meal.

By this time there were always two rival camps in neighbouring zaribas. Behind one wall of heavy sacks the soldiers cooked their savoury flour. Within another semicircle Mohammed and Yusuf, with the guide and a black camel-boy, brewed strong sweet tea, while the two girls were provided with a little camp beside the Arabs' shelter. Mohammed was always kind to them, providing them with some of his own flour and dates, together with the occasional loan of a blanket, but otherwise nobody troubled about them except when it was a question of cooking or washing clothes. True, when the length of our stay permitted the pitching of tents, the Beduins always contented themselves with the zariba, leaving to Zeinab and Hauwa the use of their tent, but the girls accepted as a matter of course that, after riding all day, they should cook and wash and clean and generally see to the comfort of the Arab retinue.

We wanted to break camp after the evening meal, but though the sandstorm had abated the wind was still cold. Abdullah pointed out that we should walk all night and arrive too tired to work in the morning, which would be waste of energy, as all the firewood for the journey had to be collected in the vicinity of Buttafal. We therefore crawled into our sleeping-bags under the shelter of the

palm fence at 7 P.M., and were up again while it was
still dark.   The same cold wind stimulated the blacks to
brisk action, and there was a great deal of running about
and singing, but the sun rose while the camels were still
being loaded and we did not start till seven.

We had camped on the very edge of the Jalo oasis.
The last palms were behind us, and in front lay the
flattest country I had ever seen.   To the rim of the near
horizon stretched an unbroken expanse of yellowish,
gravelly sand.   We thought we had crossed flat, monotonous country before, but on December 23 we rode
across a drab-coloured billiard table whereon was not a
blade of grass, a bird, an insect or a mound.   It was as if
we were at the end of the world and the round horizon the
edge off which we should presently fall!   The only objects
that marred the extraordinary monotony were a few
scattered skeletons of camels which had died at the end of
a long march from Kufara or Taiserbo.   Occasionally a
bleached thighbone had been stuck upright in the sand
to mark the direction.

It was a cool, bright day with a north-west wind.
Persistent neglect had practically cured my foot, so I
was able to walk for a couple of hours with Abdul Rahim.
He waxed enthusiastic over the extent of the Senussi
influence in Bornu, Senegal, the Sudan and Wadai,
giving me a list of the principal zawias.   "Only in
Wadai there is none," he said, "for the Sultan said to
Sidi Ben Ali, 'We will always be your friends and allies,
but if you build a zawia here the next thing you will do
will be to come and conquer us!'"   The commandant
was in a loquacious mood and reminiscences flowed from
his lips.   It was he who had been sent by Sidi Ahmed to
kill Mukhtar, the Senussi officer in the pay of Turkey,
who had attacked Bomba in Egyptian territory without
direct orders from his master.   He was at Jaghabub when

Sidi Hilal quarrelled with his uncle and, under sentence of death, fled to Tobruk in forty-eight hours. The young Sayed had described the horrors of the 250 kilometres ride to me at a dinner in his house at Jedabia when, amidst his rich carpets and brilliant clothes, he could laugh at the memory of aching bones and failing strength.

Abdul was conversant also with the doings of Ramadan Shetewi, the great Arab leader who for many years held the Italians at bay in Tripolitania, but who was killed a few months ago in a fight with the Orfella. It appears that his alliance with Sayed Ahmed was but lukewarm, for on one occasion, when he provided a bodyguard for a German mission which was taking a large sum of money to the Sayed in Cyrenaica, his men had orders to kill the unfortunate Teutons as soon as they were out of sight of Misurata. Ramadan Shetewi took the official gold and the mission's private wealth was divided among the murderers.

At noon Yusuf pointed to the faintest rise in the distance. "Behind that hill is Bir Buttafal," he said, and with visions of another green spot on our wonderful map, we hoped to see at dusk one palm and a few tufts of brushwood. Not a single blade of grass marks the slight hollow. There is not a stone nor a stick nor a tuft of green sage in all the wide expanse of thick, soft sand. The day we arrived there was not even a hole. Before we had time to ask where was the well, Abdullah and two of the blacks apparently went mad. They flung themselves on their knees and with rhythmic cries began burrowing rapidly, flinging the sand vigorously over their shoulders. Only when they had sunk to their waists and the heap around them began to grow dark and moist did we realise that they were actually digging out the well, which had been entirely filled in by the gibli of the previous day.

On Christmas Eve the whole party devoted themselves to washing their clothes, with surreptitious drinks of the sweet Buttafal spring, the first good water we had tasted since we left Jedabia. Zeinab and Hauwa laboured patiently to reduce the retinue's flowing garments to their pristine whiteness. I had to disguise myself in a jerd while my own red tobh was in the tin pan that served as a laundry. The blacks, stripped to the waist, their top-knots bobbing above their shaven heads, pommelled and pounded beside the well. By the afternoon the desert was spotted with patches of white, whose snowiness rapidly disappeared beneath stray drifting sand. However, there was a general feeling of cleanliness in the air, and we were glad when Musa She-ib appeared from the direction of Jalo, with three donkeys and a camel in search of the waters of Buttafal which could be sold in Jalo, where the wells are brackish and salt, for half a mejidie a girba. We are glad to have an excuse for "fadhling," so we pressed the kind old man to stay for a midday meal and, sitting round the fire in the largest zariba, we made green tea while Abdullah cut goat-hide thongs for a new pair of sandals, Hassanein mended the watches of the party, all of which had stopped in the sandstorm, and Mohammed made primitive rope out of the palm fibre.

That night we watched the camels being fed by moonlight. It struck me at the time that it was a stupid plan to put all the dates in one large heap, as the greediest camels devoured more than their share and the slowest eaters got little. However, I daren't argue with Abdullah about what was obviously his own job. After the animals had eaten there was a great argument as to whether they should be watered that night or the following morning. Finally it was decided to let them drink at once and it was amusing to see the way they rushed to the well.

Only two at a time could approach the shallow pan, which the Beduins kept filling and refilling, shouting monotonously, "Come and drink—then you will be strong! Come and drink—then you will be strong!" which changed when the camels became violent into a chanted, "See how your drinking splashes me! See how your drinking wets me!"

One realised the loneliness of the desert that night. The four tents and the animated group at the well were infinitesimal specks on the desolate, limitless waste, silvered by moonlight into an unbroken sea without ripple or bourne. How easily even a mighty caravan might vanish in the Libyan desert and no more trace be left of it than of a few ants crushed under foot on a sandy court. I longed for even one lonely palm to break the awful monotony. It was the aching solitude of Nature pitted against the pathetic energy of man and Nature had no need to fight. She could leave the struggle and the stress to the human midges who would traverse her trackless silences, and when their pitiful vitality and force were spent in battling with her winds and her droughts she could bury them "noiselessly in her fathomless drifts beneath the white serenity of her moons." First the fuel failed. Then the food failed. Then the last water dried.

> "With the faith of little children we laid us down and died,
> Follow on! Follow on! By the bones upon the wayside
> Ye shall come into your own!"

On Christmas Day the camp was astir by 3 A.M. Everybody was prepared for prodigies of endurance in the way of an immensely long march. Therefore, when I plunged briskly out of my tent while the moonlight was still clear, I could not understand why there were no chants or shouts, no cheerful rushing about with the

cumbersome bales.   Arabs and blacks alike were standing
about in sorrowful groups.   Mohammed, with a plaid
rug wound over the fleece-lined mackintosh, was cleaning
a ruthless-looking knife.   Even the camels had the most
depressed possible expression.   One of the nagas lay
beside the fire with drooping head.   It appeared that she
was the direct cause of the agitation, though most of the
animals were suffering severely from their unaccustomed
date meal followed by a heavy drink.   The naga appeared
to be *in extremis*.   Foam frothed from her mouth and
nostrils, her neck was twisted into a stiff distorted curve,
her sides were labouring painfully.   I could not have
believed that even the most acute indigestion could reduce
an animal to such a state after so few hours.   "She
is going to die," said Yusuf. "Prepare the knife!"
"Wait!   Wait!" exclaimed Abdullah.   "I will try
burning her first!"   Apparently there are but two
remedies in the desert, bleeding and firing.   They had
already tried the first without effect, as it was too cold
for the blood to run.   They now pushed the unfortunate
animal on its side and laid a hot iron on its abdomen.
It protested much less than it usually did at being loaded,
but the warmth presumably galvanised it into action, for
it managed to struggle to its feet and wander off with
the others, a sorry-looking, hunched-up group, one of
which appeared dead lame.

   During a wasted morning the friction between the
two hastily formed zaribas became intense.   The blacks,
incensed at the abuse which had been showered upon them
for riding the camels between Aujela and Jalo, now
got their own back.   They said that the Arabs knew
nothing at all about a caravan and could not even feed
the animals properly.   At noon the miserable naga got
much worse, and Mohammed, Abdullah and I spent the
whole afternoon sitting by her side, trying desperate

remedies from massage to soap! When we left at 5 P.M.
she was obviously dying and we prepared to face the
problem of the seven days' waterless journey with one
camel the fewer. We argued about what luggage we
could best dispense with until Yusuf calmly announced
that, as we had waited an extra day at Buttafal, there
would not now be sufficient dates to last a week.
Mohammed said that we must announce the death of the
Sayed's camel to the kaimakaan at Jalo, which meant
an extra two days' wait.

We held depressed councils, at which I insisted on
an immediate start, but apparently the camel shared the
sacredness of its master, and even its body could not be
left at Buttafal. "Very well," said I. "We will send
someone back with the news, but we must leave here at
dawn. We will give all our eating dates for the camels
and that will make up for to-day's rations."

Then the real difficulty appeared. The friction between blacks and Beduins was so strong that both parties
feared that it would eventually come to a fight, and
neither wished to decrease their number. When I
suggested a Sudanese going, Abdullah showed his hand.
"Yes, yes, send back four or five," he said eagerly. "The
journey will be easier without them," but Abdul Rahim
refused point-blank to dispense with one of his soldiers.
"The night we thought we were going to be attacked, on
the way from Jedabia, Abdullah left us and slept with
some kinsman near by," he remarked shrewdly. The
whole party was sunken in the deepest gloom, we because
the camels were already overloaded, the retinue because
each side feared to endanger its power by the loss of
a fighting man, when a black form appeared on the
faint rise beyond which we had left the dying camel.
"Mashallah!" exclaimed Mohammed. "It is the influence of Sidi Idris! A miracle! A miracle!" And

two minutes later the source of all our woe walked calmly back into camp. Its reception must have surprised it considerably, for everyone rushed out to meet it, firing revolvers and rifles into the still, starlit air, after which the blacks performed a wild fantasia to the music of a tin pan beaten by Abdullah's sinewy fingers. So ended the most unpleasant Christmas I have ever known!

CHAPTER VII

A FAULTY GUIDE ON A WATERLESS WAY

ON December 26 we made our actual start south. The day's delay in the sandstorm and the further delay with the sick camel had lost us four feeds. We had allowed half a sack of dates night and morning, so now we had only five sacks for the seven days. However, we bought the soldiers' ration for sugar, threw in most of our own, and thus brought it up to nearly the requisite amount of "alaf." As for girbas, the utmost the camels could carry was eight large ones, containing five gallons each, and eight smaller, containing four gallons each. We warned our party of sixteen that they must use only an eighth portion of the water each day. We then commended ourselves to Allah and started south at 8.30 A.M., for the weighing and exact distribution of goods, to say nothing of the quarrels between blacks and Arabs, had occupied a couple of hours.

There is no route to Taiserbo, as no one ever goes there. In the whole of Jalo we came across only two people who had visited the oasis. One said he had gone due south and arrived at the palm trees on the evening of the sixth day. The second was our own sergeant, Moraja, who had passed through Taiserbo on his way north nine years ago and he had done the journey in six very long marches. Abdullah, our keen-eyed guide, with his dark wolf's face lighted by flashes of brilliant white teeth, announced that if we headed straight for

Taiserbo in a south-westerly direction we might go too
far west and lose ourselves altogether. He therefore
proposed to go south for the first five days, within sight
of the faint landmarks on the Kufara route, and then
turn west. All day long we rode across a burning,
desolate waste, flatter than it is possible to imagine or
describe. One could see but a few miles on either side.
The whole of our world had become a flat, yellow disk,
reflecting the scorching sun-rays in quivering mirage.
The only break in the monotony was an occasional camel
skeleton. Once a great brown hillock appeared on the
edge of the disk and we thought it might be brushwood
or even a caravan, till the distorting waves of mirage
danced away and revealed it but a few huddled bones to
which some dry, brown matter still clung. We ate a
hard-boiled egg and a few dates for lunch, but clung to
our rule of drinking only morning and evening. As we
plodded onwards, for we had agreed that no one should
ride the camels unless they were ill or dead beat, Moraja
assured me that our journey could not possibly be lucky,
for we had failed to fulfil a time-honoured Arab custom
and slaughter a sheep at Buttafal. It appears that when
any member of a caravan visits an oasis for the first time
a feast is made in his honour. As none of our retinue
had seen all the oases we proposed to visit, we gathered
it would be an expensive journey!

To our surprise the blacks walked all day without
grumbling, even stopping occasionally to dance and sing.
The camel who had nearly died the previous day carried
her load gaily. "She was ridden by Shaitan," said
Mohammed gravely, "but the spirit of Sidi Idris has
cured her." At 5 p.m. Yusuf pointed out the Kalb el
Metemma, which he said was on the left, but I could see
absolutely nothing which looked like a hillock.

We saw the sun die in the flaming splendour which

is the glory of the Sahara, we marched for an hour or two
by cool starlight and then a great orange moon swung
up in the east and transformed the desert into a strange
silver sea. Across the infinite pale loneliness plodded our
little caravan and, as I looked at the white speck which
led us, I realised why there could be no atheist in the
desert. Man must put his trust in something more
powerful and far-reaching than himself. In Europe, if
there be no God to help, at least there is science and the
telephone, an express train or an aeroplane. In Libya,
where the Beduin cannot call for succour by wireless,
where there are no signposts to guide, no surgeon or
mechanic to improve his means of locomotion, no food
to be bought or picked, no anæsthetic but death, the
lonely traveller must pin his faith to some power beyond
the calm-faced guide in whose hand apparently lies the
fate of his caravan.

When Abdullah met me on the hill beside the
clustered palms of Aujela, I looked at his strong, keen
face, lined and shrewd, with steady, self-reliant eyes, and
I felt that I could trust him to lead us safely across
the waterless sands to an oasis whose size varied according
to the imagination of the speaker. When I looked across
the moonlit, speckless waste, with never a blade or stone
to break the even surface of the disk, the tiny, plodding
figure, trailing the end of his white jerd in the dust as
his energy waned after eleven hours' march without a
halt, I felt how frail a thing I relied on for my life and
seventeen lives besides. When we sit in comfortable
arm-chairs under our electric lights and talk of the
"Beduin instinct," we acknowledge the working of a
greater power than radium or steam! Europe may count
on a hundred sciences, but for Libya there can be but
one faith, one hope, "Allahu Akhbar!"

We pitched camp at 7.30 P.M., and an hour later

HASSANEIN BEY AND MOJABRAS DRINKING TEA

FLOCKS WATERING AT BIR RASSAM

SHE-IB'S CARAVAN ON THE MARCH BETWEEN WADI FARIG
AND AUJELA

OUR CARAVAN APPROACHING AUJELA

our little cluster of tents was as silent as the calm sands around us.

On December 27 we rose at 6 A.M. and got away by 8, for we had decided that the best way of doing the necessary 50-odd kilometres a day was an unbroken march of eleven or twelve hours, with a solid meal before starting and another in the evening. As the last groaning camel rose to his feet Yusuf pointed out a group of low hillocks to the east. "Those are the Hameimat on the ₁oad to Zieghen," he said.

Our plump ally was in a reflective mood that day. In spite of considerable heat, he wore the woolly lined mackintosh closely buttoned and belted, with a white cloth wound over his cheeks. "What is Allah's greatest gift to man?" he propounded to me suddenly. I felt this was a test of my faith in Islam, so I promptly replied, "The Koran." He looked at me scornfully. "The camel! If there were no camels here, there would be no dates, no food, nothing!" He paused and added solemnly, "If there were no camels here, there would be no men!"

It is curious how the desert brings out character. Hassanein became so vague that he never finished a sentence or an action. I developed a fatalism wholly at variance with my usual ideas. Yusuf showed signs of pride and dignity beneath his plump laziness. Abdullah became reserved and impressive as the dunes that guard the holy oasis, but Mohammed showed the finest qualities. All the Arabs were courageous with an enduring quiet heroism that we were to appreciate so a few days later, but Mohammed was infinitely kind and his pride was a fine, clean thing, bred of silence and religion. He made a vow never to ride, and kept it through infinite pain. He smiled when certain death was but a few hours away. He forgave without words a carelessness that nearly cost him his life. He laboured unceasingly to make everyone else comfortable, and the only time I ever saw him lose his calm, aloof patience was when his follower, Omar, had been slighted by the soldiers. As for the "blacks," they were a mixture of children and animal. When they suffered, they were sulky. When praised, they were immensely pleased. Their ideas germinated simply and slowly and were impossible to dispute. They were alternately brave and cowardly, but had no endurance until faced with hopeless danger, on which occasion they showed a rather splendid and wholly unexpected patience and fidelity.

We nicknamed the opposing camps "the black bears" and the "shepherd kings" after their first bad dispute, which took place on the second day. Little Abdul Rahim simply had not the physique to walk thirty or thirty-eight miles a day, so we were not surprised when he silently climbed on to a camel, but when the fat Moraja and various others followed his example I made violent protest. Unfortunately, Yusuf joined in, calling the soldiers "Slaves!" This fired the fuse, and for a few minutes a fight seemed imminent. The corporal seized his rifle and Mohammed pulled out his big wooden pistol. By this time, however, I was an adept at pouring oil on troubled waters and after plentifully applying praise to both parties, the atmosphere became calmer. Thereafter, however, there was open hostility between the two camps.

We camped at 7 near a group of camel skeletons, the bones of which our own camels reflectively sucked. It was the only moment in the day that Zeinab and Hauwa were in evidence, for they cooked the Arabs' evening meal over a few twigs of wood brought from the neighbourhood of Buttafal. All through the long march two little shrouded figures, wholly enveloped in coarse,

heavy blankets, huddled motionless, silent on the camels.
They never looked out of the folds. They never spoke,
even to each other. I wondered if they ever thought of
anything in particular, yet one of them, by the strange
chance of a night's phantasy, might be the mother of
the future all-powerful Sheikh es Senussi. In Islam only
paternity counts. Be the mother slave or princess, the
eldest son inherits.

On December 28 we got away at 7.40, and had to
march for eleven and a half hours before we had done
46 kilometres. The first day the camels had made a
good average of over 4 kilometres an hour, for there
was no temptation to wander in order to graze, but the
second day everyone was tired and cross, and it was
difficult to make the men drive them in a straight line.
The third day the blacks' feet began to blister. My own
foot was swollen again. It is very difficult to walk for
any length of time in the huge heel-less slippers.
Hassanein and Yusuf were both limping, and Moraja
could not keep on his legs, for all the veins were inflamed.
I was so tired I could hardly smile, but, luckily, the
unexpected distribution of a bag of dates encouraged
the retinue a little. The mirage distorted two tiny heaps
of stones into a couple of hills, and Yusuf playfully built
the last camel skeleton into an original shape with one
leg lifted high. It was not till I had laughed at its
fantastic kick that I noticed the human skull that
crowned it!

One had to divide one's attention evenly between the
two camps. If one walked for an hour with Abdullah,
and heard how our opponent's agent in Jedabia had
tried to bribe him not to accompany the caravan and
how the said agent had subsequently received the beating
he deserved, one had to devote the same amount of
time to conversation with Moraja on the glories of

the Sudan and the prowess of her soldiers. It was no easy task keeping everyone cheerful during an eleven hours' walk on no food or water. In the evening, after we had eaten our half-ration of meat and a handful of dates—for we were carrying the least possible amount of food—a pathetic procession used to rob us of much-needed sleep. We treated blistered and swollen feet, headache from the sun, toothache from dates, sores, fever and lots of other ailments before we were allowed the peace of our flea-bags—very comparative peace, for by this time we were suffering seriously from sand-rash!

December 29 saw us en route at 6.40, and by 10 o'clock Abdullah stated that we had arrived at the Wadi Farig. Personally, looking at it from every angle, I could not see the slightest depression of any kind, but everyone said it was half-way, so spirits rose high. Nevertheless, it was a trying day, for by this time nearly everyone was lame. Mohammed could hardly keep on his feet, but he doggedly refused to ride. The blacks used to walk on half a mile in front of the camels, then lie on their faces while their companions stamped on their backs, an original form of massage.

Abdullah picked up a piece of ostrich eggshell dropped by a passing caravan from Wadai. "Seventy years ago there was ostriches here," he informed us with doubtful accuracy. "What did they eat?" I asked. "Oh, food, much food!" he answered vaguely.

There was a short shower in the evening which interfered with the cooking but provided a little extra water. We were very anxious about our supply, for the first day one of our fanatis had leaked and the blacks had availed themselves of the excuse to empty it during the night. We used to arrange the girbas outside our tent and dele out the water ourselves. Several of the new girbas leaked badly and in spite of the utmost care we

thought everyone would be extremely thirsty by the
seventh day.   We ourselves drank one cup of hot coffee
in the morning and two cups of cold tea or water at
night.   We camped that day at 6.10 P.M.

December 30 we started at 7 A.M. and camped at
6.35 P.M.   It was a terribly hot day and the camels were
nearly as crocked as the men.   One had cut a foot, and
another had a raw shoulder.   Two had bad sore backs, so
their loads had to be divided among the others.   In spite
of this some of the soldiers had to be allowed to ride, for
their feet were badly swollen.   The country had changed
slightly, for faint waves of sand had marked the neighbourhood of the Wadi Farig, but the flatness of the disk
was now unimpaired, though its yellow monotony was
broken by patches of dark gravel.   This gave the mirage
a chance to build ebony hills and islands amidst its blue,
shifting waves.

December 31 we started at 6.30 A.M. and walked
till 7 P.M., doing 46 kilometres, because the situation
had suddenly become very serious.   The previous day
Abdullah had surprised us by insisting on a slightly
south-easterly course, as he had not yet seen a small
landmark on the Zieghen route.   When we had talked
the matter over in Jalo he had assured us calmly and
strongly that he had been to Taiserbo and knew the
route.   We had cross-questioned him severely, and
always he had been confident of being able to guide us
to any of the southern oases, though he had urged us
not to go to Buseima on account of the danger of being
attacked.

Now according to our map it was 350 kilometres from
Buttafal to Taiserbo.   It was generally stated by the
Arabs to be a seven days' journey, which was a daily
march of eleven to twelve hours at an average of four
and a fraction kilometres an hour.   Therefore, in spite

of Abdullah's change of direction, according to the mileage we had done, we should have been well within the oases that night. We had confidently expected it the previous evening, when we noticed a certain vagueness about our guide. "Don't talk to him, or he will lose his head," said Mohammed on the sixth day. It is looked upon as a definite disease, like fever, this losing the head on the part of the guides. It was extraordinary to see the change in the Beduin's face that day. The whole outline of his features seemed to have become blurred, while his eyes were restless and troubled. He stooped as he walked and kept asking if we thought he was going straight, so that by the end of that day we had to direct him by the map, which we had every reason to believe inaccurate. It must be remembered that while we always knew roughly where we were, we never knew where Taiserbo was. We started half-rations for the camels on the 31st and tried to cut down the water ration still more, though since the girbas had begun to leak we had dispensed with the half-cupful for washing.

New Year's Day dawned gloomily. We had two half-feeds for the camels and barely enough water for two days at less than a pint per day per person. We were, however, a little cheered up when, as we were loading the camels, Abdullah pointed out a faint blur to the east and said it was Mazeel, some hillocks he had hoped to see the previous day. On clear mornings, about an hour after dawn, when the desert is very flat, a mirage of the country about a day's journey distant appears on the horizon. For a few minutes one sees a picture of what is some 50 kilometres farther on. The Arabs call it "the country turning upside down." On January 1, the seventh day of our march, we saw this mirage for the first time—brushwood and hillocks quite clearly to the south, yet our guide turned deliberately west of it. My camel was ill after his unaccustomed date-feeding. Hassanein was in great pain from his blistered feet. A permanent north wind, warring for a week with a burning sun, had implanted rheumatism in my right shoulder. The firewood had given out, and there had been a sharp quarrel between the blacks and the Beduins on this account, each accusing the other of using more than their share.

Abdullah kept on his south-westerly course for a few hours, and then began to wander slightly. The blacks wanted to beat him. Even Mohammed was impatient with him. We steered almost due south. Hassanein had to ride all day and Mohammed's eyes were bloodshot with the pain of his feet, yet he struggled on. That night there were no fires in the camp, and I fully expected Abdullah would be murdered. However, when I woke before the dawn on January 2, I heard him laughing, so hoped he had recovered his head. We dared not start till "the country had turned upside down" and revealed to us what lay in front, so we occupied ourselves in finding our exact position. According to our map we were now within the borders of Taiserbo! This raised the problem of whether it were one consecutive oasis or whether it were possible to go between two groups of palms without seeing either!

At 8 A.M. the mirage showed us one sharp dune very much to the west. I wanted to go straight there, hoping by sunset to be able to climb it and have a good view of what lay beyond, but both Abdullah and Moraja insisted that no such dune lay anywhere near Taiserbo. "If we go as much west as that we go straight to Hell," said the guide decisively. With the ever-present danger of going beyond Taiserbo into the uninhabited western desert it was impossible to argue. With only one day's water and no fodder we dared not risk everything so boldly, but I there and then made up my mind that Taiserbo was smaller and much farther west than is generally supposed. I believe if we had gone to that dune we might have reached it. At that moment a thick, icy mist came down and blotted out everything, so I decided to go south for five hours, in which case, according to Jalo information and our map, we should have gone right through Taiserbo and possibly be able to recognise some landmarks near Buseima.

It was a terrible walk. Everyone knew that, humanly speaking, they were going to die of thirst within a day or two. Nearly everyone had blistered feet, and no one had had enough to eat, yet everyone laughed. "It is evidently the will of Allah that we die," said Farraj politely, "but no one will die before Sidi Abdullah." I doubt if the guide heard. He trailed along with a blank, dispirited stare, first edging west, then east. Mohammed was tottering on swollen feet. "I think that I would rather die beside my luggage," he said placidly. "Doubtless Abdullah and Yusuf would like to wander about to the end, but I do not know this country, Hamdulillah it will be quick!" Thereafter everyone spoke of death, and I was amazed at the way they calmly accepted its advent. The only thing that stimulated them was the demise of the guide. "By Allah, Sidi Abdullah shall go first and show us the way!" said the toothless one. "When I am certain of death I shall shoot him," said Sharki firmly. "But he called you a fool yesterday," reminded Farraj. This worried Shakri for a moment. Then he cheered up. "I will call him a fool first, and then I will shoot him," he said. Amidst this cheerful conversation the mist suddenly lifted and revealed nothing but the same flat, pale sand devoid of faintest shadow of grass or brushwood to give hope of an oasis.

It is amazing how desperation affects one. That morning Hassanein could not put his foot on the ground, but when he realised that his end was imminent he walked for eight hours without feeling pain. Mohammed also forgot his ills and I found myself wondering how soon I should awake from this realistic nightmare. When our southern course produced nothing but fanciful blue lakes and pools—for a burning sun now added to our woes —we took council and, ignoring Abdullah, decided to march east-south-east till water and camels gave out. There were several chances of salvation on this new bearing, we thought, for we might hit the most easterly end of Taiserbo if it were anywhere near its mapped position, or we might find ourselves in the recognisable country south of Zieghen or among the dunes near Buseima. We supposed these places to be too far away to reach with the camels, but if we could get anywhere near we could send a messenger for help and lie down to await his return. We knew there was a little water in the tins of vegetables, and hoped that if we kept very still this would keep us all alive for an extra day.

It was a terrible afternoon of mirage. I do not know whether weariness had affected our eyes, but on every side we saw hills, dunes, brushwood, and always they were the same dark patches of gravel. "It is a simple route to Taiserbo," had said the kaimakaan at Jalo, "but one mistake means destruction!" Had we really made the one mistake? Curiously enough, I felt no anger against Abdullah, even when he suddenly acknowledged he had not been to Taiserbo for twenty years. In fact, an odd fatalism had absorbed us all. The Beduins began discussing other disasters on these terrible southern routes.

One man had died within fifteen yards of the water he had failed to find in time. Another, whose water had gone bad on the Kufara route, had been found dead beside his camels, one of which he had killed for its blood. The blacks took an impersonal interest in these gruesome tales while they walked on with stolid calm. I gave them our last bag of dates, but warned them it would probably make them very thirsty. They replied with extreme cheerfulness that they did not want to drink in the least. They were really splendid that afternoon. They sang and laughed and cheered each other on. Little Abdul Rahim stalked on ahead with a grim smile, his rifle over his shoulder, his weakness forgotten. The only really dispirited member of the party was Abdullah, who trailed along at the heels of the caravan with downcast head. Once, when a low rise appeared to the south, he walked briskly towards it in hopes of a further view, but returned an hour later more gloomy than ever. The hot midday hours dragged along intolerably slowly. I did not feel very thirsty myself, but we had all drunk so little lately that our skins had become extraordinarily dry and parched. Our lips and gums were cracked and sore. The camels had had only a half-ration of dates the previous day and nothing that morning, so they were ravenous. They tried to eat the stuffing of the baggage saddles, and ran to every dark patch of stones in search of grass.

At 3 p.m. some faint dunes appeared on the south-east horizon. We expected Abdullah to recognise them, but his demoralisation must have been complete, for he showed no interest in them. Yusuf and Moraja began speculating as to whether they could be the "hatia" which ran between Zieghen and Taiserbo. If so, there might be vegetation on the farther side and the mystery of our position be solved. Nearly everyone ran on ahead, and only Abdul Hafiz and Omar were left to drive the camels, who were stumbling badly. It was their ninth day without water, but this mattered less than the scarcity of food. For an exhausting hour everyone struggled along at their best pace, limping, wavering, with parched mouths and bloodshot eyes, before which danced the tantalising sheets of water and cool, dark mirage hills. Suddenly Yusuf, who was on ahead, flung himself on his face and embraced the earth, afterwards executing a wild, bareheaded dance, during which he waved his long kufiya on the end of his stick. We rushed to join him and found him lovingly stroking a little mound covered with dry, brittle sticks. "It is brushwood-hattab," he said simply. "Inshallah! There is more beyond." Two other mounds appeared shortly with a little coarse, green shrub, over which the camels fought and struggled till the last scrap had disappeared. By this time sunset was near and we had to force our unsteady, aching limbs into a run to reach those elusive dunes in time to catch the clear, far view devoid of mirage that always comes at sunset. It was a pathetic race of the halt and the lame in which Hassanein and I were out-distanced. We saw the others clamber up the dune—we saw them stand gazing eastwards—and then we saw them sink motionless in silent groups. I think at that moment I felt our death warrant was sealed. I turned hopelessly to my plucky companion. "It is no good. They would have danced if it had been the 'hatia.'" "Yes, they would have made a noise," he said dully.

We crawled up to the top of the ridge, a series of wavy, curling dunes running north-west to south-east, expecting to see the same level, monotonous country that lay behind us. Instead, we were amazed to look down over a few lower dunes to an entirely changed tract. On every side were uneven mounds and hillocks covered with decayed scrub, leafless and brown, but a few hundred yards in front was a cluster of huge green bushes.

We could not understand the apathy of the soldiers, who were dejectedly rolling pebbles down the slope. "Surely there is water there," I exclaimed impatiently. "Wallahi! But that Abdullah does not know!" said Farraj. "He says only that it is not the Zeighen country." As I ran down the dune the camels literally rushed past me to the patch of green. But they did not eat. Apparently the great feathery bushes were not fodder, and the only other things among the mounds were a couple of skeletons to which the hooves and chest pads still clung. "This place is El Atash—the thirst," said Abdullah suddenly. "There is an old well here, but its water will kill you! It is salt and bad."

At the time we were obliged to rely on his statement, but since then I have discovered that he was entirely mistaken. The water at El Atash is brackish, but quite wholesome and the well can be dug out at any time. It is only filled up with sand because travellers never come there unless they have lost their way and are driven to the disused well by thirst—El Atash! There was plenty of brushwood, so we built enormous fires to cheer ourselves up, but we could cook nothing without water. The blacks ate macaroni dry and the Arabs tried flour, though we offered them our tinned meats. The soldiers had a cupful of water each, but the Beduins had none, so we had to share our last hoarded bottle with them. We dared not eat our meat ration because of the salt, so we sucked malted milk tablets and eagerly drank the water from some tinned carrots which were cool and damp. Then we tore up the baggage saddles to give the straw stuffing to the camels, for we thought we could manage one more day's march by riding.

The morning of January 3 was misty. Ripples of white fog blurred the landscape, while we silently loaded the camels, using blankets, tents, anything soft as pads

to support the panniered luggage. We ate a tin of
spinach because it was wet, but it was a hollow-eyed
procession that started due east along the "hatia" in
the hope of hitting one of the wells in the neighbourhood
of Zieghen. Abdullah had held out many hopes the
night before, but now all he would say was "Inshallah!"
We left El Atash at 7.30 and toiled laboriously round
the small mounds which looked so oddly like graves.
Three green ones gave the camels a little respite, but
there was no sign of the "gherds" (dunes) that generally
mark the presence of water. The whole retinue spread
out in a straggling line across the horizon, marching east,
and every faint rise was passionately scanned and discussed. At last Mohammed said, "If you cut my throat
now you will not find one drop of blood," referring to
the Arab idea that when a man is in fear of death all
the blood in his body rushes to his head. "It is time
that Sidi Abdullah dies," said Farraj firmly, his finger on
the trigger, and then, of course, the unexpected, the impossible, happened, and a faint dark blur appeared on
the horizon.

I have no recollection at all of the next two hours.
Whether I walked or rode or ran I do not know. What
happened to the others I have no idea. My whole being
was concentrated on those green mounds, which continually vanished and reappeared until at last they con-
solidated at 2.30 P.M. into a few clustered palms and some
"gherds" covered with stubble. I remember tottering
down a hollow and seeing some nude black figures madly
scooping up sand, and then a silent little group crouched
pitifully on the edge of the freshly dug pit that meant
life or death. The water came very slowly, for they had
chosen a bad place in their hurry, but it came. Oozing
through damp sand, the first muddy pool brought all the
primitive emotions to our hearts—joy, relief, gratitude,

too deep for words! An hour or two later life had become normal again and the deepening water brought us only the idea of a hearty meal and a bath in the biggest receptacle in the canteen.

I wonder how many readers will understand the tale of those three days, because being lost in Europe means merely an appeal to a map or a passer-by, but in Libya there is often no well for several hundred miles, and, perchance, two caravans a year or none at all! A few, just a very few, will comprehend: quiet men with tired, keen eyes—an Italian after whom a Tripolitanian "gebel" is named, half a dozen Frenchmen scattered over the great white desert south of Insalah, any Australian who has been bushed without water and certainly one or two Englishmen in strange, sunburned corners of our ruthless Empire!

We camped near the largest clump of palms within sight of the blessed well, and all afternoon I lay on my camp bed with my "zemzimaya" beside me, drinking every few minutes and when I could not drink any more I would shake it now and then to hear the delicious clutter of the water inside. In spite of all this joy we were not really out of the wood yet, for the "hatia" contained practically no forage. The camels were all feeble after their long journey and the fast at the end of it. They had to be driven here and there, from small bush to smaller tuft. It was a laborious business for our tired men and I had to leave my water-bottle once or twice to see how matters were progressing. Abdullah and Abdul Hafiz were very anxious that night, for the camels would not drink properly, so we tore up some straw mats, soaked them, and gave them to the beasts. I wanted to try them with rice, but Abdul Hafiz said they would die if they ate it.

Our guide had recovered some of his calm when he

realised that we were camping at El Atash in the Zieghen
district, at least a day and a half to two days' journey
east of the elusive Taiserbo. I was delighted when I
understood this, for fate was obviously giving me a
chance of accomplishing my old desire for travelling to
Buseima by the uncharted route which had tempted me
at Jalo.

I explained this to the retinue, and was met with
blank dismay. They wanted to go to Zieghen and then
safely by the caravan route to Kufara. They assured me
that Buseima was most dangerous, that a particularly
savage portion of the Zouia tribe dwelt there and attacked
every strange caravan at sight. I gathered that while
Kufara is a large and imposing group of oases round the
belad of the holy qubba, a big desert market and the
centre of the whole Sahara trade, besides being the headquarters of the Senussi Government and the sacred
headquarters of its religion, Buseima, although very
sparsely inhabited, is also to a minor extent a "business
centre," for caravans from Wadai and Jalo visit it.
There is no zawia there and no Government official.
The Zouias fiercely assert their independence and refuse
to admit the complete authority of the Sayeds in order
to avoid paying taxes in money, although they pay great
respect to the Senussi family and to their wishes. They
have never seen a soldier within their boundaries, and
on no account allow a stranger of any race or sect to
enter their country.

"If they do not kill us in the oasis," said Yusuf dole-
fully, "they will lie in wait for us outside among the
dunes and murder us on our way to Kufara." I said that
I thought we could massacre a few Zouias first, but even
Mohammed was frightened. "It is a bad country," he
remarked. "Why did not Allah allow us to reach
Taiserbo in safety? There is a zawia there and I have

heard of the sheikh, Sidi Mohammed. His brother was with me at the Jaghabub zawia."

I asked about the tribes in Taiserbo and was told that it was the second largest oasis, but unimportant and sparsely inhabited, that many of the date-trees belonged to the people in Buseima, that there were a few Tebus and some Zouias, of whom the larger part were Senussi. "There are different parties there," said Moraja, "but they are all good people—nahs taibeen. Beyond Taiserbo is a country of fighting. No stranger may go there. There is much danger. If we escape the Buseima people we shall fall into the hands of the Tebus of Ribiana or of wandering Tuareg bands."

In spite of these gloomy prognostications I pointed out that the camels certainly could not go five days to Kufara without food and that I had no intention whatsoever of trusting Abdullah's ideas as to the location of Taiserbo. Instead, I made the guide and Moraja each draw his idea of the famous gebel at Buseima. They both outlined in the sand a long, low, square-topped ridge. "Very well," said I firmly. "At sunset we will climb to the top of the largest gherd here and see if we cannot locate that mountain!" Having once and for all put our decorative but useless map out of our heads, we were able to reason out that Taiserbo lay to the west, ran north-east and south-west and could not be more than 25 to 40 kilometres in length, while I pinned my faith to due south for Buseima.

The desert had nearly killed us in her most ruthless mood, but when we mounted the sandy gherd and saw the red splendour fade into cold mauve and grey of the sand, while the evening star blazed as if it were a drop of liquid flame in a sapphire cup, we forgave her, especially as due south, just exactly where "instinct" had suggested to us, a faint black ridge rose, low and square,

THE MOSQUE AT AUJELA, WHERE IS BURIED THE CLERK
OF THE PROPHET MOHAMMED

DESERT WELL AT JALO

THE AUTHOR WITH THE TWO SLAVES—ZEINAB AND HAUWA

OUR CAMP AT BUTTAFAL

over the horizon. I took some bearings for fear of mirage and ordered an early start next morning in spite of wild protestations and appeals.

As a matter of fact, everyone was so tired that we did not get off till 7.30. The camels groaned plaintively and continuously, refusing to rise from their knees. I had insisted on filling girbas enough for a four days' march, though Abdullah said it was only two, and with no saddles it was difficult to balance the packs on rolled blankets and canvas. All that day was a weary succession of changing loads. When one camel sank wearily down and refused to move, we dragged off his load and placed it on another. No one rode, however blistered were his feet. Some of the blacks had raw toe joints, but we dared not risk the camels further. After about three hours we left the little mounds and sparse sticks of the "hatia" and the unbroken sands lay in great flat waves before us. We stopped at the last moment to pick the brittle wood for our evenings fires, and then marched on steadily till 6 P.M.

The "gara" of Buseima appeared suddenly at 12.30. It looked like a solid, black ridge on the horizon, but we knew it was more than a day's journey away. The camels wandered and lagged and stumbled. I doubt if we did more than 2 miles an hour. In the afternoon the sand waves developed into hard dunes, low and round-backed. We could no longer make straight for the black mark in the distance, but had to swerve eastward to avoid the higher dunes. About four I thought the camels could not go another step. Several of them lay down at the same time, but somehow we got them to their feet again, chiefly by dint of song! The reiterated refrains of the Sudanese had a great effect on the weary beasts, but never had the barraking cry "Adaryayan!" "We have arrived at the house, oh sick ones!" sounded more welcome. It was the cool, pale hour that precedes night when we encamped in a great hollow among white dunes. The stars were triumphing over the last glowing rays of the sunset and the mysterious mountain that had fired my imagination for so long lay, violet-hued and sombre, to the south.

Next morning, January 5, we again started at 7.30 and plunged immediately into a maze of dunes, great, curved, hard-backed ones, with a few soft patches in the hollows into which the camels sank, protesting. They walked rather better than the previous day in spite of a continual series of ascents and descents. Perhaps it was the sight of the strange, sinister ridge in front, coal-black against the surrounding white sand. Perhaps it was the very cold south wind which blistered our faces as we moved into it. At any rate, at 12.30 we arrived at the mysterious gebel which had first appeared as a solid, even ridge with a flat top, had then added to itself a sort of squarish, sugar-loaf hill at each end and now turned out not to be a ridge at all but a chain of cliffs, some square, some roundish, but all of sombre dull black stone with faint reddish patches. To my eyes, uninitiated into the by-ways of geology, it looked like a vast volcanic eruption, for passing east of the main body of the hills, we entered a veritable inferno of desolation. Right in the middle of the white, curly sand dunes lay a tract of about 8 kilometres of scattered black stones. Their brittle sheets of ebony matter stood up in lines—it looked as if all the old slates in the world had been flung in careless piles in this dreary region. Experts later informed me that the black stone was Nubian sandstone impregnated with iron and manganese, nothing volcanic at all. The other stones were sandstones of lighter colour, fossilised wood, and flints.

For two hours we stumbled and clattered over this

blistered, black waste, picking up specimens of as many
kinds of stone as possible and then, as we clambered up
a rough bank between two of the sombre sheer-cut hills,
the long line of Buseima palms spread before us with
the thin silver strip of lake—real water, no mirage—that
had seemed to be but a fable of Jedabia imagination!
Till we reached the stony track by the gara we had
marched in very businesslike formation—three soldiers
ahead, the camels in the middle, and scouts flung out on
the highest dunes, while everyone had rifle or revolver
ready.   Abdullah, himself a Zouia, had mocked the
blacks with "Look out, you soldiers, for now you are
coming to the land where men fight!" and therefore
every slave was athirst for battle and revenge!

CHAPTER VIII

THE LAKE IN THE DESERT

WHEN we drew level with the hills Abdullah decided to go on ahead and explain our harmless design and see if it would be possible for us to camp in the oasis. I was amused to see that even he would not go into the belad without his rifle, while the rest of the retinue implored me to take only food for the camels and then go on to Kufara, but I was not going to be cheated of my lake and my mountain, the first I had seen in Libya! I drove them protesting down the stony slope to where the desolation ended in a little sandy wadi full of huge palm clusters and coarse brown vegetation, half grass, half moss. White Abdullah tested the feelings of the two villages, one at either end of the long strip of palms that border the lake, we set up our tents in the usual camping-ground and I turned the opening of mine to face the mountain, now purple and ruddy in the afternoon sun.

The soldiers, still overwhelmed with visions of a night attack, urged us to avoid the green clumps, to whose welcome shade we clung, and pitch our tent in the open on the edge of the stony waste, but we refused, and soon Abdullah returned with news that the brother of the sheikh el zawia at Taiserbo lived in Buseima and was coming to see us. Our guide brought with him a pale-faced sister with great velvet eyes, and heavy silver necklace mixed with many leathern amulets. She gave us a kid-skin full of very good large dates, for her

148

husband owned palms and gardens in Buseima, and the
retinue began to cheer up.

We were just preparing coffee and rejoicing in our
first really clean date—for up to then all we had eaten
had been plentifully flavoured with sand—when Sidi
Mohammed el Madeni, the brother of the Taiserbo
sheikh, with Sidi Omar and Sidi Bu Regea, arrived,
prepared to welcome us most hospitably in the name of
the Sayed. It appeared that the brother of the former
was in Kufara at the moment, so we should have missed
him had we arrived in Taiserbo. Abdullah made tea
and I made coffee, and we all sat round a little zariba with
our backs to the sun and our feet to the startling cliffs.
"Fadhling" had begun again, and this time we learned
many things, all because when we asked if the water
were good, Sidi Mohammed said, "In the Nasrani well
it is very sweet!" "Nasrani? Did a Christian make it?"
"Yes; many years ago a Christian came here, flying
from Kufara, where he had lost all his belongings,
and he dug that well." At last we had found Rohlfs'
traces! In great excitement we followed the lead the
sheikhs had unwittingly given. After an hour's conversation we discovered that a man called Korayim Bu
Abd Rabu had protected Rohlfs in Kufara and saved his
life by escaping with him to Benghazi, and that his son,
Hamid Bu Korayim, was then in Kufara. They recognised the name of Bukr Bu Guettin as the man who
wished to murder Rohlfs and said that his son, Mansur,
was now living in Jedabia. They knew nothing of the
German's southern journey, but with regard to his statement that he had gone from Jalo to Taiserbo in four
and a half days, they said it was quite possible, as in
olden times the Zouias always used to ride the waterless
stretch without stopping and eat their meals on their
camels. Sidi el Mahdi and the Senussi family had started

the fashion of travelling more slowly and camping by the way.

The curious thing was they all said that when Rohlfs escaped from Kufara and passed through Buseima in his flight, he was alone with Korayim, whereas he speaks of having three Germans with him. The name by which they recognised the Teuton explorer was Mustapha Bey. Oddly enough, Sidi Omar and Bu Regea proved to be nephews of Haballah el Abed, mentioned by Rohlfs as the head of the Ait Anira, part of the Zouia tribe at Kufara, and a descendant of the last Tebu sultan, while Abdullah turned out to be a near relation of the same chief.

We tried to discover where in the Kufara oasis the fight had taken place. "There was no fight," they said. "The man was a Nasrani. He came without the permission of Sidi el Mahdi, who was then at Jaghabub. He deserved to die. His caravan was eaten up by Bu Guettin and the Zouias and he did not go to the belads at all." "Where did he camp, then?" I asked. "We do not know," they said. "We were young then. Senussi influence had only just started. There were but four ekhwan in Kufara, but the Nasrani did not go into the country." It was impossible to pin them down to details, but they evidently believed that the gallant Teuton had camped on the outskirts of Kufara and been obliged to retire after the loss of his caravan. To our amusement neither Abdullah nor our two visitors were proud of their connexion with the Tebu sultan. "It was before Islam," they said. "The Tebawiya were infidels—Kufara!"

We asked if there were any of these savages left in Buseima and were told that the Tebus were rapidly dying out and while some had been converted to Islam and continued living in Kufara and Taiserbo, the remainder had ensconced themselves in Ribiana. Our

Informant added that when the Zouias made their voluntary submission to Sidi Ben Ali es Senussi the Tebus were already their servants or slaves, for they had been originally conquered by the Fawai tribe, who had been forced to give way to the Ghawazi, who in their turn had fallen before the prowess of the fighting Zouias. This tribe originally came from the Fezzan, where some of the stock still exist in the Aulad Bu Hassan.

We went to bed that night feeling really truimphant, for the shadows that for so long had veiled the strange Libyan oasis were being gradually rolled away. At the same time we realised how difficult it is to dig out even recent history from the cautious Arab brain. We were anxious to open a Tebu tomb, but in order to do so we had to talk for nearly an hour about Egyptian mummies, so that we could ask if perchance the infidels who used to live in Buseima had buried their dead in the same way. I must acknowledge that Sidi Mohammed el Madeni was the most intelligent and broad-minded Arab whom I have met. From him we learnt much of the history of the spread of the Senussi influence through the Sahara, and he offered to show us all over the oasis on the following day.

We woke late on January 6 and found both our watches had stopped, but the sun was strong, so we imagined it must be about 8, and hurried through a breakfast of coffee, dates and unleavened bread in order to begin our voyage of exploration. Our start, however, was delayed by a furious quarrel between the blacks and the Beduins as to whose duty it was to re-make the baggage saddles and fetch water for the camp. For once I discarded soothing words and rated them all so soundly that in a few moments the toothless Farraj was creeping off in one direction with a girba and Shakri positively running to the wadi in search of "leaf." Earlier in the

morning there had been another squabble as to who
should go to the village for the festal sheep. We now
learned that the Sudanese dared not approach the village
singly. They had spent most of the night on sentry
duty of the most primitive kind. They had made a fire
and sat well within its light, so that no lurking marauder
would have had the slightest difficulty in shooting them
at all. They also talked at the top of their voices, which
disturbed our sleep and naturally after such unusual
energy they were feeling cross and tired. The arrival of
the black and white sheep, led by the undismayed Omar,
cheered them up somewhat, and we left them already
making plans for its division.

It is generally impossible to buy food in the desert
oases. There are no regular customers and no suq. Each
family produces enough for its own consumption only.
Thus neither bread, eggs nor milk were forthcoming,
though we were reported rich. Dates are always an
exception to the rule. A mejidie buys a great sackful
and though Buseima and Ribiana do not pay taxes in
money, they feed the Sayed's camels free when they
happen to pass through. They also pay a percentage of
sacks of dates yearly to the Government. An official
comes from Kufara to collect them. Faqrun offered us
some of those that were stored ready for removal. "You
are the Sayed's guests. You have a right to them," he
said. Though there was no fodder or grass for our beasts,
there were plentiful date rations. We had bargained
endlessly over the sheep with a strong-minded female in
the attractive Buseima dress—white tobh with scarlet
girdle, a black cloth wound closely round the face like
a nun's coif and the barracan of rose and saffron just
doubled and flung over her head like a great shawl.
Finally, we bought it for fourteen mejidies, and a small
boy suddenly appeared with ten eggs, for which he asked

a mejidie (fivepence) each! Abdullah contributed the
most bitter goat's milk I have ever tasted, mixed with
fresh laghbi—the juice of the palm, which ferments after
twenty-four hours and makes a very potent liquor. The
stern Senussi law decrees that anyone getting drunk on
laghbi shall be flogged and fined.

After all disputes were settled we mounted the two
least weary camels and started picking our way across
the waste of salt that lay between our camp at one end
of the semi-circular strip of palms and the village at the
other. It was difficult going, because the salt was caked
in hard and uneven formation, but it was a wonderful
morning, vividly clear and cool in spite of a brilliant sun.
To the east of us lay the chain of cliffs, no longer black,
but purplish red, against the pale dunes beyond. To the
west was an iridescent blue lake about eight kilometres
long, very salt, so that no fish can live in it, but exquisitely
translucent. Beyond it was the border of massed palms
and the faintly coral sands, for the reddish dust from the
gebel tints the neighbouring country.

Half-way across the salt waste we were met by Sidi
Mohammed, and before we left it the whole male population of Buseima had joined us. Our amusement may be
imagined when we discovered that it numbered about
a score! Including men, women and children, I don't
believe that there were more than fifty human beings
in the danger spot that all our fully armed retinue were
mortally afraid to approach! Thereafter we had the
profoundest distrust of the far-spread tales of marauding
bands and murdered caravans.

I also came to the conclusion that the Senussi influence
was much more firmly established in the smaller oasis
than is generally supposed. Sidi Mohammed had kissed
the Sayed's letter and touched his eyelids with it and the
important Faqrun family, about whose loyalty our retinue

had entertained the gravest doubts, had only waited to welcome us until they were certain we were under the protection of Sidi Idris. Once assured of this, the two brothers Faqrun, Maihub and Salah, met us most amicably and showed us the ruins of a Tebu village on the north-west shore of the lake. The Tebawiya must have led cramped existences, for their houses are tiny and of an odd formation, a series of small, round constructions like immense native ovens. Some of them had three or four of these round "rooms" clustered together without regular order, like the cells in a honeycomb. They were made of stones and quite hard mortar, and were window-less unless there had originally been some windows higher up. Unfortunately they were all roofless, the highest walls being about 15 feet 8 inches. Only one door gave access even to the biggest clusters.

Before we came to these ruins we passed east of one of the smaller round hills of the Gara and faint traces of a Tebu fort were pointed out to us. There had been another on the main cliff of the gebel opposite, so the Tebu must have been a warrior race. These forts would have been impregnable, situated on the top of almost perpendicular rocks, commanding a view of the surrounding country 50 kilometres on every side and, moreover, showing a very good idea of defence, for they must have utilised various ridges of rock as walls and barricades. On the main gebel are some Tebu tombs, but they are difficult to find among the mass of stones. These primitive people were buried in a sitting position exactly as Rohlfs describes the one he saw in Taiserbo, but generally they have sheepskins wound round them. Apparently they had no knowledge of textiles and wore only skins.

The main village of Buseima, at the north-west end of the lake, with well-kept and well-fenced date gardens, in which grow a few vegetables and fig-trees, stretching to the water's edge, was another surprise to us, for it contained but six houses, square buildings with solid, well-constructed walls, and regular, neatly finished yards, with strong wooden doors.   They looked neat and comfortable, and had none of the crumbling aspect so common to Arab villages.   Here we left the men of Buseima after they had promised to come and share our woolly sheep with us in the evening.   Sidi Mohammed continued the tour of the lake to show us the Bir Nasrani, a tiny hollow at the roots of a great clump of palms.   We had brought our fanatis to fill, as this was supposed to be the best water in the oasis and, while two blacks were slowly scooping up the cold liquid, we "fadhled" in the shade and drew maps in the sand, locating the elusive Taiserbo where "each man sticks to his village and never goes beyond it; so no one meets them or hears about them."   Ribiana, we found, lay a day and a half's journey due south, through bad sands, which put it in the middle of Kufara (Kebabo) according to our map.

After leaving the well we skirted round the whole of the outer shore of the lake and wondered if we had wandered into fairyland by mistake.   It seemed incredible that after fourteen days in the intolerable sands, unchanging and characterless, we should be in an iridescent setting of turquoise, emerald and amethyst.   Buseima is the loveliest oasis I have ever seen, with its strange, ruddy hills—jewels purple and crimson reflected in the silver salt mirage which girdles the bluest lake in the world. All this colour is clear-cut against the soft, pale dunes. It is seen through a frame of drooping palm branches with perhaps a rose-hued figure, scarlet sashed, guarding a flock of goats by a dark pool among high green rushes. Time stood still for us that day as we wandered slowly on from green of the palms to gold of the sands and so back to our tents in the wadi.   We had eaten nothing

since the date and damper breakfast, so we urged Faraj
to cook some part of the sheep—which now hung in neat
portions in the thickest palm clump—as speedily as
possible, but certainly our day was out of gear, for the
sun set as the smiling black triumphantly produced our
lunch—a raw-looking leg of mutton in a small frying-pan
with two minute, sandy, poached eggs balanced on top
of it!

Later the two Faqruns, Sidi Mohammed, Sidi Omar
and Bu Regea, came to partake of our sheep flanked by
two enormous bowls of rice. Everybody ate out of the
same dish with their fingers, scooping up the food swiftly,
without speech, but with loud sucking noises. Afterwards we drank so much green tea that sleep became
impossible, and with the stars for lamps and the palm
clumps for walls, we sat round a little fire and talked
slowly with long pauses. We were told that when Sidi
Idris passed through the oasis he camped for two days
under an immense cluster of palms within six feet of the
blue lake and the spot was now regarded with awe and
reverence. We informed our guests that the Emir had
lately gone to Italy to visit the King. Sidi Mohammed
seemed puzzled that the Holy One should have established
such a precedent. "Why did not the King come to see
the Sayed?" he asked, "for it is the visitor, not the host,
who confers honour in Arab land."

Finally the question of departure arose and we
discussed the possibility of going to Taiserbo first,
thinking from Rohlfs' description that there must be
some interesting Tebu ruins there. Taiserbo was supposed by the adventurous German to have been the seat
of the Tebu sultanate and he suggested that some ruins
at Diranjedi might have been the stronghold of the
reigning potentate. For this reason we were anxious
to see the second largest of the desert oases, in spite of

the fact that geographically and commercially it was described as uninteresting. Kufara is the centre of the Sahara world; Buseima produces the finest dates in Libya and caravans come from Jalo to fetch them; Ribiana is apparently the haunt of the most lawless human element in the neighbourhood. We were told that there were five hundred Tebu there, but it was probably incorrect.

Taiserbo is outside the trade circuit and contents itself with a peaceful, self-centred existence. We heard the number of its inhabitants put as low as fifty and as high as two hundred. With regard to its size, it was generally supposed to be between 25 and 30 kilometres long and about 10 kilometres in breadth. It lies from north-west to south-east, with its northernmost end but a point or two west of due south of Jalo. It comprises eleven so-called villages of which the largest is Gezira, containing ten houses. The traveller from the north should arrive at Ain Jelelat or Ain Talib, within a kilometre of each other. Two kilometres south of these wells is Gezira, where there is the Senussi zawia, whose sheikh is Sidi Mohammed el Madeni, brother of our friend with the same name. South of Gezira lies Mabus el Awadil and Mabus Gaballa, some 2 kilometres apart. Sixteen kilometres east of Gezira is Kusebeya, the most easterly point in the oasis. Eight kilometres west of Ain Jelelat is El Wadi and a kilometre farther on is El Abd. On the extreme West is Tunisi. At El Wadi is the Kasr Diranjedi, where there are some old Tebu buildings, one of which might have been a castle or a palace. El Wadi is the most populated part. There are other Tebu ruins at Dahwa, Ain Jelelat and Gezira.

There are clusters of palms round all the villages, with patches of "halfa" (half grass, half moss) in between.

A band of "hattab"—small mounds with some brush-wood and fodder—surrounds the whole oasis. Some of the smaller villages contain but two or three houses. The larger dwellings are made of sand and stones, and the poor ones are merely shelters of woven palm leaves with small, square courts of palms.

Most of this information came from the Sheikh el Madeni, whose people had originally lived in Jaghabub, where they had a violent quarrel with another family of ekhwans. Blood had been shed and Sayed Ahmed Sherif had arbitrarily ordered the emigration of the Madeni to Taiserbo, where two brothers now lived. The one we met had quarrelled with them, and been banished to Buseima. It speaks well for the prestige of the Senussi family that the Madeni are still their loyal ad-herents, though poor Sidi Mohammed spoke of Kufara and Jaghabub as centres of civilisation and culture and Buseima as the back of beyond.

We spent hours drawing sand maps in the firelight, while a waning moon gleamed pale in the amazing sky of Africa, sapphire blue, yet soft as the azure veils of a Circassian bride. Occasionally the toothless Farraj challenged an imaginary passer-by with a sharp "Min?" Occasionally there was a rustle in the palms, which Shakri said was a cat who wanted to investigate our temporary larder. Before that night I had no idea how exciting it was trying to make geography. For a year I had worked and plotted to reach Kufara because the thought of this holy oasis, nucleus of the greatest Islamic confraternity, rigidly guarded from every stranger, the centre of the mighty influence against which every European Power has battled in turn, stirred my imagination. As I gradually learned more about this group of desert cities, Hawari, Jof, Boema, Tolelib, Tolab, Zuruk and the holy Taj, and realised how they represented the spider at the

heart of the web, whose threads were the long caravan
routes spreading out in every direction from Tripoli to
the Sudan, from Lake Chad to Egypt, the commercial
side of the problem fascinated me. Kufara controls the
desert trade of half the Sahara. So few of the old routes
are open now and others are almost impracticable for
lack of wells, but there are infinite possibilities in the
future. Camels need not remain for ever the only means
of transport in Libya. Cisterns of water might be stored
at various known posts, as is done between Jalo and
Jaghabub, where the Sayeds have caused water to be kept
in great stone jars for the use of travellers.

That night at Buseima, when our guests departed,
we returned to the tent athirst for map-making. We
shut the flaps and drew out our secreted apparatus. We
ruined many sheets of paper and lost our compass in the
sand a dozen times before we produced the first rough
chart of the desert oasis, but we felt the effort was worth
while when we saw the wells we had added to the 1915
Egyptian Survey map. "Let us hope we shall have
saved the next European quite a lot of trouble!" said
Hassanein, unconsciously adding sand to his already
ruffled hair.

Sidi Mohammed spent the night in our camp. I
thought it was to avoid the long walk back in the dark,
for he lived in the farthest away of the two villages. In
the morning I discovered he had done it as a precaution.
Apparently the tales of danger were not so absurd as
we had thought. The Faqrun men had said to Mohammed, "Wallahi! If it had not been for Sidi el Madeni,
we would have killed you all!" It remains a complete
mystery how they proposed to do it, but there could be
no further doubt about Buseima's dislike of strangers.
A pale-faced woman had slipped out of the bushes to
talk to Moraja as he went out of the camp. The sergeant

had Arab blood mixed with his Sudanese and the figure in blurred reds and fawns was of his kin. "Why did you bring these Egyptians here?" she asked angrily. "We do not want strangers. Make them go, or they will suffer!" The morning of January 7, therefore, everyone had a new panic. It was in vain that we asked them if they were afraid of a mere handful or of shadows. They resurrected all the old stories and, with frantic glances at the deserted dunes, they implored us to depart at once.

The pitiful thing was that Mohammed's spirit was utterly broken by the last three days of thirst. "Allah has given me a new life," he said. "I dare not risk it again." We were quite used to the cowardice of Yusuf and Abdul Rahim, a pathetic little wisp of a man who had no physique and no fighting spirit, but I was very sorry for Mohammed. He had been my greatest ally, always ready for work or for risk. Now his mind seemed to have suffered as well as his body. I wondered whether he would be of much use to us in the future. As I poached eggs on a sweet-smelling fire and made coffee in the "Nasrani water," which tasted so sweet but which made one's mouth terribly dry, I wished the retinue could absorb a little of the scene. The only things that moved in the purple and gold of rock and dune were the little grey and black birds, like water-wagtails—the "abu fasada" of Egypt. I suppose one should make an exception for the insects, for there were several kinds of beetles, as well as long, sandy locusts and actually mosquitoes, though the latter were either particularly merciful or abhorred the European as much as did the other inhabitants of Buseima.

After breakfast we climbed to the top of one of the rocky cliffs. Moraja assured us that it would take the whole day. We completed the ascent in three-quarters

CARAVAN ON THE MARCH BETWEEN BUTTAFAL AND TAISERBO

THE MOUNTAINS OF BUSEIMA

CARAVAN IN DUNE COUNTRY NEAR BUSEIMA

THE FIRST MEETING BETWEEN THE FAQRUN FAMILY
AND OUR PARTY AT BUSEIMA

of an hour, probably about 100 metres. Our camp level
in the wadi was just under 380 metres. The view was
marvellous. The whole oasis spread below us, with the
great gap in the cliffs through which we had come two
days before and beyond, on every side, were the waving
lines of creamy dunes, growing steeper as we looked south
to Ribiana or south-east to Kufara. Two spots of black
broke the monotony of pale curves—outlying blocks of
the Buseima Gara.

On our way back we explored a good many ruined
Tebu houses scattered here and there on the rough salt
waste between our camp and the cliffs. The walls were
still in good condition and the houses were larger than
on the farther side of the lake. The biggest round bee-
hive room measured 8 feet 6 inches in diameter. I left
Hassanein to tell the retinue that we would start the
next morning and to listen to their elaborate plans for
defence upon the way, while I went with Abdullah to visit
his relations in the neighbouring village. His sister lived
in a low hut made of palm branches and a little square
court in front, with a wall of the same waving leaves.
There was nothing inside the one room except some mats
of plaited fronds, a few woven grass bowls full of dates,
a couple of yellow gourds, a kid-skin of water, and some
rather doubtful blankets. The whole life of these people
depends on the palm. Their houses, mats, bowls, food,
drink, baskets, string, shoes, stuffing for camel-saddles,
all come from it.

Several women gathered round me in the cool darkness. Most of them were pretty, with pale olive faces
and pointed chins. The dark eyes of a Latin race looked
out between heavy, black-fringed lashes, their features
were finely cut and they had the most beautiful pearly
teeth I have ever seen. They told me it was the effect
of dates and the thing that most interested them in me

was a gold stopping! They thought it was a new form of jewellery and everyone in turn was called upon to inspect and poke my unfortunate tooth. "If we have gold," they said, "we make it into necklaces and ear-rings. Why do you wear it in your mouth?" They insisted on unwinding my cumbersome red hezaam, which I had always rolled round my waist, and swathing it very low on my hips, which gave me the immensely long-bodied effect of all Arab women. They showed me all their jewellery—huge silver ear-rings, necklaces and amulets—and asked me why I had no tattoo marks to show my tribe. Altogether we spent an amusing hour in the dark palm-room, varied by drinking sour goat's milk out of bowls made of palm wood, and eating dry, black dates almost too hard to bite.

From Buseima there are two routes, one due south to Ribiana, described as a day and a half through very big dunes, a hard road that no guide likes to face, and another slightly south-east, taking three and a half days, of which two are difficult. From Ribiana it is possible to continue through the same high dunes to the Kufara group. By the more direct route one arrives at Hawari and by the longer one at Tolab. We took the straight road without hesitation, for our camels had by no means recovered from our last disastrous journey. Two of the nagas were expected to foal at any moment and all looked extremely thin and weak. Abdul Hafiz shook his head over them despondently. "Allah is great," he said, "but so are the dunes!"

We left Buseima at 8.20 on January 8. Bu Regea walked with us to the top of the first sand ridge, from where there was a marvellous view of the whole oasis, palms, lake and mountains, the latter like ruddy amethysts in a gold setting. The "Fatha" was solemnly repeated on the summit of a sharp rise; then, after many good

wishes and blessings, we plunged sharply into the maze
of dunes. The strange little scene stuck in my mind
because of the treachery that we knew underlay it. The
preceding evening, after they had eaten our food, one of
the Faqrun family had said to Yusuf, "Wallahi! Had
we but a force equal to yours, you should not now depart,"
while the loyal Sheikh el Madeni had urged Mohammed
to leave the oasis as soon as possible.

The morning of our departure a spy arrived from
Ribiana, saying, "The Bazama family have just returned
from Jedabia, and they tell us that strangers are coming
to this country. We cannot believe it is true that the
Sayed has given permission to any stranger to visit
Kufara. I have been sent to discover the truth." Now
the aged ekhwan who originally intended to accompany
us on our journey, Haji Fetater, had warned Abdullah
that the Sayed should not allow the Bazamas to go to
Ribiana until we had returned in safety. Amidst all the
complications of our departure the warning had been
ignored, yet when the spy's words were repeated to us we
felt at last we understood the situation. Ever since we
had left Jedabia there had been a strange undercurrent
that we could not understand. We met with much hospitality and friendliness, yet always an odd distrust
dogged our footsteps, while queer, impossible rumours
spread before us. There was the robber band that laid in
wait for us near Bir Rassam. There was the change of
front at Aujela. Even in Jalo there was a faint uneasy
shadow, which Hameida Bey Zeitun explained by saying
that some of the sheikhs were old-fashioned and ignorant.
Then came the actual enmity of Buseima, with all the
rumours and warnings that terrified our retinue and were
disregarded by us. The culminating point was the arrival
of the spy, whose tale gave us every reason to suppose
that we should be attacked on the way to Kufara, for he

made exhaustive inquiries as to the strength of our party and the retinue we were taking.

It was Mohammed who elucidated the mystery. He told us that the Bazamas were an old and highly respected Senussi family, who had been ekhwan since the ancestor, who was sent to Kufara by Sidi Ben Ali, was one of the original four who were to instruct the Zouias in the faith of Islam. There had been an ancient dispute about the possession of some land in Ribiana between the Sayeds and a member of this family, but Sayed Ahmed had settled matters amicably by making them sheikhs of Ribiana. Unfortunately, they had lately evaded the payment of "Onshur" (the tenth part) to the Government, on the grounds that they had not enough servants to till the lands. Sidi Idris had just removed them from office and appointed another man in their place. Consequently the whole Bazama family were in search of revenge. What better opportunity could offer than the murder of the Sayed's guests, who were, moreover, generally supposed to be engaged on an important Senussi mission?

Now we could trace all the threads to one spinning-wheel. We had attributed the robbers to chance greed, the affair at Aujela to the meanness of a surly Zouia who did not wish to feast the travellers, the rumours of danger in Buseima to the strained imaginations of the retinue. As a matter of fact, we probably owed our continued existence in the first place to our disguised flight, which misled Jedabia. Later on, Hassanein's eloquence the first night in the She-ib's tent at Aujela; at Jalo, the loyalty of the kaimakaan; at Buseima the smallness of the population doubtless saved us from disaster; but what about Kufara? The Bazamas might have much influence there, and in a large Arab oasis there are always factions only too glad of an excuse to squabble. The sacred character of the place and the fierce fanaticism of the older Senussi would give our enemies every chance of fomenting the distrust which the advent of the first strangers in their history must naturally arouse. Mohammed and Yusuf were exceedingly troubled. For the hundredth time I imagine they wished they had never started on this southern journey! The story invented by the Bazamas, the one most likely to unite every faction and family against us, was that Sidi Idris had sold Kufara, Ribiana and Buseima to Europeans, and that Christian strangers (sometimes I was reported to be the Queen of Italy!) were coming to gain all information about the country, so that the Europeans could occupy it with greater ease! Unless this amazing rumour could be rapidly discredited, every man's hand would be against us and our lives not worth the fraction of a centime!

We calculated that the spy would waste at least half the day "fadhling" at Buseima, after which it would take him a day to return to Ribiana. We expected that more time would be wasted there in organising the attack and so hoped, by moving speedily, to arrive at Hawari without a battle. It would not matter much, in case of attack, whether we were victorious or not, for in the former case we should have started a blood feud and the relatives of the slain would lie in wait for us on our return.

Unfortunately, the dunes made rapid progress impossible. The camels slipped and fell going down them; the ungirthed loads were flung off in all directions. The beasts had to be urged up them slowly and laboriously. We were obliged to wind round the largest and our course that day was an infinitely slow zigzag. We rose to a height of 580 metres, with great waves and ridges of dunes running irregularly on every side. At 3 P. M. we arrived at an almost flat stretch with one very high pointed dune measuring nearly 100 metres high at the farther side. We clambered up this and had a wonderful view over the turbulent sea of sand. Behind us the great cliffs of Buseima appeared just sunk among the dunes. On the western horizon rose another long, square-topped formation, dark as the gara we had left. This was the mountain of Ribiana. It appeared to me at least 60 kilometres away. To the east were clearly visible the Fadil hills and the Hawaish between Zieghen and Kufara, mere little blots of indigo among the curly sand ridges. At 5 P.M. we were forced to camp because one of the nagas was foaling. She walked up to the last moment and an hour later she appeared to have recovered, but, alas! the foal was reported dying, which depressed the Arabs intensely, for camels are gold in their eyes, and gold to them is Alpha and Omega and a great deal else in between!

The Sudanese amused me greatly that evening. "Don't be afraid! We will defend your life," said Farraj cheerfully. With memories of their various panics in Buseima, I replied, "Don't you worry about defending my life. I can do that all right. Keep your minds fixed on defending your own!" This was a new point of view and elicited the doleful answer, "But I don't want to fight without a reason. There is a little girl I want to marry when I go back!"

January 9 was a very cold morning, so the retinue dawdled hopelessly over their meal. The Sudanese prefer the fiercest sun to a touch of cold, which literally freezes them. We started at 8 A.M., and made better progress than the previous day, in spite of the fact that the foal, having completely recovered, had to be carried in a sort of pannier on the mother's back. The dunes were very uneven in size. Sometimes for a kilometre or two there was a stretch of mildly undulating sands and then we would come to great massive dunes like small mountains, from the top of which one had a view of the four black, rocky chains, roughly east, south, north and west. At 10 A.M. we climbed to the top of the Seif el-Biram, which the Arabs say is the highest on the route. It is called the "Dune of Firepots," because the Zouia women, flying south before the Turkish occupation of the northern oasis, took their clay cooking pots with them on their camels. As the beasts crawled down the precipitous slopes of the mighty dune the vessels fell off and were all broken! To a certain extent our caravan repeated the experience, for most of the baggage collapsed and a strange woman who was travelling with us—a pale girl-widow, who had left her baby in Buseima because her husband's family refused to give it up and had claimed our protection to go to Kufara to join her own people—turned a complete somersault over the head of her surprised camel. Luckily the sand was soft! It became distinctly pinkish as we went farther south, a pale coral colour. Unfortunately, another naga took it into her head to foal, after we had done only 28 kilometres and we were forced to camp at 3 P.M. Luckily there was no doubt about this foal's health, so we avoided the gloom of the preceding evening.

Yusuf and Abdullah sat with me while the tent was being erected in a wide open space, splendidly open to attack, but the fatalistic spirit of the desert had made us careless. They told me stories of Sidi el Mahdi, who is supposed among the Beduins to be still alive and a mystic wanderer in the Sahara. Some day he will return to lead the Senussi to further glory and power, "Inshallah!" They say that he disappeared suddenly at Garu on the way to Wadai and another was buried in his place in the holy morabit in Kufara. As an instance of his continued existence they quoted the experience of some Arabs seated round their camp fire amidst the starlit dunes. To them came a stranger who asked them for news of the Mahdi. "Our lord is dead," they replied; "the Sayeds at Kufara say so." "He is alive," said the stranger, "Huwa fi Wasst." The Beduins translated this to mean that Sidi el Mahdi was in a town called "Wasst" in Algeria, and they rushed with the news to Kufara. "Why did you not hold the man?" asked the sheikhs. "That was the Mahdi. He is alive. He told you he was 'fiwasst,' 'between you.'" The play on the Arabic words is clumsy in English. "Fi-wasst" means "between," "in the middle of," while "fi" means "in," and "Wasst" might be the name of a place.

The previous night we had camped with a feeling of unrest and apprehension. Everybody clung to his rifle and I remember Hassanein and I had a fierce dispute over an ancient musket, left behind by a soldier who had deserted at Jalo, reducing our army to nine, inclusive of commandant and sergeant. As a matter of fact, the weapon which really filled the Beduin soul with terror was Hassanein's useless target pistol. Its long barrel thrilled them and we overheard Abdullah telling a friend that Ahmed Bey had a revolver which could shoot people an hour away!

The second night the desert had stuck in her claw again—fatal anæsthetic which makes one utterly careless of the future—"What matter dead yesterday and unborn to-morrow, so that the day be good?" In truth the days are generally extremely trying, for there is either a blazing sun which burns through the thin cotton barracan over the wound handkerchief, or a bitter wind which pierces every bone in one's body. Sometimes there were both together and then one side of one is frozen and the other baked! One's skin split and blistered under this treatment, but there was only one hour I shall never be able to forgive the desert. This was the moment when, at 5 A.M., one crept shivering out of one's warm flea-bag into pitch darkness, placed one's feet gingerly on icy cold sand, fumbled with numb fingers for a candle and matches, and proceeded to drag on cold, stiff garments from each of which fell a shower of sand. Meanwhile, with chattering teeth, one had to call out loud, cheerful greetings and hearty good wishes to rouse our improvident following, although one's mind contained nothing but venomous invective! However, the nights were good. On that particular one, Shakri, being sentinel, stationed himself clear-cut against the starlit sky on the top of the highest dune and, in case his presence were not sufficiently obvious, he played mournful little tunes on a wooden flute.

Next day, January 10, we started at 6.30 A.M., after the usual breakfast of half a plate of rice with a dozen dates and a cup of coffee. It is amazing how one gets accustomed to much work on little food. We walked for eleven and a quarter hours, doing 44 kilometres as the crow flies, with only a handful of dates at midday. Moreover, when we reached camp there was always map-drawing and writing to be done before we thought of supper.

That day Abdullah and I started off briskly in front of the others, for it was very cold and the sun had not yet risen above the dunes. We were soon stopped by the sight of something white a little to our left. Upon inspection it proved to be a pathetic reminder of the desert cruelty we had escaped just a week ago. Three human skeletons lay in a huddled group, half-covered with sand. "Thirst," said Abdullah grimly. It must have been a fairly recent tragedy, for the men's white clothes were in good condition, and the skin of the hands was still yellow and dry. The strange woman bent over them pityingly. "Three men were lost on their way from Ribiana to Kufara," she said. "Their baggage was found but they had disappeared." The soldiers, however, said they were probably blacks, for they had many Sudanese hejabs on them. We found some leather amulets, a fox's foot and the complete bones of a bird, but I would not let the men disturb the desolate scene further. With a "Rahmat Ullahi Allahim!" we passed on to join the caravan.

The foals were being carried in panniers, one on each side of the biggest naga, and occasionally we had to stop to let them feed. Otherwise we made good pace, for the dunes were gradually getting less steep. At 8 A.M. we mounted the last big rise and saw before us a sea of low coral waves, for the sand was getting steadily pinker, with the black mass of the gebel in front. Great was our excitement, however, when, with binoculars, we were able to follow this chain, apparently with scarcely a break, to very near the position of the Ribiana Gara. In fact, the whole horizon seemed to be enclosed in a semicircle of irregular violet hills, stretching from the Fadil and Hawaish to the north-west and west with scarcely a break where Kufara lay, to the long chain of the Gebel Neri. From the map we had seen we had supposed the hills to be in small, regular groups. This marvellous view of a land enclosed by strange cliffs was so unexpected that it was like discovering a new country. From that point the ranges appeared to run in a complete half-circle from north-west to south-east. With blazing eyes Hassanein began tracing his sand maps. "Don't you see the Hawari Gara is a continuation of the Gebel Neri?" he said. "Yes, and the Ribiana Gara is a bit broken off the other end," I answered with rising excitement. "Do you know, the Hawaish mountain was originally called the

Keid el Adu, 'vexation of the enemy,' " he continued, "because no one could break through it?" "To enter the enclosed land," I interrupted. "Of course, these oases are all linked in a circle by the black hills. Taiserbo alone has no gara—she lies outside."

From that moment I have always thought of Buseima, Kufara and Ribiana as the mountain oases of Libya. Some day, no doubt, geologists will come and prove our theory false or true, but for me the palm gardens isolated in the middle of red sands, each with its guardian crag, will ever be an island country within the arms of the strange dark mountains.

The name Hawaish means a great beast; therefore we questioned Yusuf and Abdullah closely about these mountains. "No one ever goes there," they said. "The jinns live there!" "Does anyone ever go to Gebel Neri?" "No; they are afraid." "What are they afraid of?" "They do not know." "Have they seen anything?" "No. When they go near the mountains they have a feeling." "Are there men there?" "No. There is no water nor food. Men lived there long ago and drank rain water." "They may be there still, then?" "No. There are jinns." "What do they look like?" "Nobody has seen them." "How do you know they are there?" "In the morning one can sometimes hear a loud noise as of many birds." "And no one has seen anything?" "They have seen bones." "What kind of bones?" "They do not know. They are afraid." Pressed on this point, Yusuf said the bones were big and drew a picture in the sand which might represent the vertebræ of anything from a man to a camel! I repeat this conversation verbatim in order to show how difficult it is to draw information from a Libyan Arab!

CHAPTER IX

TREACHERY AT HAWARI

IN the afternoon we left the dunes behind and emerged on flat, rolling country, with broad sand-waves ahead and the purple crags of the Neri running south in an irregular mass of peaks and square-topped ridges, with dark stretches of stones and lava in between. The sand was now the colour of mellow brickdust, with occasional streaks of purplish red and scattered patches of stones of all colours, like those I had picked up in Buseima. Some of the ground looked almost like mosaic work in blues, mauves and reds. Hoping to arrive at Hawari on the morrow, the caravan moved briskly through the sunset, when the land turned an ugly hot brown and the aching cliffs tore the orange sky with sombre violet crests. We barraked beneath the first big, round sand wave, from where we could see the dark gara of Hawari—a continuation of the Gebel Neri—and while we triumphed in our success as geographers, the retinue developed a beautiful new panic!

They had heard that one man had left the Bazama caravan at El Harrash and gone on to Kufara. Abdullah suggested that he would have spread all kinds of libel about us and Abdul Rahim grew pale beneath his ebony! The pitiful thing was that Mohammed had so completely lost his nerve that he too was terrified. He had changed very much in the last week. He no longer looked out upon the world with his old, frank, boyish glance. His eyes wavered and fell. He never laughed or sang these days. I think that he was really the only imaginative

and sensitive man in the party and therefore he alone
had conjured up visions of what dying of thirst really
meant. Also his reserved pride had been violently
wounded by the attitude of Buseima, though he would
never acknowledge it. Unfortunately, that morning he
had seen the skeletons and drew on his vivid imagination
for details and comparisons. This completed his demoralisation. He joined with the guide and the soldiers in
imploring us to go past Hawari by night and arrive at
Kufara proper before dawn, so that by the time anyone
woke up in Taj we should be established in one of the
Sayed's houses, presumably in a state of armed defence.
In vain we argued and protested. They all foresaw a
well-organised attack the moment the inhabitants of
Hawari perceived us. To do Yusuf justice, he was the
only one who declared this was nonsense. "There may
be robbers," he said, "but how could they openly attack
the Sayed's slaves?" We found an unexpected ally in
him when, sitting round the camp fire, we tried to instil
a little courage into the retinue while at the same time
insisting on staying in Hawari.

It had been an exceedingly hot day and feet had
blistered anew, which perhaps accounted for the mental
depression. Yusuf was our most reliable barometer.
When he discarded the fleece-lined waterproof and strode
along in his fluttering white shirt and a skull cap, as he
had done that afternoon, we knew it must be almost
torrid. I never saw Mohammed walk without my
plaid rug wound over the top of the torn woolly waterproof!

January 11 I saw the sun rise from the top of the
immense dune that had guarded our slumbers. The
dull sand turned slowly pink as the purple cliffs of the
Gebel Neri came into view in low, irregular masses to
the south, while a little to the east of them appeared

the solitary black rock of the Hawari Gara. It looked at least a day's journey away. Abdullah said we should reach it by midday. As we marched towards it I tried to draw out more tales of the desolate mountain on our right, for I was intrigued by the description of the sounds heard therein, "a noise of birds." Hornemann, the first modern writer to speak of the Tebu oasis, says that the people of Aujela described the speech of the inhabitants as "like unto the whistling of birds." Curiously enough, the Tebu women I met had extraordinarily high-pitched, sweet voices, which sounded rather like clear warbling. Moraja and Abdul Hafiz both volunteered the information that "footprints" had been seen near the haunted Gebel. "Footprints of what?" I asked. "Well, they are like snakes!" they replied. The anti-climax was too great. I could not bear my jinn or prehistoric savage to turn into a serpent!

After two hours we left the pink sands and passed into the waste of stony ridges and small hills on the outskirts of the mountains. The colours were quite extraordinary. Occasional banks of vivid vermilion lay between patches of loose black stone, with here and there scattered blocks of grey, rose and mauve, at the foot of the smaller cliffs. All round us the basis of the sand was fawnish red and as the stones grew thicker we found odd hollow tubes and balls, heavy and black, but filled with sand. The largest balls measured more than a foot across, the smallest about an inch. The blacks were delighted with these new toys and broke open the solid ones to see the sand run out, after which they used them as cups and candlesticks. I had never seen the formation before and did not know what it was. We passed the Hawari Gara at noon. It does not stand out particularly from the rest of the Gebel Neri, as it is but one cliff among many in the neighbourhood, but a few hundred yards beyond,

the ridges of stones and red sand rise sufficiently to
allow one to look, as it were, over their edge on to
a country of paler sand beyond. Here reigned our
old enemy, the mirage, so it was difficult at first to
distinguish the false from the true. On the far horizon
loomed the purple hills of the Kufara Gara. Somewhere beyond those peaks and cliffs lay the mysterious,
elusive oasis that was no near and yet always just
beyond our reach. Up till that moment we had considered Hawari as a part of Kufara, but Yusuf, pointing joyfully to a pale sand wave just before the distant
hills, said, "Do you see the white sand? Before we
come to that, below it, are the palms of Hawari, but
Kufara is 'bayid,' beyond the Gebel."

For a couple of hours we straggled across uneven
country, dotted with rare patches of stones and mounds,
with ever more and more tantalising points appearing to
the south till we wondered if the mountains ever ended.
Nobody waits for anyone else in the desert. Everyone
walks at his own favourite pace. If you cannot keep up,
you drop behind and your companion does not stop to
ask the reason. If you pause to shake the sand from a
shoe, he does not halt with you. It is against the custom,
unless you are ill. The Beduins often speak of the long,
waterless routes as "The roads where we do not wait for
a dying man. An hour for a camel, two for an Arab,
then we leave them!"

At last a stronger sand wave than most gave us a
sudden perfect view of Hawari, a long, very narrow strip
of palms running for about 12 kilometres very nearly
north and south, with two little isolated groups of palms
at the southern end. All round it lay a band of very
red sand, broken into thousands of small mounds of
"hattab," the little dry sticks we had seen before. A
third naga started to foal, but we ruthlessly left her to

the care of Abdul Hafiz and pressed on, so that we
entered the oasis at 3 P.M.

Against the wallflower sands the thick, low-growing,
heavy-foliaged palms looked almost grey. There were
few tall ones, so it was easy to cut great clusters of yellow
dates, which were very sweet and tasted of honey. I did
not like them very much. The retinue began to panic
frantically, chiefly because a group of blacks we passed
cutting dates amidst a picturesque circle of goats and
blue-robed women, asked, "Where is the caravan with
the Christian? The Bazamas sent news of it."

We went straight across the southern end of the oasis
to the palm gardens of the Sayed, which were kept in
excellent order with neat leaf fences, many wells, rows
of newly planted young palms and continuous patches
of vegetables, brightest green amidst the monotonous
brick-red sands. The whole of this portion of the oasis
was inhabited by the Sayed's slaves and we saw numbers
of blacks, men, women and children, working in the
gardens or driving small, pale grey donkeys laden with
dates. We camped on the edge of the village and Abdul
Rahim nearly had a fit when he saw me wander off to
photograph the houses, gleaming white between the
palms. He ran after me almost foaming with terror.
The general state of nerves was beginning to get boring.

The houses of Hawari are almost like European
buildings. They are exceedingly well constructed of
sand bricks in regular lines, square, solid, flat-roofed,
with windows, but many of the yards have quite low
walls, all of which are neatly coped. We had scarcely
put up the tent when the sheikh of the zawia, Musa
Squaireen, arrived to inquire our business. He was soon
followed by the leading Zouia headmen, among them
Musa Gharibeel and Mansur Bu Badr of the Gebail.
Soon a circle of a dozen were sitting round our hastily

GARDENS AND LAKE AT BUSEIMA

THE AUTHOR ON A CAMEL AT BUSEIMA

ZOUIA WOMEN AT BUSEIMA

AT BUSEIMA: TEACHING THE FAQRUN FAMILY TO
USE FIELD GLASSES

built zariba, while Mohammed's faithful follower, Omar, hurriedly made coffee. The tribesmen were slightly depressed at first and we wondered if it had anything to do with our arrival, until it appeared that one man had made a bad bargain in buying slaves from a Wadai caravan a few days before. He had paid 400 mejidies (about £70) for a man and two women, and now the man was very ill. "It was bad business," he said sadly. They all repeated the same formula, "The Sayed's orders are above our heads," and added that our visit was welcome, saying, "Your coming is a blessing. May Allah bless our Sayeds and those who come from them!" Yet Abdul Rahim started the rumour that night that we were prisoners and were not to be allowed to move till permission arrived from Kufara.

We were too sleepy to inquire into the truth, but the following morning gifts of sour leban and milk arrived, together with a couple of chickens, so we thought that probably the Zouias, while paying all honour to the Sayed's guests, were anxious to show how impossible it was for strangers to penetrate their well-guarded borders. Yusuf and Mohammed implored us not to move from the camp, which they had pitched in an unsheltered, torridly hot and fly-ridden spot to avoid robbers in the palm groves. "Wait till the big men come to see us," they said. "Then you can walk with safety." This was palpably an excuse, for Hawari is only a little village suffering from its nearness to a big centre. The whole life of the country depends on the town beyond the mountains. The big sheikhs and ekhwan live in Jof and Taj. In Clapham or Tooting one does not expect to find Ministers of the Crown. So in Hawari everyone says, "There is nothing here. All things come from Kufara." The important sheikh of the place, Bush Naf, was at the moment in Jof. For this reason we had sent on Abdullah as a herald of our coming to present our credentials to Sidi Idris's wakil and to prepare a dwelling for us in Taj.

That morning we over-ate on eggs, dates, fresh bread made with yeast—oh, but it tasted good—and goat's milk. Then, while Hassanein lazed—he called it absorbing the spirit of the desert—I hid two kodaks in the folds of my voluminous barracan, veiled my unfortunately white skin and went off to explore the town. The corporal and the largest Farraj offered to escort me, but they were not happy till they realised how little interest we aroused. We saw many well-kept gardens wherein grew vegetables, peaches, barley, thorn-tree figs. In each of them were one or two Sudanese working the primitive wells, sometimes with the aid of the delightful little grey donkeys, the cleanest things I had seen in Libya. We walked all through the village, encountering no opposition, but of subjects for photographs there were few. The big, square houses, with their complicated yards and outbuildings, were dotted here and there among the scattered palms or over the broad bare spaces of sand. There were no winding streets or passages as in Jalo and Aujela. A small, insignificant mosque, a low, square building with a row of windows, a little zawia established by the great Sidi el Mahdi, with a "qubba" that looked rather like a horse trough with an upright stone at each end (a former muezzin of the zawia), made a group at one end of the village. We climbed one of the vermilion dunes, half-covered with the feathery grey bushes we had first met at El Atash, in order to get a better view for a photograph, but the scattered houses were too far away.

On our return we passed one or two buildings with mud porticoes, whose arches could be seen above the walls of their yards. Some women came out to talk to me in high, clear voices. They were practically unveiled and wore straight, dark red tobhs, unbelted, so they made an attractive group under a large thorn-tree between high sand walls. One and all they asked for medicine, and when I returned to my fly-filled tent a group gradually gathered outside with various tales of woe. The most important entered and sat uncomfortably on my folding bed, from which they soon slipped thankfully to their accustomed crouched-up position on the sand. My treatments were simple, consisting chiefly of boracic powder and quinine, but the recipients tied the pills carefully into corners of their barracans and departed with blessings.

Suddenly a blaze of colour obstructed the view beyond my tent flap. The smallest of the grey donkeys, almost covered with a gorgeous striped mat of reds and blues, and still further obscured by the voluminous draperies of a small, huddled figure in the vividest scarlet I have ever seen, was led up by a tiny urchin in a tattered white shirt, while another beat from behind. "The mother of Sheikh Musa has come to visit you," announced one of the Farrajes. The flaming folds disengaged themselves, trailed into the tent and crumbled into a red heap on the sand, from which emerged the oldest, frailest Arab woman I have ever met. She was bent and wrinkled beyond belief, toothless and almost blind, yet she carried on an interested conversation about the Sayeds and finally offered me a Moslem rosary blessed by Sidi el Mahdi.

As the heat was terrific I was glad when the visit came to an end and only wished we had fixed our departure for that afternoon instead of for the next morning. Hassanein suggested our wandering down to the other end of the oasis where there is another small village, Hawawiri. We borrowed a donkey from the reluctant sheikh el-zawia, who told us we should be killed before we were out of sight of the belad, and called for a guide to show us the way. At that moment there were half a dozen Zouias seated round our zariba, but none of them moved. I began to understand the sufferings of Rohlfs when I looked at the cruel, anæmic faces of these Arabs. Brave they may be, but they had not the keen, fierce looks of the warrior Beduin. They had small, cunning eyes that shifted restlessly, long, mean faces with thin lips and generally a fretful scowl between the brows. The Zouias are known as a bad tribe and these people certainly looked untrustworthy to the last degree. When we offered a bribe of tea and sugar one of them got up to accompany us, but none of the soldiers would come. Moraja and Abdul Rahim hid in their tent and Yusuf said he was lame. We were just starting off alone when Mohammed sprang up and slung on his gun. "They are a pair of eagles!" he exclaimed. "I will not be less brave than they." After we had gone a few hundred yards there was a soft thud-thudding in the sand behind, and the big Farraj, who had become our sort of personal slave, together with the corporal, silently joined us.

Our progress, however, was almost instantly stopped by a band of young men and boys rushing wildly after us. "Do not walk! Do not walk!" they yelled, and pointed to a large group of white-clad Arabs marching rapidly towards us. We turned to meet them. "For God's sake do not go!" said Mohammed. "There is bad work here. I do not understand it. Let us go back to the camp!" He followed gamely, however. The Arabs were all armed and they looked very angry, for they were gesticulating and talking in loud voices. I always wore my revolvers underneath my hezaam. I managed to get them out under the folds of my barracan and wondered with an odd, fierce pleasure how many shots I could get in. The corporal pretended to busy himself with the donkey, but our Farraj came on, his rifle ready. The Zouias surrounded us, a wild, threatening group. "You

shall not move from here till orders come from Jof!"
they shouted. "We have been warned about you. We
know. No strangers shall come to our country. They
die quickly here!" Hassanein suddenly had one of his
inspirations. "You wish to show that you are brave and
will defend your country to the last, but you should
behave thus to strangers, not to the guests of the
Sayed!" he said angrily. They were puzzled. They
expected us to be frightened and impressed. Instead,
we were angrier than they. If you can make an Arab
talk he generally forgets to fire.

While loudly arguing we led the way to the camp
and soon there was a large "megliss" seated outside our
tent. Some Tebus joined the Zouias. They were coal-
black like the Sudani slaves, but with more refined and
intelligent faces. Most of them do not talk Arabic, but
their head man explained the situation to them and to
our surprise they ranged themselves on our side. "The
guests of the Sayed are welcome to our country," they
said. The Zouias, headed by Bu Badr, were angrier than
ever. "Why does not a messenger come from Jof?"
they asked. "Sidi Abdullah went last night and he
promised to send back news. We told him you should
not follow until permission came."

We looked blanky at each other. We had not told
the guide to send back a messenger, and he had breathed
no word to us of such intention, nor of his tribesmen's
threats. "It is a plot," said I grimly. "Yes, but
where, why——?" murmured Hassanein vaguely.
Mohammed leaned forward triumphantly. His eyes
shone, his voice was strong. I think in that moment he
recovered his self-respect and we our old ally. "I understand it all," he cried. "Wallahi! I will never stroke
my beard again till I have settled with Abdullah who has
betrayed us. You men of Hawari, you are fools and you

have insulted the Sayed's guests because you are like the
foolish woman in the suq who buys the first thing that is
offered to her!" He whispered to Hassanein in Arabic
too rapid for my comprehension, "By Allah, hear and
believe, for I speak the truth!" shouted the latter above
the babel of angry voices. Even Sheikh Zarrug of the
Hawaij ceased from exclaiming that if no messenger
came from Jof on the morrow the Zouias would know that
we had deceived them and it would go hard with us.
"You get no news here and you believe the first-comer,"
continued Hassanein. "Abdullah told you that you must
prove to the strangers that you were brave and strong lest
they think that anyone can enter your country easily. Is
it not so?" They acknowledged uneasily, some ever
with crooked smiles, that this was the case. Then they
remembered the point which changed a bluff meant to
impress strangers into a grim reality. "Abdullah was to
send back a messenger if the ekhwan approved of your
letter and would receive you. It is a short journey and
none has come."

At these words smiles vanished and the pale, cruel
faces grew more cunning and suspicious. The Tebus
grouped themselves behind us. It might be a good battle,
I thought, and wondered if the Zouia rifles were modern.
A fight is always stimulating and not like that awful,
helpless day of thirst when one could not war with nature!
"Of course, no messenger has come," said Hassanein
triumphantly. "None will. You have been fooled and
so have we. To-morrow you would have prevented our
going. There would have been a fight. You are brave
but so are the slaves of the Sayed. Perhaps his guests
would have been killed and Abdullah would have been
saved. Do you know why?" Then followed the story of the
guide who had lost his head and his reputation at the same
time and I suddenly grasped Abdullah's neat little plot.

If none of the caravan returned to Jedabia, or even if the two strangers, chief witnesses against him, disappeared, he would be saved. He knew full well that no one would employ him as a guide after the story of his Taiserbo mistake became known. His future depended on our lips being sealed. His best chance lay amongst his suspicious Zouia kinsmen, always distrustful of strangers, fanatical and warlike, yet the caravan could not be attacked while he was with it. Therefore he suggested going to prepare the way for us at Taj. When we agreed, it was easy to arouse the *amour propre* and suspicions of the Hawari Zouias. "Show your courage by not letting these doubtful strangers cross the borders of your land. If their story is true and the sheikhs of Jof will receive them, I will send back a messenger." He had never the slightest intention of dispatching anyone to rescue us from the ever-growing hostility at Hawari, and he calculated that in a day or two we should make an attempt to escape and be promptly fired upon. The blacks would be obliged to defend us and, after the general carnage, the story of his failure would be buried with the slain.

Mohammed having discovered the plot, Hassanein rose nobly to the occasion. His words poured forth with all the subtle rhetoric that sways the Beduin mind and when their brains were steeped in this river of speech he suddenly flung down Sidi Idris's letter. "Do you wait for orders from Jof when your Sayed sends us here? Is this the insult that you pay him when he trusted you to help his guests?" There was an uncomfortable pause. The shifty eyes of the circle would not meet ours. Sheikh Saad, the feki of the town, who had been the spokesman against us, murmured incoherent words. Mansur Bu Badr sent hastily for a sheep. The group began to split into twos and threes. A party was forming in our favour. Musa Gharibeel exclaimed, "He is speak-

ing the truth. We have made a mistake." For at least
an hour arguments raged on every side, but we ignored
them and planned low-voiced revenge with Mohammed
in the tent. It was delightful to see how the man had
taken hold again. "Wallahi," he repeated five times
running. "May I never see my wife again if Abdullah
does not get his reward from the Sayed!"

From the pleasant task of plotting the guide's downfall we were summoned by a smiling Yusuf. "Your
words are flames," he said to Hassanein. "The people
are feeling very foolish and they regret what they have
done." I felt it was Hassanein's triumph, so left him
to receive the apologies of the Zouias with condescending
coldness, but even this did not content them. Musa
Gharibeel and Bu Badr insisted on wishing me personally
a good journey on the morrow. "I shall be glad to rest
in the house of Sidi Idris," I said coldly. "He told me
it would be an easy journey, but I think he has been
mistaken." The Zouias were silent.

Yusuf told me afterwards that Abdullah had insisted
that the caravan was to follow him to Jof the next day
without waiting for any news from Kufara. To make
things quite certain he had told the men of Hawari that
we were looking for gold in the mountains and we would
return with an army to conquer the land and take the
treasure it contained!

When it was dark the slave-girls, Zeinab and Hauwa,
crept into my tent. "We thought we should all die
to-day, but now we are happy. The people are bad here,
but we have been saved!" they said. Our greatest
triumph, however, was the moment when a very meek
Zouia deputation woke us up to ask us if we would care
to go to Hawawiri on our way to Kufara on the morrow.
They dared not approach the tent themselves, so sent
Yusuf to offer their olive branch.

CHAPTER X

FEASTS IN THE HOLY PLACE

JANUARY 13, therefore, should have seen the successful termination of our long journey, instead of which it saw us prisoners in earnest until a furiously ridden white donkey appeared on the horizon, amidst a whirl of tarboush tassel, rifle and long legs ending in bright yellow slippers, each swinging wildly at different angles. All this because Abdullah over-reached himself. In order to make our destruction certain he went to the kaimakaan at Jof and warned him that we were two Christians from Italy disguised as Moslems and that we were learning all about the country in order to conquer it later on. "It is impossible," said that official loyally. "They have letters from the Sayeds." "What is writing?" said Abdullah. "They have cheated the Sayeds, I tell you. Ever since they left they have been secretly making maps. They had watches on the feet of the camels, and the Sitt held a watch in her hand all the time [my compass]. They hang a strange thing on their tent—a weapon to kill us if we come near [the barometer] and they have spectacles which make the country look big while it is far away." He drew such lurid pictures of our nefarious designs that the kaimakaan was determined at all costs to protect his beloved Sayeds from the consequences of their mistake. "They must not leave Hawari," he said firmly. "In a few days they must go back. The honour of our princes will thus be saved." Abdullah agreed warmly, believing that in a

185

few days what was left of us would hardly be worth sending back! Then the blow fell. "You must take an order at once to Yusuf and Mohammed Quemish." In vain the guide protested, pleaded, argued. The kaimakaan was firm. It was then the afternoon and there was plenty of time to reach Hawari before night. The energetic official hustled Abdullah out of the town and the plotter saw his neat little plan for our destruction in jeopardy.

He knew that Mohammed was intelligent and that Yusuf was known to many people in Kufara. Both were loyal. Therefore, unless we were killed fairly quickly, in the general inquiry his own perfidy would come to light. He had meant to ensure that we were not immediately invited to Jof. He had no desire to return to us even with an order for our detention, for though it might make things uncomfortable for us temporarily, in the long run he was bound to suffer. Therefore he spent the night in the mountains and only arrived at our camp at 9 o'clock, hoping that by this time we should have come to blows with the Zouias, for he had particularly instructed Yusuf to start off with the caravan at dawn.

I do not know which was more aghast at seeing the other, Abdullah or I! At that moment, of course, I knew nothing of his work at Kufara. I only felt that we had jumped to wrong conclusions the preceding day and when, with restless eyes downcast, he murmured that we could not leave Hawari yet as they were preparing a house for us in Jof which would not be ready for several days, but that the slave-girls were to go on at once, I felt that something was seriously wrong. He tried to avoid presenting the note to Yusuf and Mohammed in front of me, but I would not leave him, so the paper, which was presumably meant to be private, was read before me. It ran, "You will see that you do not stir from Hawari until you receive further orders."

Abdullah murmured something incoherent about going
to the village and the remark galvanised me into action.
Once the Zouias knew of that message we should be
prisoners.   It, therefore, behoved us to send someone
reliable to Taj to find out what had happened before the
suspicious tribesmen set a guard round our camp.
Mohammed was the only possible person and he loathed
the idea, for had he not the written order of the Sayed's
wakil that he was not to move? However, he yielded to
persuasion. Perhaps the long miles trudged side by side
through hot sands under a hotter sun, the precious water
shared, the jokes over our aching feet, the first cold nights
when we had divided our blankets and coats, above all,
the day we had torn up the baggage saddles together and
distributed the straw to our starving animals with little
hope that we could ever provide them with another meal,
all bore fruit. "Wallahi!" he swore. "I shall discover
the truth." Abdullah almost lost his self-control. He
burst into the tent with the cowardly Abdul Rahim, while
Hassanein was penning a tactful letter to the kaimakaan.
Angry protests flowed from his lips. He threatened to
fetch the Zouias. The little commandant stuttered feeble
futilities. Mohammed wavered.

At that moment I saw the dream of so many scorching days and weary nights fading like the mirage of noon.
The object I had striven for, laboured for, for which I
had studied Arabic during gay London summers, for
which I had plotted in Cyrenaica, for which I had pored
over route maps and charts from Khartoum to Tripoli,
for which I had waded through ponderous tomes from
Ptolemy to Behm and Duveyrier, balanced trembling in
the scale of this man's mind. Every nerve and sinew,
still aching from our almost intolerable journey, spoke of
the strenuous effort made. Surely this must weigh
heavier than Abdullah's guile. It did! Somehow the

dark-faced guide, the cringing commandant, ceased to
exist. Hassanein called for a donkey for our messenger
and pushed the cleverly worded letter into his wallet.
Then for a moment Mohammed and I were face to face,
and I looked straight into his keen, boyish eyes, wringing
his hand with a few words of intense confidence and knew
instantly that he would not, could not, fail us!

Thereafter it did not matter that we could not
leave the camp, that Abdullah's face was thunderous,
that the soldiers hid in their tents with the exception of
the large, faithful Farraj, who offered me pathetic little
gifts every hour to cheer me up, raw onions, parsnips
and dry cut grass which makes a kind of liquid
spinach! I had to pretend to be ill and lie on my bed all
day behind the harem curtain to escape the distrustful
Zouias, who peered into the tent every two or three
minutes to see that we had not escaped. It was a distinctly trying time, for angry councils were held at
intervals outside the camp, but we were not invited to
attend them and the friendly Tebus were absent, though
once a bronze maiden with wide brown eyes, a cheery
smile and a large white pea-nut stuck in a hole in her
nostril, crept to my guarded quarters and offered me
four eggs with many kindly "Keif halak."

In the sunset came Mohammed, smiling, triumphant,
breathless, having ridden 20 kilometres to Taj over
a strange country he had never seen before, without track
or guiding mark, argued with a justly suspicious kaimakaan anxious to defend the prestige of his princes, convinced him of our good faith, learned the whole story of
Abdullah's treachery, remounted his white donkey and
plodded back over the rough sands to our rescue—all in
eight hours. Certainly Mohammed justified that day my
long-established faith in the Beduin race and their future.
He brought a letter of enthusiastic welcome to "their

Excellencies the honoured guests of the Sayeds," asking
them to proceed to Kufara on the morrow and to bring
blessings and honour to the town by their presence
therein.

The mentality of Libya is as changeable as its
barometer. That night, the men who had wished to kill
us a few hours before, sat amiably round our camp fire
and actually told us of their own accord the stories that
had preceded our coming. They varied extremely, for
whereas most of them put us down as the heralds of a
conquering army one said we were cousins of Rohlfs who
had come to make inquiries as to his treatment. "I
remember that Nasrani well," said old Zarrug. "He
came with a Zouia caravan." "How many other
Nasrani were with him?" we asked, remembering the
Buseima tale that on his return, at least, the German was
alone. "There were none. He came alone with his big
horse and a cook called Ali." The sheikh was quite
definite on this point. He told us that "Mustapha Bey"
had gone to Hawawiri to avoid the larger village and
then, skirting to the east of the Kufara dunes and hills,
had camped outside Boema, where he was promptly
made a prisoner.

January 14 produced about the most unpleasant
specimen of desert climate. The sun, no doubt, was hot,
but a cold, strong wind blew from the east, raising
clouds of sand and making progress difficult. Nevertheless, we sent the caravan direct to Kufara and ourselves
started for Hawawiri. The Zouias meekly allowed us
to go anywhere we liked, but they did suggest that
perhaps we were tiring ourselves unnecessarily, for
there were only three houses in the farther oasis, as all
the palms were owned by people in Jof and Boema.
However, we felt we had to visit the place as a lesson
to the soldiers, who had refused to accompany us the

previous day. Therefore, muffled to the eyes in the thickest blankets and jerds we could find, astride two minute, barebacked donkeys, we plunged into the east wind and laboured down the whole length of the narrow Hawari oasis.

The village of our captivity proved to be unexpectedly large, for more houses were scattered continually along the strip of palms. When we asked the number of inhabitants, the only reply was the one word which denotes any form of size, long, big, great, powerful, plenty, numerous, etc., "wajid"—but I imagine that there must be a population of two hundred or more. There was a gap between the palms of Hawari and those of its little companion, which was only a few square kilometres in size, and whose three houses were surrounded by a few huge fig-trees. The figs were nearly all small and hard, but the villainous-looking Zouia, brown-haired and green-eyed, with very low brow and narrow skull, who accompanied us, knocked down a few little purple ones from the top. They were very good and comforted us for the awful wind, which froze us even at midday, as we tramped over the stony gherds that lie on the way to Kufara.

The red sand continued, mixed with more and more patches of black stones, while little rocky ridges rose into low dark hills or big mounds, increasing in size after Hawari was lost to sight beside her vermilion gherds. Each time that we mounted a faint ridge and saw black hills in front of us we said, "Those are the last—behind those is the secret of the desert." A dozen times we were disappointed as a further waste of stones and rock obscured our vision. Finally, when from quite a high hillock we saw nothing but mounds and low hills where the boulders had almost conquered the red sands, we began to wonder if Kufara were a huge joke by which the African mind retaliated on European curiosity. By every map the oasis is a solid flat block of green just beyond the Gara of Hawari and we had already walked 35 kilometres at least beyond that imposing cliff and apparently could see half as far again in front with not a sign of a palm. "Look! The sand begins again on the horizon," I said. "It is much paler and there are more hills." "If Kufara is beyond those, I shall give up and send home for an aeroplane," answered my companion firmly.

Thereafter we covered our faces in our jerds and struggled on blindly, so that the Sahara gave us her secret suddenly and when we saw one of the most wonderful views in the world spread almost at our feet, we first blinked and rubbed our eyes to see if we were asleep and then cursed ourselves as fools for not having guessed that the explanation of the mystery was—a wadi!

For this reason one almost falls over the edge of the last black cliff into the soft pale sand of the oasis before one realises it is there. They say anticipation is better than realisation. They say that success is tasteless and that it is only the fight which thrills, but I am not ashamed to confess my excitement when a whole new world seemed to be revealed to me. To the east where the cliffs ran out a little, the sacrosanct village of Taj perched clear-cut against the sky, high above the oasis it guarded. The massive block of the zawia rose above the group of strong, dark houses, square, solid, all built of blocks of black stone with red sand mortar. The endless blind walls gave away no secrets, but here and there within the courts rose the triple arched porches of some big dwelling and already there were blotches of white that told of watchers for our arrival.

This is the holy place of the Senussi, where are the houses of the Sayeds and the blessed qubba of Sidi el-

Mahdi, with clustering colleges and mosque all looking like grim fortresses, for Taj boasts no blade of grass nor speck of green to relieve the monotony of black rock and red sand. Below it, east and west, runs a wide, flat wadi, its pale, faintly pink sands broken by a great mass of palms and green gardens, acacias, figs and feathery bushes, all surrounding a curly, vividly blue lake—this to the west; while eastwards beyond the guardian sanctuary on the cliff are more dotted palms and then a broad splash of emerald round another lake, while the whole enchanted valley is encircled with low amethyst hills or gherds. Scattered here and there upon the rose-petal sand are villages whose strong, dark walls look as if fortified against more formidable weapons than the peering eyes frustrated by their windowless secrecy.

Jof lies in front by the side of the greenest gardens, east of the first blue salt lake. Beyond it Zuruk is hidden amidst her palms. Tolab and Tolelib are too far away to be visible, for they lie at the western end of the oasis, where emerald and coral blur together at the foot of the strange purple hills. To the east is Buma, on the way to the second lake, with a smaller village, Boema, close beside, and beyond again more palms, till the pale sands rise to the dusky cliffs that shut in the secret oasis from the south.

We gazed and gazed as if afraid the whole glorious view might fade before our sun-burned eyes and leave us lost in the desolate, dark waste that lay behind us. Then suddenly we felt how very ill and tired we all were, for the one well at Hawari to which our suspiciously guarded followers were allowed access contained very bad water and we were all suffering strange pangs. "Wallahi!" said Mohammed. "It is beautiful and I am grateful, but how I want to sleep!" And he wound himself up in his jerd and flung himself down on the

THE FOUR EKHWAN WHO RECEIVED US AT TAJ

HASSANEIN BEY TALKING TO EKHWAN AT TAJ WHILE
THE AUTHOR PHOTOGRAPHED THEM

THE KAIMAKAAN AT TAJ

nearest patch of sand. I followed suit, with a blanket
over my head and one by one the foremost of the retinue
sank down beside me, so that when the lingering caravan
caught us up it had to wake half a dozen exhausted
explorers before we could make a dignified entry into
the Holy Place.

Abdullah came out to meet us, for he had taken
Zeinab and Hauwa the previous night to Sayed Rida's
house, as it was not meet that the personal slaves of the
Sayed should be looked upon by the people. He tried
one last shot when he saw me riding a camel. "Get
down! Get down, Khadija!" he shouted loudly so that
the interested group of loafers might hear. "You cannot ride into this holy place!" We were still nearly
half a mile from the nearest house, so we ignored him,
but when we came to the last hillock we dismounted, I
covering my face completely, and with the army of nine
in battle array behind us we marched towards a very
dignified group who came forward to greet us.

Except for the Sayeds themselves and the ekhwan I
had met for a moment at Jedabia, I had so far talked
only with merchants and Government officials, a few
sheikhs of the smaller zawias and the Beduins. Now
we were meeting the great men of the Senussi, important
ekhwan, shrewd statesmen as well as religious chiefs.
They welcomed us with grave, calm dignity, that uncon-
scious, simple dignity that the West can never learn of
the East, for rank in the former is a ladder up which
all men may climb, but in the latter it is a tableland
apart. It is such a remote world, so utterly unattainable
by those who do not inherit it, that the sheikh may
safely invite the camel-driver to "fadhl" with him or
the ekhwan unbend to the bread-seller. Men talk of the
democracy of the East because there appears to be but
one distinction—the free-born from the slave, yet even

the black Sudani girl may be the mother of a Mahdi!
There is no shadow of democracy in the untainted East.
There is only heredity. A man lives by the glory of
his father and his father's father and when he may
not take pride in them it is to the glory of his tribe
he clings.

With the grave, massive figures in spotless white
jerds, under which gleamed the richest colourings, orange,
red and purple, in splendid embroidered jelabias, we
entered the first big house on the edge of the cliff. It
was the dwelling of Sidi Idris, so a great honour was
done us. Along one side of the big central court ran
one of the high arched loggias we had seen from
the hill and this opened into an equally long room,
immensely high, thickly carpeted, its white plaster
walls decorated with texts from the Koran and small,
regular alcoves wherein were unglazed windows protected by green shutters, over which hung immense
glass balls like those we put on Christmas trees. The
ceiling was covered with gay chintz and a row of
huge ornate lamps, with more pendant green and blue
balls hung from it. We found ourselves seated in a circle
facing the open door with four of the reverend ekhwan.
In the place of honour was Sayed Saleh el Baskari, a
cousin of Sidi el Abed, his wakil and the acting
kaimakaan of Kufara, in daffodil yellow and black, with
purple lining to his wide sleeves. He had a broad,
intelligent brow and dimples in his bronzed red cheeks,
a long, drooping black moustache above a firm-lipped
mouth and tiny thin beard. His eyes were kind and
his smile frank, but he was the typical Eastern statesman of few bland words to hide much thought.

Next to him sat Sayed Abdil Rahman Bu Zetina, a
small man with broad, grey beard and dark, reflective
face, level brows and fine-cut nostrils. He might be a

philosopher, a divine! Then came the mighty Mohammed Bu Fadil, brother of the absent kaimakaan,
enormous of person, in pale saffron yellow, with a
primrose kufiya wound round and round his head above
the turban, so that much of his plump, shining face,
with wide-lipped smile and humorous eyes, was hidden
in its folds. The fourth was a very old man, long and
lean, with pointed, trailing beard, shrunk, hollow cheeks,
parchment coloured as his robes, but something of the
seer burned in his still vital eyes. He, Sayed Osman
the judge, had known the wonders of Sidi el Mahdi,
and the passionate faith which makes martyrs was in
him. The little council read and re-read our letters
and expressed calmly and graciously their satisfaction.
Then the subject of our detention in Hawari came up,
and with it smiles. "You did not choose your
messenger well," they said. "Had you heard the
stories of Abdullah you would have sympathised with
our hesitation. We did not like that talk ourselves.
However, we will now relieve you of him." The tone
was decided. We wondered what would happen to
Abdullah. Justice is tactfully slow in the East, but
when it comes it is final.

Immediately after our visitors had left, while we were
putting up gaily painted canvas partitions in the long
room, black slaves appeared, bearing a banquet in many
blue bowls on an immense brass tray. This was placed
on a vermilion cloth on the floor and beside it we sat
cross-legged, dipping our fingers first into one dish and
then into another. "This is the real joy of Kufara,"
said Hassanein, voraciously devouring most of a lamb
cooked in "mulukhia," a sort of thin spinach sauce.
I was silent from pure joy—and a wonderful vegetable
which I discovered at the bottom of one of the messes
of thick, buttery gravy and meat. I hoped Hassanein

did not know it was there, so I encouraged him to continue with the pseudo-spinach, but he pounced upon it suddenly. "Bamia! We have it in Egypt," he exclaimed, and thereafter it was a race! There is practically no sugar in Kufara. It costs three mejidies an oke, so there were no sweets to our banquet, but a great brass bowl and a long-necked ewer were brought to us to wash hands and mouth in and, as we shook the five weeks' conglomeration of sand from our flea-bags, we were blissfully happy.

I feel that one should not acknowledge it, but certainly January 15 stands out in my mind as a day of food! I have described so many fasts ,that I remember feeling an intense pleasure in writing my diary that night, while Hassanein concocted warm letters of thanks to be sent back to Sidi Idris and Sayed Rida by a north-bound caravan.

I had scarcely woken up and blinked at the unfamiliar sight of a red and blue carpet when Sayed Mohammed el Jeddawi (who had come from Jedda some forty years ago, a follower of the sainted Mahdi, and was now wakil of Sidi Idris and Sayed Rida) appeared with an offering of a bowl of sour curdled milk and a palm-leaf platter of marvellous stoneless dates, huge, soft, clean, golden things which melted in one's mouth—such as Europe has never known! We were warned that at 9 A.M. there would be a banquet for the whole party in the house of Sayed Saleh, so we arrayed ourselves in our cleanest garments, not a very imposing spectacle, for I had to wear a jerd belted with a scarlet hezaam, as my only barracan had served forty days without washing!

Slaves came to show us the way and we followed these cheery black personages through a winding sandy path between high walls, across a wide space before the massed buildings of the zawia with the high, square

block of Sayed Ahmed Sherif's house. I began to see
that there were few houses in Taj, but all of them were
large, intricate buildings with a maze of courts and
passages. As a matter of fact, in the holy place, beside
the clustered houses of the Sayeds, which occupy about
a third of the town, and the many dependencies of the
zawia, only the important ekhwan live. Therefore, one
saw but two classes of people among its dark walls.
Many slaves in strips of bright colour, or imposing and
generally portly figures in immaculate white turbans and
silk jerds over straight tobhs or jelabias in all imaginable
colours. I noticed one delightful and massive old man
in a garment the colour of blood oranges with what
looked like a white shawl bordered with vermilion round
his shoulders, but it was difficult to see clearly through
the one tiny little chink I allowed myself in my thick
white draperies.

In the desert I had been as careless of my veil as
my namesake Khadija, Mohammed's first wife, a lady
of forceful character, in whose service the prophet took
a caravan to Syria before he espoused its owner some
twenty years older than himself. In Kufara, however,
the greatest care was necessary and I had to learn to
endure a more or less perpetual headache from the heavy
folds and also to make swift photographs from between
them. The faithless Abdullah had taught us one thing
at least—to hide our cameras and note-books with more
care!

Sayed Saleh's house was like the maze at Hampton
Court. However often I went in, I do not think I
should ever be able to find my way out again. A
resplendent person with a dark green cloak, much braided
in gold, flung over his khaki uniform met us in the
second court, where we left our soldiers to be royally
feasted in one of the rooms leading off it. After that

I counted three more courts and five passages before
Mohammed and Yusuf were spirited away to their
separate banquet. Still our guide went on past various
pairs of yellow shoes discarded at several entrances. At
last, after two more yards and several passages, we
entered the central court, with broad, matted and
carpeted verandas running along two sides.

Hastily removing our shoes, we went to meet our
stately host, who beamed his welcome and waved us
across the wide space between the arches into a long,
high room whose walls seemed to be entirely hung with
clocks, barometers, thermometers and other such objects.
I cannot tell how many instruments there were, but I
counted fifteen clocks, most of them going. At either
end was a row of the huge painted, carved chests that
the great folk carry on their long caravan journeys and
in most of the alcoves, which were hung with rugs, were
tea-caddies of every size, shape and colour. A large
pianola bore reels of *Pagliacci* and *Carmen*. Thick dark
carpets were piled on the matted floor, with rows of stiff
cushions round the walls, but the thing that interested
me most, after the meagre rations of our journey, was
the fringed, scarlet cloth in the centre of which reposed
a round brass tray laden with food and flanked with all
sorts of bowls and bottles.

Our host wished us good appetite. "Bilhana!
Bilshifa!" "With pleasure and health!" He then
vanished and a slave lifted an exquisite silver and brass
ewer to pour water over our hands into its companion
bowl with a fretted cover. Another brought minute
cups of black coffee strongly flavoured with red pepper.
Then we sank cross-legged beside the tray, wide-eyed
with wonder at the array before us. Arab hospitality
is prodigious. Everyone gives of his best, but only a
very great man could provide the Arabian Nights' feast

which was offered us. It brought back memories of
Sayed Rida's marvellous dinners at Jedabia, especially
as it was to him and to Sidi Idris that we owed our
welcome in Kufara, the most loyal and devoted of all
the Libyan oases, for it is the keynote of the Senussi
faith. I heard Hassanein repeating rapidly the vital
points of the speech he intended to make to the
kaimakaan concerning our return journey and I almost
shook him. "Never mind those details now!" I
exclaimed. "How long do you think they will leave
us alone with this food?"

There were twelve dishes of lamb cooked in different
rich sauces, with a monster bowl of strange oddments,
which I imagine also belonged to the private life of a
sheep, floating in rich gravy. There were a score of
poached eggs on silver plates and fifteen vegetables and
green sticky mounds of "mulukhia" which hid all sorts
of intricate delicacies. Then there were bowls of curdled
milk, which I had begun to like, or powdered mint
leaves and of an unknown liquid which I thought was
sweet-scented vinegar, with bottles of water, because
the Senussi law forbids strong drinks. When we paused
for breath a slave brought us another bowl, this time of
bitter lemon juice, to renew our appetites and when
at last these failed, a second cup of the peppered coffee
appeared before the ceremony of washing hands and
mouth in the carved ewer. Then fly-whisks were given
us and we leant against the hard, stiff cushions, feeling
beautifully replete, until our host joined us and we did
business in the Oriental fashion, while he made three
series of tea, the first bitter, the second scented and
the third with mint. He had an elaborate silver tea-set
spread before him and he warmed the teapot himself
on a little brazier, while we skirted round the subjects
nearest our hearts, approaching, retreating, avoiding

obstacles or shadows of such and winning his obvious approval by the tactful way we left the matter of our future travels in his hands. As I regretfully relinquished my third empty glass a slave poured scent over me, strong and sweet, and another offered me a silver incense burner over whose warm perfumed smoke I might dry my scent-drenched hands! In all the generous-hearted East I had never met this last pretty custom before.

When the due proportion of business for a first visit —a very minute amount it would appear to Americans —had been discussed, we bade farewell to our host and returned to our cool house on the cliff. Since I said this was a day of food, let me add immediately that about midday the delightful wakil appeared with an enormous basin of "couss-couss" about two feet in diameter. On the top of it reposed most of the jaw of a sheep and the whole mass was encircled by a continual line of sausages and a phalanx of hard-boiled eggs. Now, if there is one thing on earth I love it is "couss-couss," but for once I looked at it almost indifferently. Hassanein suggested various desperate remedies, such as instantly walking round the wadi, but I would not be parted from my "couss-couss." I looked at it lovingly and, after a violent argument with Farraj over the possibilities of heating a quart or two of water for a bath, found energy enough to eat a pathetic little hole in one side of the floury mess.

The climax to our day was at sunset, when we were summoned to another huge banquet at the house of the ever-hospitable Sidi Saleh, who was determined to honour the Sayed's guests by every means in his power. The memory of that last meal is somewhat blurred, but I believe the centre dish was the larger part of a sheep on a mountain of rice, flanked by bowls of hot, very sweet milk. As we waited for our host to join us in

order tactfully to brush the antennæ of business, I com-
plimented Hassanein on the thoroughness with which
he had assimilated the grave, aloof dignity of a Sheikh
el-Alim.   He looked at me blankly.   "It is not dignity.
It is torpor!" he said.

Of course, there were other moments in the day.
The most delightful little person about nine years old
came to see us after we returned from the kaimakaan's
morning feast.   He had the largest and most velvety
brown eyes, surrounded by a thick fringe of curly lashes,
with a faint shadow of kohl to accentuate their beauty.
A prince and the son of a prince, little Sidi Omar had
all the dignity of his race.   He was garbed in a long
purple silk jelabia, opening over a rose-coloured
embroidered jubba, while his little pale face was framed
in a miniature white kufiya under a purple tarboush.
He insisted on accompanying us as we wandered round
the sacred village, giving us grave advice.   "Sitt Khadija,
cover your face now," he would say as the snowy trap-
pings of a bulky ekhwan appeared at an unsuspected
door, or "Sidi Ahmed Bu Hassanein, you must salute
So-and-so; he is the son of So-and-so."

From the edge of the cliff, where the last houses
almost overhung the steep descent, there was a glorious
view of the whole wadi.   One could stroll east of Taj
and look across pale sands, broken by green of barley
and wheat, to the lake amidst palms and the narrow
end of the valley where the hills close in.   One could
gaze straight south over the Sayed's gardens to the solid
walls of Jof rising in tiers on slight mounds with the
famous ancient zawia standing a little apart and in the
far distance the line of Zuruk's palms, where a wide
break in the guardian dunes gave a glimpse of flatter
sands.   To the west the view was limited only by one's
eyesight.   A few large isolated houses lay beside the great

mass of palms, which swept round the second streak of blue water beside a dry salt marsh and away, ever widening to the far horizon where lay Tolab and Tolelib in a dark blur as the valley ran beyond the strangely luminous hills.

When we started to stroll down one of the steep defiles that lead from the rocky tableland to the smooth sands below, Sidi Omar's brilliant smile disappeared. "Do not go down alone," he urged. "The Zouias are bad people. Perhaps some of them will ask you questions—why you have come to their country and for what business?" Therefore, we stayed that day on the plateau and I took many photographs beneath the shadow of my heavy draperies. For once I was grateful to the Moslem veil, for Hassanein used tactfully to lure our companions away to look at a view and I would wander shyly and slowly, with the uncertain gait of the harem women, to the desired point of vantage, whip out the 3A kodak from my enormous sleeve and snap some aspect of the enchanted valley before aimlessly straying back. I risked a lightning snapshot at the main block of the zawia while Hassanein greeted a learned sheikh, but I felt it was dangerous, because there were a few students lingering round the door beside the round tower in the wall and they must have seen the flash of the lens between the white folds of my girdled jerd.

CHAPTER XI

THE "CITIES" OF KUFARA

ON January 16 our battles began again. Unfortunately Hassanein was ill, but he dragged himself up for a last effort. Perhaps success had gone to our heads a little, for not content with visiting Taj and Jof, the religious centre and the seat of Government, we had lately made plans for exploring the oasis to its farthest limits. In vain the unfortunate retinue pointed out that it would be another case of Hawawiri. "The Zouias are in the two 'cities,'" they urged. "There is nothing in the villages. You can throw a stone into Buma from these walls, so why tire yourselves further?" We felt that this sudden thought for our comfort had an ulterior motive, so we pursued the subject. "I should like to see the people," I said to Yusuf. "You will see them all in the suq at Jof. Every week they come in to buy and to sell. They are savages, the Zouias who live on the edge of the oasis, and they are poor people without interest." "Well, I should like to see the western end of the wadi." Yusuf looked puzzled. "But you can see everything in Kufara from this mountain," he said with some truth. I was reduced to retorting that I could not see the actual houses of Tolab and Zuruk. Our fat retainer had a distinct sense of humour. "Nor could you see the houses of Hawawiri from our camp!" he reminded. "I want to meet the heads of the Zouias and if I go to all the villages I can talk to them." Yusuf seized upon this happily. "They can come and see you and then you can ask them about their people."

Thus word went forth from the kaimakaan that all the tribal headmen were to come to Taj to meet the important strangers and the hour and place appointed for this most solemn council were "four hours before sunset in the house of Sidi Idris." We had anticipated battle, because Abdullah had been absent for twenty-four hours and we learned too late that he had been making a tour of the small villages, expounding the treacherous stories which had failed in the Senussi centres, but we did not expect quite such a disastrous meeting. The fifteen sheikhs who appeared nearly two hours late at the rendezvous, were weak and convinced that if they carried out their designs they would be acting against the wish of the Sayeds whom they respected and honoured. Yet so great was their long-cherished loathing of the stranger, which had been fostered by years of isolation till it was as much a part of their creed as the Shehada or the Zakah, that they were determined at all costs to prevent our penetrating farther into their country. One gradually absorbed something of the mentality of this strange, distrustful people as one sat amidst the circle of gloomy, suspicious faces.

For generations the Zouias have been known as a lawless tribe. Originally they came from the Fezzan by groups of families, each owning a particular headman, but they never seem to have possessed one supreme chief. The two most famous of the ancient sheikhs were Abdullah Shekari and Helaig, though it was Agil who met Sidi Ben Ali es-Senussi in Mecca and told him of the strange enclosed land in the centre of the Sahara which the Zouias had conquered from the enfeebled Tebu. The great ascetic had already set flame to the religious imagination of North Africa from Morocco eastwards, but he knew nothing of southern Libya. Yet he told the half savage tribesmen that in a wadi near Taiserbo would be found an irak tree, from the wood of which the Arabs make their primitive form of tooth-brushes. The tree was duly discovered, the miracle announced to the tribe and, later, Agil went north again to Gebel Akhbar in Cyrenaica, to offer the allegiance of his people to the great Senussi. Kufara, the original sultanate of the Tebus, had become since the Zouia conquest some two hundred and fifty years before, a danger spot to every caravan, for it was a regular stronghold of brigands who lived by plunder.

It was a definite custom that all travellers, especially merchants, passing through the oasis, should pay "darb," a duty which varied according to the value of their merchandise, otherwise the caravan would be attacked and plundered.

Before the coming of the Senussi there were only palms in the oasis and the tribesmen were content with the most primitive clothes, hardly better than those of the skin-clad Tebus. It was Sidi el Mahdi who introduced the jerd and the jubba.

The dawn of civilisation came with the ekhwan sent by Sidi Ben Ali, but the Mahdi made Kufara the wonder-land it is to-day and by extensive planting started the cultivation of grain, fruit and flowers. Sidi Idris owes some of his influence among the Zouias to the fact that he is the great Mahdi's son, though his own strong personality counts for much in a land where striking individuality is rare. Under the Senussi government the Zouias were obliged to give up their organised brigandage, but with such a long history of murder and plunder behind them—half the tragedies of the Sahara may be laid at their door—it is not to be wondered at that they are still lawless and wild. Every man fears them and only a power as great as the Senussi could hold them in check. They were practically infidels before they made their submission to Sidi Ben Ali, having very nearly lapsed from Islam, though, as they come from Yemen, they probably formed part of the armies who followed Beni Suleim in the eleventh century, from Midian through Syria and Egypt to Cyrenaica where some tribes settled, notably the Abidat, Hassan, Faied, Brahsa, Hohsa, Abid Auwaghir and Mogharba. With the fierce religious fanaticism which they absorbed fresh from the fervent ascetics who were enthusiastically preaching a new, pure Islam, were mixed the hatred and scorn of all who had not received this teaching. "He who is not with us is against us," was interpreted literally and the land was closed against the stranger, be he Christian or Moslem.

It was easy, therefore, to understand the attitude of the white-robed figures who crouched immobile round one end of the long room. They felt that they were defending not only their jealously hidden country but their religion from the strangers whom they hated and feared. In their hearts they could not believe that the greatly revered Sayeds had authorised our journey. Continual distrust and suspicion are bad daily companions. They had marred and lined the brooding faces round us till there was little left of the frank, fearless Beduin. On one side sat Hamid Bu Korayim, son of the man who had saved Rohlfs, his dark, narrow face set in mute obstinacy. In front of us was Sheikh Suleiman Bu Matar, the only spot of colour in the group, for he wore a brilliant orange robe under his jerd, and Bush Naf el Ghadad, an old man with a grey beard who occasionally poured a little oil on the troubled waters. Others present were Sheikh Badr and Mabruk Bu Helayig.

The whole assembly had made up its mind to oppose
us and they would listen to no argument. "Khallas!
It is ended! It is ended! Of what use further speech?"
they cried. "If you have a letter from Sidi Idris, saying
that you are to visit all our villages by name, then you
shall go," said Bu Korayim. "You know that we have
the Sayed's permission to visit Kufara. No traveller can
set foot beyond Jedabia without it. Do you think we
should have risked certain death? We know that no one
can hope to visit even the outskirts of your country without the consent of Sidi Idris, but we are his guests!"
They changed their ground. "You have seen Kufara,"
urged Suleiman Bu Matar. "Jof and Taj are the
'markas' [centre of government]. The villages are
not interesting. There are no zawias even." Argument
was useless, for none dared give way before the others.
We saw that one or two were weakening out of respect
for the fact that we were guests of their rulers, but the
old inherited instinct welded them together. Generally
it would be impossible to get fifteen Arabs to remain
united against strong arguments for a quarter of an
hour, but we were fighting a principle as profoundly
part of their existence as food and drink. "Khallas!
Khallas!" resounded from every side and, without even
waiting for the usual ceremony of tea-drinking, the
meeting rose hurriedly. "We have spoken," they said,
"and argument is of no avail." "If you go, you go
at your own risk," added Sheikh Badr. Yet before the
last flow of protest they had read the "Fatha" all
together to show that they honoured the Sayed in the
persons of his guests!

So the strange council of impulse and reason came to
an end and, as the last white-robed figure fumbled for
its shoes at the edge of the matted loggia, Hassanein
turned to me despondently. "We have failed abso-

lutely!" he said. I would not agree. The guests had
come to us strong with a great resolve, wound up to battle
pitch, each man determined to support the others. Now
they would separate and, each alone, would have the nasty
cold feeling of wondering what he had done and what
the final result of his action would be. "Wait!" said
I. "Very soon they will feel that they have shown us
how dangerous it is to cross their borders and they will
only remember in whose house they met us!"

Later in the afternoon a Mojabra merchant, Tawati
Haifan, cousin of our old friend She-ib, and one of the
ekhwan, Sayed Mohammed Semmen, visited us, partly
to welcome and partly to console us for the behaviour of
the Zouias. "They are bad people," they said. "They
have always been like that."

Then sunset came and with it the summons to dinner
in the house of many courts. The Wadi of Kufara is
always beautiful, but at sunset it is magical, for the
girdle of strange hills glows with wonderful mauve and
violet lights and the oasis lies half in shadow where blend
the emerald and sapphire of palm and lake, half in flame,
where the burning sands reflect the glory of the sky. It
used to make me catch my breath with ever-new surprise
as I came out of the discreet little door in the wake of
the ebony slave, who took a great interest in the state
of my appetite and never could understand why I could
not cope with three separate breakfasts sent me by as
many hosts.

I never realised more fully the remoteness of Kufara
than when, after the deft-handed slaves had spirited away
the huge, brass tray, and with it every trace of our meal,
we sat motionless beside our host in the long shadowed
room, while he silently and very slowly made his carefully
prepared tea. The many high-walled courts produced a
silence in that dim room of thick carpets and rare lights

ZAWIA TOWER AT TAJ

KUFARA WADI, FROM TAJ

BARRAKING: A TOO SUDDEN DESCENT

A LUNCH IN KUFARA VALLEY

as profound as the stillness of the desert. Words, even
smiles, would have been out of place during the little
ceremony, while rose-water or mint was being measured
gravely by the sensitive fingers of our host. Beyond the
circle of light cast by a solitary candle in a high silver
sconce were only vague forms of cushions or huge chests
looming in remote corners. Within it was a dark, thin-
faced young sheikh, all in white, from his silken kufiya
to his flowing jerd and beside him our grave, reflective
host, with a vivid green shawl bordered in purple
framing his bronzed face and drooping over a long
green jubba, which showed the richly embroidered sedairi
beneath. A jewelled hand slowly poured drop after
drop of essence into the amber glasses, while the scented
smoke of a little brazier drifted gently across the picture.
One heard Time pause to catch the shadows of thoughts
that wavered between the light and the dark, so mystic
was the silence. Then suddenly and startlingly clear
came the sound that perfected the harmony—the cry of
the muezzin for the evening prayer!

Next day a small and somewhat forlorn party
descended one of the steep defiles into the wadi. It
consisted of Hassanein and myself, mounted on microscopic yet exceedingly unruly donkeys, the Commandant
of the Gendarmerie, resplendent in pale grey uniform
slashed and faced with red and an immense tasselled
kufiya, with four fully armed soldiers and a most picturesque Zouia sheikh, Mohammed Teifaitah, the only
tribesman who was brave enough to accompany us. He
was splendidly mounted on a white Arab horse, curved
of neck and long of pastern, with a scarlet saddle, bow-
pommelled, five different coloured saddle-cloths, and
silver stirrups rather like sharp coal scuttles.

Kufara is narrow at the eastern end and with a break
in the southern wall of cliff, where a broad space runs

out beyond Zuruk, it widens gradually as it goes west. The main mass of palms begins between Jof and Taj and sweeps west to Talakh, but there are several isolated groups, of which those of Boema and Buma are the largest. We rode first eastwards, along the foot of the cliffs and I realised as we ambled through thick, pale coral sand that if one wishes to keep the impression of an enchanted valley one should never leave the heights. There are beautiful spots in the valley, where palm and tamarisk and rush blend their shades of green besides some unruffled lake, but it is from above that one grasps the whole wonder of water and wood and decorative dark-walled towns, set in the close circle of jewelled hills.

As we neared Boema, its few houses, large, square or oblong blocks of reddish-purple, standing just below the northern cliffs a little apart from its gardens, the sheikh grew very nervous. White figures came out to look at us and he urged us away, but I wanted a photograph! Let no one imagine it is easy to manage a wild, toy donkey, keep one's face completely hidden and secrete about one's pocketless person two kodaks and a spare roll of films!

The oasis at Boema is lovely, for various kinds of thorn, a few dark green olives, tamarisks, acacias and the feathery grey trees described as "firewood," all mingled their foliage with the clustered palms. A kilometre away is Buma. At one end of the oasis are a few poor dwellings of the slaves who tend the gardens, some of them made of palms, some of uneven sand bricks. At the other there is a village of the usual dark houses, while a lovely turquoise lake, bordered with high rushes, lies in the centre. On the southern shore, where there is a stretch of rough, dry, salt waste, we found the ruins of a large Tebu fort. These ancient people chose their sites well, for this high, round honeycomb stood on the very edge of the water, its grey, broken walls one with the salt stone that surrounded it and made passage difficult from the land. There were one or two of the small, round oven houses scattered near the lake and we wondered if Buma had been the capital of the old Tebu Kufara—then called Tazerr—for this fort was bigger than anything at Buseima, but roofless and windowless as usual.

From the plantations of pumpkins, radishes, parsnips, onions, with neatly irrigated patches of wheat and barley, we drove our escort south down the long, flat stretch of gravelly sand to Zuruk, a long strip of palms chiefly owned by Sidi Idris and other Sayeds. There is no village in this southernmost oasis. It is inhabited only by the Sudani slaves who look after the dates. We stopped at a palm-leaf fence to ask a huge ebony figure in a tattered white shirt for some dates. He dived into his plaited leaf "tukel," reminiscent of the Sudan, and reappeared with a gourd full of large, dry, purplish dates mixed with the lemon-coloured unripe ones that the Arabs eat to quench their thirst. We rode the whole length of Zuruk's palms, for by this time the Zouia had laid aside his suspicions and was becoming confidential. We asked him how long ago his people had come to Kufara, and he replied, "My father, my grandfather and his father have all lived here, but before then the tribe came. Sheikh Mohammed was fifty-six, so we gathered that the conquest had taken place some hundred and fifty years ago. It is a pathetic thing that the Tebus are disappearing from the wadi even faster than the traces of their odd round houses. Only a few years ago there were about five hundred of these dark-skinned, round-faced people, with smooth hair, broad nostrils and wide mouths, but devoid of the thick negroid lips. Now there are between fifty and a

hundred. Nearly all of them live in a palm-leaf village
with a few round mud hovels on the outskirts of Jof.
They are more pastoral in habit than the Arabs, so, in
spite of their debased position as employees of the
Zouias, they own a good many goats and sheep and a
few camels.

There is practically no pasturage in the wadi, only
a little coarse grass or rushes by the lakes and sparse
tufts of the brown, mossy hattab we saw at Buseima.
Therefore there are very few flocks indeed and milk
and meat are luxuries except among the prosperous
ekhwan of Taj. Fresh water is not plentiful, for there
are no springs. There is absolutely no rainfall. Sometimes for eight consecutive years there is not a single
shower. All the gardens are irrigated from wells, but
slave labour is abundant. Yet Kufara in summer must
be a veritable Eden. From her grapes she makes the
sweet vinegar we drank at banquets and from her roses
the essence dropped into our tea, as well as the heavier
perfume used in braziers. She has olives for oil,
almonds, lemons, figs, melons and peaches. Her leather
comes from the Sudan and the shoemakers in Jof
fashion delightful red heel-less shoes of soft, pliable hide
without nails, but with thongs to bind round the
ankles. The Tebus make baskets and rope from the
palm leaves, but there is no weaving. The rich clothes
of the princely ekhwan, which were our envy and
admiration, came from Egypt. "Before the war there
were many caravans. One came nearly every day"
(which means that one was nearly always within the
confines of the oasis, perhaps a weekly arrival). "Now
there are very few," said Sheikh Mohammed.

We learned that when a caravan came from the Sudan
it consisted of 150 camels, belonging to perhaps a dozen
different merchants, who brought ivory, feathers, sandal,

leather; but smuggling of slaves had been difficult since the stringent French law had decreed that the whole caravan should be confiscated if one slave were found in it. As a matter of fact, we had been thirty-seven days on the route from Jedabia and we had not met a single caravan from Wadai, nor did any arrive while we were in Kufara; but this may have been partly due to the fact that the Beduins prefer travelling in summer, when they march all night and sleep most of the day. They can go farther this way, without suffering from the intense cold of the winter dawn. Also the winter is the foaling time for camels in Libya, which makes travelling precarious.

There is a large market in Jof twice a week, to which people come from as far off as Hawari and Tolab to barter pigeons, eggs, fowls, girbas and foodstuffs. Slaves are not now sold in the public square on Mondays and Thursdays, but many a human bargain is arranged in the shuttered houses around it. For 100 mejidies one can buy a man and for 200 a woman, but young girls of fourteen and fifteen fetch up to 250 mejidies (nearly £50). "These be high prices," said the Zouia despondently. "But the people in Barca have bought many slaves lately and there are fewer caravans." We learned that the Tuaregs of the west had regular slave farms, where they bred and sold human beings as we do cattle. "You can see sixty slaves in one farm," said our guardian sheikh. As an instance of how uncivilised were the Zouias before the coming of the Senussi, he told us that a certain Sheikh Mohammed Sherif went to Benghazi, the end of the world, and came back with an oil lamp which was looked upon as a miracle by the tribesmen of Kufara. By the power of a little kerosene he ruled them for years, giving judgments and discovering malefactors by interpreting its light.

Deep in conversation we skirted the rough, rocky

ground to the south of the broad belt of Jof palms and came to Talakh, at the end of the emerald maze where Sayed Ahmed owns many gardens. A whole colony of slaves dwelt in clusters of "tukels," within neat palm-leaf fences and there were some biggish houses of sand bricks, on whose flat roofs masses of dates were drying in the sun. The afternoon was far advanced by this time, but the Zouia was anxious to show us the beauty spot of the oasis, so we rode through the thickest palm groves between mounds of grey bushes until quite suddenly we came to a little round lake, whose still water reflected every frond of the palms drooping round it under the shadow of high amber banks which shut in the pool on every side, so that duck sported on it peacefully without fear of onlookers. It was a lovely picture, with the rose-red hills in the distance, but we were glad to turn our donkeys' heads homewards and still gladder when the massive houses of Taj appeared on the most precipitous cliff in the distance.

The names of the villages in Kufara are interesting, for whereas Taj means very suitably "a crown," and Jof "inside," Zuruk and Tolab are the names of two tribes which are still to be found in Egypt. Sheikh Mohammed told us that they had helped the Zouias to conquer the unfortunate Tebu and had received the places bearing their names as their share of the spoil. Later, however, they had grown tired of the remote valley and of the endless disputes between Zouias and Tebus, which lasted till the coming of the Senussi, and had returned to their own country.

January 18 saw the virtual end of our pilgrimage. As we took leave of Sidi Saleh, after our third cup of mint tea, he asked us if we would like to visit the Zawia of the Asayad. Daily we had passed the massive block of buildings from which generally issued the sound of the

chanted Koran. We knew that inside those formidable
walls was the qubba of the Mahdi, a symbol only, for the
Senussi believe their saint still living, but nevertheless,
the goal of all Senussi pilgrims and the object of almost
as much veneration as the tomb of the Prophet. In the
course of slow, dignified conversation, with the correct
proportion of prolonged silences, we had delicately approached the subject of visiting the revered shrine, but
no other sanction than "Insha-allah" had been vouchsafed us. Time and date are never suggested in the
East. Thus we had to wait patiently till the kaimakaan
was satisfied that the suitable moment had come.

We passed through the large, low mosque which
joined the zawia. Rows of great, square, whitewashed
pilasters supported the heavy wooden palm trunks forming the beams of the flat roof. It was utterly unadorned
and the "mimbar" was of the simplest description, without paint or carving; yet for a moment, as I stood on the
threshold of the holy of holies of a great warrior confraternity, austere and fanatical, I forgot the troubles and
dangers of a long journey. I understood something of
the awe and reverence of any other shoeless pilgrim, who,
after much travel, steps at last from the white mats of
the mosque into the dim chamber where he will kiss the
sacred qubba. For the first time I realised the great
peace which comes at a journey's end, yet the long,
narrow room was unlike our Western idea of a shrine.
Nearly the whole of the floor space was occupied by the
graves of members of the Senussi family, oblongs of
desert sand, with a stone edging and an upright slab at
either end. A narrow carpeted pathway ran round these
to the farthest corner where stood the qubba of the Mahdi
—an ark-shaped wooden framework covered with a red
cloth.

As befits a creed which forbids all luxury, the simplicity of the room was striking. There was nothing to impress the pilgrim except his own passionate reverence. His worship must of necessity be a thing of the spirit and not of the senses. Yet that low dim chamber in the middle of the Sahara is in its way as impressive as St. Peter's at Rome, or the Temple of Heaven in Pekin! Cardinals and mandarins may bring mixed motives to their worship, but the fierce-eyed Beduin in rough white burnus, worn wooden rosary hanging from sun-dried fingers, prays with a strenuous simplicity and earnestness that must impress the very atmosphere with the sincerity of his devotion. Thus I felt as, hands raised to Heaven, I murmured the "Bismallah Arahman Arahim" under keen watching eyes; but when we passed out into the sunlight the impression faded and one's guard was up again!

First there was a fight with the blacks who had become hopelessly unruly. Having been only remarkable for their absence when there was any real danger, they now devoted their time to eating, sleeping and talking of their prowess. We, therefore, decided to send them back to Jalo by the main caravan route and go on ourselves to Jaghabub. This time the retinue protested in vain. We had suffered too much from their fears coming in to wish to return through the continual minor panics of the Zouia country. The Jaghabub route is considerably shorter, for it cuts off the angle of Jalo and, above all, it is utterly unknown to Europeans. As it necessitates at least twelve days without water, some 600 kilometres, it is rarely attempted except by very large well-equipped caravans, who can afford to lose a few camels by the way, or by the Senussi family, who can send camels laden with water on ahead to fill some reservoirs especially placed for the purpose.

We had seen the dangers of travelling with a

moderately large and inefficient retinue, so we now determined to try the other extreme. We proposed to take with us only Mohammed and Yusuf, a guide and perhaps a camel-man. We should have to take four camels for water alone and another two at least for fodder, before we could think of luggage and provisions. The latter are easy, for it is no use providing for more than seventeen days at the outside after leaving Hawawiri. If by that time the traveller is not safely in Jaghabub he is dead, for there are no wells on the route after leaving Zakar, three days from Hawawiri. Altogether it would be an exciting journey and, looking at the blank white space on our survey map, where not even Zakar was marked, we longed to put a long red line across it. Caravans from Egypt should logically do the Jaghabub route unless they go direct from Siwa, which means an extra half-day without water. The alternative is seven days to Jalo, one to Buttafal, then seven to Zieghen and a further five to Hawawiri. The worst point of the more direct route is that there are four days of bad dunes just before reaching Jaghabub. However, anything was preferable to trying to keep the peace between Beduins and Sudanese for three weeks, with the accompanying tale of sore feet and overladen camels, water squandered, fuel all used during the first few days and doubtless a delay at each well.

We spent most of the morning arguing with the soldiers, who all apparently wanted to get married at Jaghabub, probably on the reward they hoped to get for accompanying us there. Then visitors began to arrive, which proved that the mental atmosphere was changing. The chilly, doubtful feeling I had predicted was beginning to trouble the Zouias who had so stormily swept from our presence two days before. The dark Hamid Bu Korayim was the first to come. He had been one of the loudest to denounce the strangers. Now he said: "I wanted all the men to come out to meet you with drums, but there was dissension. What you said at the meeting was true, but it would not have been good for me to have agreed with you then. I was obliged to support the others, for we had arranged what we were going to say beforehand." This was a poor specimen of Arab mentality, but he was followed by an entirely different type, Suleiman Bu Matar, old and much-travelled, very devoted to the Senussi family. At the original meeting he had been calm and suave, only saying that we should waste time by going to the villages. Now he said with very quiet dignity, "Your words were wise, but you must not judge the people here by your own countrymen. Egypt is the mother of the world. The villagers here are very ignorant." He then offered to accompany us to the other end of the oasis.

Thereafter the retinue were somewhat less frightened and we went to Jof without difficulty. We rode along a little causeway which crossed the big, curly lake in the midst of the Jof palm gardens and when we came to the rough, salt marsh on the farther side, we found the ruins of a whole Tebu village. Some of the houses were amazingly small but very well preserved—the hard mortar smooth and always polished on the outside—looking exactly like round clay ovens. As at Buma, on the very edge of the water was a castle. It appears that the Tebus fought only with spears, so a strip of water was a good protection against attack. Therefore, wherever there is a lake in the Kufara or Buseima oases, one is pretty certain to find the ruins of villages and primitive forts. The Zouias won an easy victory because they had guns and gunpowder. Jof is a large native town stretching for about a kilometre in a line of solid, long walls without door or window. At one end is the

old zawia established by the ekhwan of Sidi Ben Ali. It
is an insignificant building, very low, with a dark, bare
mosque, large and very well kept, and in a further room
a qubba of the daughters of Sidi el Mahdi. This tomb
is enclosed in a green wooden frame and hung with
quantities of ostrich eggs. It is much venerated and in
one of the courts we saw some pilgrims from Wadai,
fierce-looking blacks with rosaries and long palm staves.

The whole life of an Arab town goes on within the
high, impenetrable walls. Otherwise they are cities of
the dead. I doubt if we saw a dozen figures in the streets
of Jof till we came to the Tebu settlement, yet it has a
population of some seven hundred. The women literally
never set foot outside their houses. The whole time I
was in Taj I never saw a woman except one or two
elderly black slaves. It must be an extraordinary life
within a few square feet bounded by blind walls. The
ladies of the Sayeds' families can visit each other perhaps,
as in Taj the houses of the Senussi family are adjoining.
But I have never been in any Eastern town where life
was so reserved and aloof. Presumably the men gossip,
but if so, they do it in each other's houses, for one never
sees a group in the streets. Very occasionally one notices
a grave figure with brass ewer or humble teapot, per-
forming the necessary ablution at sunset before saying
the obligatory prayers, or perhaps a reflective grey-
bearded individual standing at an open door. The great
difference between the Senussi towns and any other desert
city is the entire absence in the former of the cafés, which
usually form the centre of life and movement. They
vary in size and splendour, but, from Omdurman to
Tuggourt, one finds in every village at least a mud-walled
room with rough benches and little tables, or, in the
more primitive places, merely a raised ledge running
round the walls, where all the menfolk gossip over long-

stemmed narghilehs, while generally a dancer performs some variation of the *danse du ventre.* In Libya, smoking, drinking and dancing-girls are forbidden by the Senussi law. Therefore the café has no *raison d'être* and the towns are silent, apparently deserted, infinitely discreet!

We rode all round the scattered masses of Jof's houses, meeting She-ib's brother, Ahmed el Khadri, a well-known Senussi clerk, who greeted us warmly and was delighted to get news of his family. Then we climbed the little group of gherds beyond the town and looked down upon the Tebu village whose headman is Sa-ad el Tebu. Very primitive were the dwellings after the solid Zouia buildings, for the greater part were just palm-leaf huts. The men were generally tall and clad in sheepskins, the wool worn inside. Their food, when they travel, consists of powdered locusts and powdered dates mixed together. The women wore only one long dark piece of stuff, wound round them like a barracan, but generally tattered and somewhat inadequate. The young ones were distinctly pretty with charming round faces, wide, long-lashed eyes, almost black skins, but without any of the swollen negroid characteristics.

As we rode back across the wadi I discovered the right adjective for the cliffs of Kufara. Of course they were amber, a rich, mellow amber, which detracted from the green of the palms, so that the gardens of Jof took on a wonderful silvery-grey appearance against the burnt gold of the hills.

That night, while meticulously measuring the just proportion of tea, sugar and spice, the kaimakaan offered to show us an original letter of Sidi Ben Ali es Senussi to the people of Wajanga on the road to Wadai. I think our enthusiastic interest pleased him, for he at once detached an immense key from his belt and gave it

to a slave, who brought a casket not much bigger than
the key.   This was placed solemnly in the circle of light
on the dark-piled carpets and in the almost tangible
silence that seemed to reign within that house, Sidi
Saleh reverently drew forth a single sheet of rough quarto
paper, three-quarters of which was covered with minute,
old-fashioned Arabic.   I give the literal translation in
the appendix because the letter is of historical importance
as it announces the Senussi's intention of accepting the
allegiance of the Zouias, of coming to Kufara with the
tacit understanding that his rule would be accepted so
far south of Wajanga. It was an exceedingly interesting
document and one fully appreciated its value in the
exotic house of Sidi el Abed in the middle of the legendary
oasis.

CHAPTER XII

THE FLIGHT FROM TAJ

THEREAFTER we settled down for a day or two to the reserved and placid life of Taj. We got up shortly after sunrise and while there was yet no sign of movement among the dark, discreet walls we wandered miles along the cliffs, trying to get the exact positions of the various oases and villages. The latter are almost invisible in some lights, as they are made of the sand and stones amidst which they stand. We found that the wadi narrowed to a strip to the north-east beyond Boema, while to the west it widened out into a wide expanse of hattab, high mounds covered with sticks and leafless bushes. To the south-west these hillocks rose from twelve to twenty feet and then beyond Tolab, which was too far away to be seen from our cliffs, the hattab gradually merged into the flat desert.

One morning we explored the whole of the salt marsh, from whose hard, grey, stony matter the Tebus had built their houses. We found the remains of a whole village, though some of the houses were but broken circles on the ground. The main fort had one chamber sixteen feet in diameter and the highest bit of wall existing measured eleven feet, but round it was a crumbled mass of walls and smaller rooms, or separate buildings perhaps, as each was neatly finished off with perfectly rounded surface, like the damp clay pots one sees made on a rotary wheel. I think the Tebus must

have found the salt, hard sand especially good for their
very enduring mortar, for their ruined villages are to
be found only on marshes, as at Buseima, Buma and
Jof. When we heard that there were Tebu remains in
Taiserbo and actual Tebus in Ribiana, we instantly
concluded that there were marshes in these two oases
and the idea proved correct.

When we returned from our matutinal walks we had
enough appetite to cope with Sidi Saleh's prodigious
hospitality. Every morning on the stroke of nine a
light tap came on my green and yellow door and there
was Durur, with smiling ebony face, ready to lead us
by sandy path and intricate court and passage to the
wide, carpeted loggia, where waited our kindly host to
wave us into the long, dark chamber redolent of roses
and cinnamon. After we had gravely washed our
hands in the Damascus basin, we crouched cross-legged
beside the immense brass tray and there was a moment
of thrilled expectation while another slave lifted the
lids of a dozen dishes. Sometimes there was a small
carved tray, inlaid with silver, on which stood half a
score of bowls of sweetmeats, stiff blancmanges of all
colours adorned with almonds, very sweet pastes something like Yorkshire pudding, junket made of the milk
of a newly lambing sheep, all sorts of date concoctions,
couss-couss made with raisins and sugar, a white, sticky
cream flavoured with mint. Always there were bowls
of sweet hot milk and piles of thin, crisp, heavy bread
fried with butter and eaten hot with sugar, called in
Egypt "bread of the judge." Arab custom ordains
that a guest must be entertained for three days and
three nights, but the generous kaimakaan would not
hear of our getting anything for ourselves. The story
of Jedabia was repeated over again. Once we protested
about the mighty meals provided in the house of Sidi

el Abed and the next day, as a reminder that the hospitality of the East is unbounded and must be accepted with the simplicity with which it is offered, the number of dishes was doubled and there were no fewer than twenty loaves ranged round the tray, while the centre *plat* was no longer a bowl, it was literally a bath of mellow, golden rice in which lay the buttery fragments of a whole sheep. Two hours each morning were spent in that quiet room going through the various ceremonies dependent on "breakfasting." When the highly spiced and peppered coffee was finished, there were always the three glasses of green tea, hot and strong, with dignified slow conversation, punctuated by many pauses, while the brazier smoke made little hypnotic spirals, and through the open door a splash of sunlight crept over the castellated wall and lingered on the purple and rose of the carpets between the great arches of the loggia.

About eleven o'clock, scented and very replete, we took ceremonious leave of our host and departed slowly, but the instant the doors of Sidi Idris's house closed on the last "Aleikum salaam" of the departing slave, we dropped the ponderous and reflective gait suited to our exalted position and ran across the great court to shut ourselves up in the "harem," the only really private bit of the house, with pencils and paper. How we regretted, as we struggled with angles and degrees, the perverse distrust with which the Zouias regard even a compass. We used to have the most frantic arguments about our primitive maps, but Hassanein was nearly always right as to direction and I as to distance, fruit of so many long journeys in the desert, where all landmarks appear three times as near as they really are. We worked solidly till four or five, though there were nearly always interruptions—Mohammed, to say that we

A TEBU AT AWARDEL IN KUFARA

OUR CAMP AT AWARDEL

LOADING AT AWARDEL

should have to buy a camel-man for twenty pounds and
sell him again at Jaghabub, Yusuf, to say the girbas still
leaked after all his cunning treatment, little Sidi Omar,
resplendent in a wonderful yellow jubba, to hint about
the scarcity of pocket-knives in Kufara, Sheikh Musa,
from Hawari, to tell us that the men of his village were
too over-awed to visit us in the house of the Sayeds,
but were exceedingly regretful concerning their reception
of us.

So the hot hours wore away and about five we
wandered out to see the amazing sunsets over the wadi,
when for a few minutes the whole oasis was dyed in
rainbow flames. Generally, before the crimson disk had
sunk beyond the western sands, Surur was anxiously
scanning the landscape to announce the dinner hour.
We had long ago lost count of European time. We
used vaguely to calculate that the sun rose at 6 A.M. and
set at 6 P.M., but for all practical purposes we followed
the Arab day, which begins an hour after sunset. We
set our watches each evening to solar time and found
ourselves counting the changing months by the lunar
year of Islam. I never knew what day of the week
it was till Friday came, when, if we were in a town,
we joined the stream of worshippers, clad in their best
clothes, who wended their way to the mosque. In the
desert the most learned would recite the Koran and
read a simple form of prayer. While the muezzin was
crying the melodious call to prayer, "La Illaha ill'-
Allah! Haya alla Salah! Haya alla Fallah!" from
the round tower at the end of the zawia wall, we passed
between the shuttered houses, gravely greeting the few
white shrouded forms who crossed our path. As the
last appealing yet triumphant "Allahu Akhbar!" rang
out to the evening star we entered the first low door,
and the oppressive secrecy of the house shut us in.

How many cloistered lives were hidden behind the little
wooden shutters that never opened for dark-fringed eyes
to peer shyly at the passing strangers! Sometimes little
Sidi Omar ran out to kiss my hand and say, "On my
head and my eyes, I love you!" Sometimes we saw
a long row of red leather slippers before one of the
smaller porches and caught a glimpse of white figures
bent over a huge platter from which, with the right
thumb and two fingers—it is very bad form to dirty
more of the hand than this—they ate rapidly. Otherwise the house kept its secrets well and we never knew
who lived in it or how!

After the evening meal the atmosphere mellowed
with the candle-light and mint tea. Our host talked
to us of the Sayeds he served, of their great history
and their great influence. We learned that Sidi Ahmed
es Sherif was respected and revered as the supporter of
the old régime. He stood for the stern, unbending
laws of the first Senussi. His judgments were ruthlessly
severe and rapidly executed, as in the case of the
unfortunate Mukhtar. The malefactor saw only a stately
white figure, completely veiled, and from behind the
snowy cloth came the immutable words of judgment.
Sayed Ahmed broke men. He never bent them. Yet
the older ekhwan, serious and simple, venerated him
because to them he represents the power of tradition,
the inviolate Islam, fanatically opposed to European
progress. On the other hand, Sidi Idris is loved. As
the son of the Mahdi, the Senussi saint, the wonder of
whose works and words is rapidly becoming legendary,
he inherits a great power. The Beduin likes to worship
something tangible under Allah. He must feel convinced that there is one being on earth who blends
spiritual and temporal power so that he can himself
dwell in a sort of mystic security. "Inshallah, and if

our lord Idris wills it!" is an oft-repeated phrase. The
Emir has a reputation for justice and patience. The
former is as stringent and as merciless as that of his
predecessor, but it is tempered with the infinite patience
always taken to ensure the whole of the case being
examined before judgment is given. This is essential in
a land where the justice of the Koran is the only code.
"An eye for an eye. A tooth for a tooth." Drunken-
ness is punished by flogging. The thief loses his right
hand. Treachery means death. Sidi Idris is too good
a Moslem and too great a mystic not to have secured
the whole-hearted devotion of his father's followers,
while his broad-minded and intelligent foreign policy has
secured him the respect of the modern element. The
accord at Regima was one of his greatest triumphs. It
showed his power in Cyrenaica. The tribal sheikhs of
the coast, almost without exception, announced, "The
word of Idris is ours!"

The closing scene of our day will always be connected in my mind with the chanting of the Koran in
the zawia and the most brilliant clear starlight, as we
returned to our house in silence, only broken by the soft
shuffling of our heel-less slippers in the sand. While
the cold white light warred with our candles and the
melodious words of "The Book" were still humming
in our ears, visitors would gradually make their appearance: the judge, Osman Quadi, Mahmud el-Jeddawi, the
wakil, a few of the more advanced ekhwan, among whom
was Mohammed Tawati, "close friend of the Mahdi."
The last-named is partially paralysed, and the Senussi
mind, always alert for signs and miracles, explains that,
in defiance of the direct orders of Sidi el Riffi, the
unfortunate man started to journey north. Before he
reached Hawari his camel died and he himself was
stricken with paralysis.

In those dim evenings, while I made scented tea, the
talk was a little less formal. We learned how much
the Mahdi had done for Kufara, for besides giving it
flowers, fruit and vegetables, he introduced pigeons and
duck and the cultivation of grain. He built the fortress
sanctuary of Taj, where the wells are ninety feet deep,
so that water is always scarce and a girba full is a gift,
since two hefty slaves have to wind up the heavy buckets
foot by foot. The site is well chosen, but the town
depends for its life on an army of slaves, for every
vegetable or flower, every date and piece of firewood,
must be carried up from the wadi below. The fuel is
dry hattab and huge palm leaves. There is also charcoal
made in the valley. The Mahdi instituted the regular
caravan route to Wadai and encouraged a very extensive trade between the Sudan and Cyrenaica. He
"miraculously" discovered wells on the southern route
and old Sheikh Suleiman Bu Matar told how his father
had been with the saint when water failed the caravan
at Sarra, on the way to Wadai. The Senussi leader
pointed to a spot which appeared to be solid rock and
bade the men dig. Hour after hour they laboured till
the well had sunk beyond the sight of the watchers up
above. Only their faith in the Mahdi could have made
possible so gigantic a task, for the water did not appear
till the almost inconceivable depth of 120 "kamas" (the
length of a man's forearm and hand from elbow to
first knuckles). "Only a man with amazing eyesight
can see the water and the rope is unending," said
Sheikh Suleiman.

We learned a list of the prices in Kufara from a
ponderous merchant whose striped brown and yellow
jerd reminded one of Biblical pictures. Hejin (trotting
camels), all of which belonged to the Tebus, cost seventeen to eighteen pounds in gold. Sheep were five

mejidies, goats four and a half, fowls half a mejidie, and pigeons four and a half qurush. Eggs were very cheap—a hundred for a mejidie (two a penny), but sugar was two mejidies an oke (eight shillings for two pounds) and tea three mejidies an oke. Butter fetched two mejidies for three rotls (one pound). Practically no other produce is sold. The owners of the gardens keep their vegetables for themselves. Mahmud el-Jeddawi volunteered much information about dates. "This year the grazing is good in Barca, so you may buy several camel-loads for a mejidie, but when there is no grass in the north the Zouias come here with large caravans and buy all our dates, so that for a mejidie you can purchase but a few rotls!" [1] He added that many tons of the Sayeds' dates were even now rotting, as there were no camels to take them away.

"I have noticed that there are very few camels in Kufara," I said. "There are very few men also," he replied. "The Zouias have all taken their camels to Barca this year to feed them on the good grass. They do this every winter when the nagas are foaling, as there is no fodder here. They leave their families in Kufara and come back to them in the summer."

I used to get very sleepy before the last visitor departed, having generally urgently urged us not to do the Jaghabub route. They are the most depressing of Job's comforters with regard to journeys, for they always remember terrible stories of death from thirst or loss of direction, which they relate with infinite detail. Thus we learned that the Gebel Fadil, on the east of the Zieghen route, was so called because some twenty years ago one Jebail Fadil had missed the well

---

[1] The usual exchange for paper money is six mejidies for one pound, but for gold one receives seven. No paper money of any country is valid beyond Jedabia. Ten qurush make one mejidie.

at Zieghen on his way from Jalo and had perished in
the mountains with all his family. Concerning the
Jaghabub route, the most encouraging sentence was
generally, "If you miss it, you go either to Siwa or to
hell!" uttered in a tone that left no doubt as to which
was the more probable!

We had secured the only guide in the place,
Suleiman, and we had ascertained that he really had
done the journey four years before and that previous
to that he had done it with Yusuf. He was a little,
quiet old man, bent and grey, of few words. When
we asked him the length of the journey, he said,
"Wallahi! I cannot tell. My walk is twelve days
from Zakar, but I do not know your walk." We
assured him with the utmost fervour that our walk
would most certainly be twin brother to his own, but
personally I thought the whole caravan would probably
sit down and die of complete inanition. Hassanein and
I had never yet managed to walk a whole twelve hours
on end. Mohammed had nearly died in the attempt.
Yusuf had grown fat and soft again on the rich fare of
Taj, while Suleiman looked much too ancient and frail
for such a stupendous march. Our weakness was
equalled only by that of the animals, for the best had
all foaled and only the young, unreliable nagas, three
years old, and a couple of ancient camels were left,
beside the caricature and various halt and lame, who
looked as if they were dancing all the time, because they
had cut feet! However, we had become completely
fatalistic. We proposed to take vast stores of water and
put the rest of our trust in Allah.

We also proposed to leave Kufara as soon as possible.
Firstly, because our hosts were so prodigious in their
hospitality that we could not bear to take advantage of
it longer than was absolutely necessary for our work.

Secondly, because, though what may be called the party directly responsible to the Government were very kindly disposed towards the guests of their rulers, the ancient and old-fashioned ekhwan held aloof. They would not believe that any strangers could have been given permission to penetrate their guarded privacy. They were torn between their desire to do honour to the Sayeds and their horror of diverging a hair's breadth from immemorial custom. Among the Zouias there were now two factions. Many had been infected by the stories of the Bazama family and Abdullah, but a small party had gradually formed in our favour under the leadership of Suleiman Bu Matar.

There were always, however, currents and cross-currents under the surface which sometimes rippled into open suspicion. Also there had been many very persistent inquiries on the part of the most lawless elements as to the exact date of our departure and our proposed route. It was known that the soldiers would not be travelling with us, so we should be an easy prey if the tribesmen wanted to play their last card. We therefore spread the rumour that we should remain at least a fortnight longer at Taj and privately began to make preparations for another flight, this time aided and abetted by the kaimakaan, who planned to send our little caravan a day's march ahead while we were still openly in Taj. Under the guidance of a trusted sheikh we could overtake it on fast-trotting camels.

Meanwhile it was necessary that we should investigate the western end of the oasis. For this purpose Sheikh Suleiman offered himself as guide and host combined. "I will arrange everything," he said quietly. "Do not trouble yourselves. You shall travel in comfort." We rather wondered what represented his idea of comfort when he announced that we would start two hours before dawn, as it was a very long way. However, we duly rose at 9 o'clock by night Arabic (3 A.M.), and shortly afterwards a muffled thudding on the door warned us that our escort had arrived. We hurried out, clutching all available blankets, for it was extremely cold. The moon had set, so at first I thought two immense towers had sprung up in the night outside the house. A second glance revealed them as very tall hejin. They were barraked with difficulty and I mounted the most uncomfortable saddle I have ever met. It must have had the advantage from the camel's point of view of being exceedingly light, for it consisted merely of two bars about ten inches apart, across which was doubled a carpet, with an upright spoke in front and behind, but it had every possible disadvantage for the aching bones of the rider. Little did I guess that I was destined, with a few short pauses, to spend no less than seventeen hours upon that seat of torture. The commandant, Saleh Effendi, with his gold and green cloak thrown across his thickest jerd, and Hassanein mounted donkeys, which looked microscopic from my towering height. Two soldiers perched themselves, one behind the other, on the second hejin, and down into the wadi we swung, picking our way slowly till we came to the massed palms, when the party settled down to ride.

The silvery stone of the marsh was a frozen grey in the starlight and the houses of Jof but a blur on the low ridge. The leaf hedges were rustling fingers stretched out to bar our way, and the great beams of the "shadouks" (wells) ghostly gibbets in the shadow of the palms.

Outside one of Jof's blind walls we barraked, when, after prolonged knocking, a sleepy slave announced that Sheikh Suleiman was not yet ready. Arab life is very

adaptable. Within a few minutes of receiving the news
the saddle carpets had been spread in the shelter of the
wall, a fire of palm leaves (sent out by our host) lighted,
dates produced from the same hospitable source and
we had all settled down for a prolonged wait under the
still brilliant stars. I think I slept for a few moments,
my head on a stone, for when I was roused by a soft
"Salaam Aleikum!" the stars were less brilliant and
a third slender-limbed hejin was outlined against the
grey sky. We set forth briskly to the south, and soon
the long block of Jof's houses and the neatly fenced
gardens of the Sayeds lay behind us. The donkeys kept
up a sort of short amble, while the camels slipped into
the tireless swinging stride, half swift walk, half trot,
the most comfortable pace in the world. As the light
grew clearer I saw that mine was a big Tebesti beast,
palest grey, long-haired and stately, but not as finely
bred as the other two. They were the fast Tuareg
breed of piebald grey and white, with blue eyes, very
thin, like greyhounds in their lean slenderness. They
ought to be able to do the racing trot which covers
10 kilometres an hour.

Through the dawn we rode and till the sun grew hot,
always west with a hint of south. The large sweep of
Jof palms disappeared on our right. Zuruk was left on
the other side. Then, as we came into the open space
beyond, where the large mounds of hattab begin, we saw
that we were leaving the enchanted wadi behind us. We
skirted the long strip of palms which forms Tolelib.
There is no proper village in the oasis, but, scattered
through the green, one catches sight of a few houses of
the slaves who tend the palms. As we went farther
west the mounds grew to hillocks and the red sand was
tufted here and there with high grass, while masses of
grey bushes climbed over the miniature gherds. Four

hours after sunrise, while yet Tolab was far ahead, Sheikh Suleiman called a halt. A cold north wind had arisen and was finding the old tender spot in my shoulder, so I was glad when he chose the largest sandhill for our picnic breakfast. Bright scarlet rugs were spread on the lee side for the men and a faded rose-red carpet in the shelter of a smaller mound for me, as a woman could not eat with the soldiers. I fancy it would have hurt the Zouia's susceptibilities if he had been obliged to encounter feminine fingers in the common bowl.

After that meal we had an idea of what the Beduin means by travelling comfortably. A complete portable kitchen must have been hidden in the capacious brightly striped khoorgs that hung on either side of the blue-eyed camel. The most delicious odours were soon wafted from a pot stewing on a brushwood fire. A soldier brought me a long-necked brass ewer and a towel before my breakfast was shyly handed me by an ancient and dignified servitor of the sheikh, by name Mohammed, who had run beside his chief the whole way from Jof without protest, though he carried a heavy rifle. I had been given a brass tray of dates to eat and I was contemplating writing a monograph on the various uses of the date in Kufara. It is used for all sweetening purposes in cooking. Mixed with some other local ingredient it makes a sticky sort of glue. A soft date, slightly squashed, takes the place of a cork and every tin of oil is sealed that way. The stones apparently make studs for the nostrils of Tebu girls. I feel sure there are other uses, but the appearance of food prevented my thinking of them that morning among the bristling mounds of hattab.

I lifted a plaited cover of palm leaves embroidered in red and there were nearly a dozen hard-boiled eggs surrounding a mound of crisp, flat bread. Another layer of palm leaf disclosed enough cold lamb, cooked in red pepper and onions, to feed all the party liberally, while the whole was balanced upon a bowl of delicious thick soup full of vermicelli, carrots and other unknown vegetables. All was hot with scarlet strips of fil-fil. Greed and fear struggled in my mind, but the former won and all the cold north wind could not cool my fevered tongue after I had partaken of that highly spiced dish.

When a row of little tin tea-pots were heating on separate piles of ashes, I joined the party under the larger mound and we drank hot sweet tea, which tasted strongly of the inside of the girba which had been hidden underneath the saddle-bags. Afterwards there was half an hour's amiable silence, punctuated by rare remarks chiefly concerning the flora and fauna of the wadi, this being the least suspicious subject of conversation we could think of and Mohammed being visibly eager to distrust. It could not be lengthened out interminably because there are no wild animals in Kufara and I never saw a bird, though I was told that several species, chief among them the wagtail-like "abu fasada," make their appearance in March at the harvest time—the grain is a winter crop. Of insects there is a large variety, chiefly distinguished by their voracious appetites! Cleopatra's asp, a small, fawn-coloured snake, lurks among the sand and in the oasis there are several kinds of serpents, large and small, most of them poisonous. We were assured that one large dark snake measures at least 6 feet and is particularly feared by the natives. Perhaps this is the legendary beast of Hawaish!

After our excellent meal Tolab appeared much nearer and the wind much less strong. We rode on for another couple of hours and verified our suspicions that the wadi had no definite end; we had a bitter argument as to degrees, for we had not dared to bring even a compass, which for once was later decided in my favour by the setting sun. Then we turned to the scattered gardens of Tolab, where I saw roses, verbena and tiny lemon trees, all neatly tied up in fibre matting after the fashion of English gardeners. There is absolutely nothing to see in this last oasis of Kufara, whose sand-brick houses are scattered round the cultivated plots without regular order. We noticed a number of shadouks worked by small, grey donkeys and were hurried away by our host to get a glimpse of the far-distant Gebel Neri, as he had become quite interested in our exploration. These mountains are wonderful landmarks for at least two days south and north, but when we passed them on the way from Buseima we had no means of judging their height. We thought they might rise 150 to 200 metres above the surrounding country, which would make them 750 to 800 above sea level, but this was only a guess.

Two and a half days' journey north-west of Tolab lies Ribiana, behind a gara twice as big as that of Buseima. We were told that the population consists of about a hundred Zouias and Tebus. There is an old zawia founded by the four original ekhwan sent by Sidi Ben Ali. The sheikh is Abu Bakr. There is a salt marsh between the mountain and the strip of palms some 18 kilometres long, at the southern end of which is the zawia, while at the northern end is a village of about ten houses. This information we gathered from Sheikh Suleiman as we rode round the western end of Tolab and turned homewards through the waste of low hattab towards Tolelib. Thereafter the hours seemed interminable. Nothing ever got any nearer, while the saddle bars felt like knife blades. The only break was when we dismounted for the Asr prayers. Eventually we entered the northern edge of Tolelib's palms and were only too thankful when, just before sunset, the tireless Zouia called a halt beside an immense sandbank and the morning meal was repeated.

"We will take a glass of tea to refresh us," said our host modestly, but very soon another savoury mess was being stewed in the capacious pot, while Saleh Effendi produced fresh mint leaves which had been given him at Tolab. This time everyone ate swiftly, plunging great chunks of bread into the basin of stewed vegetables and meat, but once again I was provided with a separate meal tastefully arranged on wicker plates. In half an hour we were in the saddle again, but the animals were tired and the sunset blazed behind us before we drew near the dark shadow of Zuruk. A three-quarter moon mingled her silver light with the red of the flaming west and the amber sands reflected the most extraordinary colours, which changed in the unreal light like the transformation scene in the pantomime. The pace was just too quick to walk in the soft, deep sand, so I had to cling to my painful saddle for another three hours. In starlight we had left Jof. In starlight we returned to it, steering by a glazing fire set to guide us to the gardens of Sayed Rida, from where Mahmud el-Jeddawi had asked us to bring some sacks of dates, probably for our own journey. The scene of the early morning was repeated, for the Sayed's black slaves, fantastic figures in tattered sacking or shreds of cotton, brought bundles of palm leaves for a fire and poured a great pile of hard golden dates on to a huge woven platter. We crunched these as we rested our aching bones on hastily spread carpets, while more and more ebony figures joined the group and just the heads of the camels solemnly chewing the cud came into the circle of wavering firelight under the stars.

The last hour's ride was very slow, for the hejin were

unaccustomed to carrying loads, but it was done to the accompaniment of marriage music from the town and wild "ulla-la-een" of women, mixed with firing of guns and beating of drums. "He is taking a very little girl. She is only thirteen," said Saleh Effendi of the bridegroom. I thought of the woman-child in her stiff, heavy draperies, clinging shyly and desperately to the veil which she would so soon have to raise for an unknown man, the stranger to whom her parents had given her!

Yusuf and Mohammed were waiting for us at the top of the cliff—two unrecognisable figures entirely muffled in immense woollen jerds. With the usual Arab cheerfulness they had come to the conclusion that we had already been murdered by the Zouias!

The attitude of the two men had been very characteristic during our stay at Taj. Both knew by this time that the object of the expedition was to write a book about the country. Both believed it must be for the good of the Senussi since we travelled under the Sayeds' protection, but after this they differed. Yusuf felt that he had accomplished his duty when we arrived safely in Kufara. He was delighted that we were well received and hospitably entertained by the Government, for he thought that we should be impressed by the generosity of the Sayeds. Mohammed felt instinctively that we did not need impressing and all he wanted was that the work of Sidi Idris should be successfully achieved. Both were conscious of the undercurrent of unrest. Yusuf, treating us as strangers and himself as one of the people of Kufara, explained to us with perfect justice that the position was largely due to our own mistakes. Often we had trusted the wrong people. Often I, alas, had forgotten the nice shades of Moslem feminine behaviour in my thirst for knowledge. Mohammed swept aside all these points. He counted that Sidi Idris and he and we were all pitted

for the moment against those who hampered, con-
sciously or unconsciously, the work of the Sayed. Therefore he used to encourage us in friendly fashion, gather
news for us, explain exactly how we should treat such
and such a rumour and urge us to persevere. Yusuf
always laboured to vindicate the honour of the Sayeds.
Mohammed, knowing that no vindication was necessary,
laboured to accomplish through us the task he had been
given so many weeks before in Jedabia. The one thought
in terms of couss-couss and padded camel-saddles, the
other in something he vaguely termed work, but which,
of course, should logically have been the pencils and note-
books he distrusted!

The day after our long expedition to Tolab was
El Gumma, so, luckily, breakfast—a mighty bowl of
pigeons, eggs and carrots—was sent to our house and
we stayed indoors till it was time for the noon prayers,
announced by the muezzin and by a runner who knocked
at the outer door of each house with his cry of in-
vitation ever repeated. Hassanein clothed himself in
the cleanest jerd and departed to the zawia with the
devout Mohammed. I slipped into an outer room beyond
the mosque, for there was no place in the latter for
women, and watched the impressive scene, discreetly
hidden behind a pillar. All the ekhwan were present in
their most resplendent silk jubbas, with snowy veils
above their many-coloured kufiyas. They made splashes
of vivid red, orange and green among the coarse white
jerds of the Beduins. After the last "Azzan," with
sound of fife and drum, escorted by a guard of soldier
slaves in their gala attire, khaki with sundry embroideries,
the kaimakaan arrived in state with Sidi Mohi ed Din
and Sidi Ibrahim the sons of Sayed Ahmed Sherif and
Sidi Senussi, son of Sidi el Abed. His usual grave
dignity was accentuated as he mounted the "mimbar," a

massive figure in striped rose and purple silk, with embroidered blue jacket underneath a gorgeous, many-
tasselled kufiya, stiff with gold thread, over his spotless
white turban, from which depended the finest silk and
wool veil. In delivering the usual Friday speech he
asked the prayers and benediction of Allah for the four
earliest Caliphs, Abu Bekr, Omar, Othman and Ali, and
for twelve other sainted followers and friends of the
Prophet. After the prayer a solemn procession, headed
by the sons of the Senussi Sayeds, passed in ponderous
silence save for the rustling of bare feet on palm mats
to the dim inner chamber to salute the qubba of the
Mahdi.

If it be possible for Taj to be more dignified and
impressive than usual, it achieves that effect on El
Gumma, for all day one catches glimpses between the
dark walls of the richly garbed ekhwan moving slowly,
silk jerds carefully raised above the sand. After the Asr
prayers the deputation of four who had received us, the
Judge, Sidi Saleh, Sidi Ahmed es Senussi and Sidi Omar,
came to bid us the city's formal farewell, though we
were not expected really to leave for several days. The
visit was meant tactfully to imply that we were now free
of official receptions and banquets, though Arab hospitality could only be satisfied by privately sending large
meals to our house while we remained in Taj. We lured
the judge and the portly dignitaries into our sunlit court,
but they were terrified at being photographed. We had
to treat them like children at the dentist's and keep up a
flow of laughing conversation about the painlessness of
the operation, while they huddled pathetically together
for comfort and support!

Later in the day we were visited by Hasan and
Husein Bazama from Ribiana. Relations of the men who
had spread so many false reports about us, they doubtless

CAMP AT MEHEMSA: YUSUF, MOHAMMED AND AMAR

THE AUTHOR ASLEEP ON A CAMEL

JAGHABUB

WELL IN ZAWIA AT JAGHABUB

came to Taj in the first place to discover how much of
their kinsmen's tale was true. Finding us the guests of
Sidi Idris, they decided the larger part must be incorrect.
Hasan was dark and lean and altogether too reminiscent
of Abdullah to please me, but his brother was a nice little
plump person, kindly disposed towards the world in
general and most unusually truthful for a Beduin, for
when his elder brother tried to sell us a camel he
remarked, in a small, plaintive voice, "He is a *very* old
camel."

By this time we had learned how to make Arab tea.
It must have been a good brew that day, for the brothers
verified all Sheikh Suleiman's information about Ribiana
and urgently invited us to visit it. We politely refused,
having seen quite enough of these lonely strips of palms
with a few deserted, dark red houses. They seemed
slightly hurt, so we explained that our camels really
could not be expected to do an extra week's travelling
before the long Jaghabub trip. As a matter of fact, we
were very much troubled about our caravan. Five of
the nagas had foaled and could not be taken away from
their offspring. We had given the soldiers six camels for
their homeward journey via Zieghen and Jalo and they
complained bitterly about the inadequacy of the number.
Moraja had married the pale, dark-eyed woman who had
travelled with us from Buseima and he wanted to take
his wife back to Jedabia with him. Abdul Rahim very
naturally refused, as already they had insufficient transport. The sergeant was furious and threatened to stay
behind, but we were no longer interested in their troubles,
having quite enough of our own.

The girbas we bought in the suq were too new to be
safe and we were desperately afraid of losing our water.
Suleiman, the guide, suddenly announced that only the
Asayed ever went to Jaghabub and that, as nobody had

travelled that way for more than three years, the one well at Zakar would not only be filled up, but probably covered by a dune! As the water was very far away it might take three days to dig down to it. Worst of all, we had only seven camels. Four of these must carry water and two fodder. This left only one for food for six persons, their luggage and tents!

We tried to hire Tebu camels at an exorbitant price, but found that nobody would let their beasts go north in mid-winter, for the camels have very thin coats in Kufara and generally die when they reach a colder climate. I explained that there had been no difference in the temperature of Aujela and Taj, but was told that the Jaghabub route would be bitterly cold and the winds almost intolerable. With this pleasant thought in mind we suggested buying a couple of camels, but there was none to be sold except the ancient Bazama beast, already shivering. "He will die on the way," said Yusuf, hating to make a bad bargain. "I don't mind if he does, providing he will last four or five days beyond the Zakar well. We shall have drunk his load by then and shall not need him any more," I said. "Do you think he will break down before then?" Yusuf would not commit himself. "One could see it in his eye if he meant to die in two days," was all he vouchsafed.

Our friend Mahmud el-Jeddawi bestirred himself energetically on our account and, after searching most of Jof, he triumphantly produced the most amazing camel I have even seen. It looked as if a portion of it had been left out in the making. We all walked round it in mystified silence to discover what was missing. It had the self-satisfied expression of a short, plump, curry-loving Indian colonel and most certainly there was something odd about its shape. I looked at Yusuf appealingly. "It is very woolly." "Yes, it has much wool," he

said with polite despair. We decided not to purchase it
and were rewarded at the last moment by the production
by a Tebu of a really magnificent camel, half hejin and
half beast of burden. Its price was very high, two
hundred mejidies, but we did not even wait to bargain.
It was too necessary to us. We hated letting it go out
of our sight for a moment, but its master insisted that
we could not have it till the following day and we were
obliged to let the caravan start without it.

This time the flight was well arranged, though it was
precipitated by another of Abdullah's darts. We learned
that he had been spreading far and wide a story that the
venerated Sidi Ahmed el Rifi, teacher and adviser of
the Mahdi, had prophesied disaster to any stranger who
travelled on the Jaghabub route. "It is a sacred road
between our two holy places," he had said. "It is for
the Sayeds and their followers only. Nobody else may
go safely by it!" Whether the saying had other origin
than the twisted brain of Abdullah we did not know,
but it might have a distressing effect on the easily roused
fanaticism of the retinue. We therefore hurried the
small caravan off early one morning with the nominal
destination of Hawari, because there was a certain amount
of grazing in the neighbourhood and it would be natural
for the camels to rest there for a week or ten days before
starting for Jaghabub. As a matter of fact they skirted
the village and main oasis and camped in an isolated palm
grove some miles farther on where their presence was
little likely to be suspected.

Next day we made obvious preparations for a tour
in the wadi and then, just after sunset, while all the
devout inhabitants of Taj were occupied with their
prayers, we slipped out of our discreet little door,
wandered carelessly round a projecting wall and found
two camels ready saddled in charge of a plaintive Yusuf,

who hated the idea of travelling in a strong north wind, bitterly cold. Muffled in coarse jerds, only our new primrose leather boots with crimson uppers laced with scarlet thongs apparent to the public gaze, we plodded out of the little town followed by Yusuf, Suleiman and a fortnight-old foal! The wind was so strong that we hardly cast a backward glance at the oasis which had shown us so much in so short a time.

It was a complete chapter of life we left behind. We felt that we had studied its pages thoroughly, but we knew that we had not read all that lay between the lines! Through a glass darkly we had been allowed a glimpse of an unsuspected civilisation aloof from our own and utterly different. For a few days we had moved amidst the friendship and enmity of a rigidly isolated religious fraternity, feeling something of their remote fanaticism, much of their warm generosity, a little of the almost pathetic simplicity which underlay their plots and counterplots. Yet we were ever strangers in a strange land, welcome to their dignified hospitality, but never admitted for a minute to the inner workings of their minds. Some glimpses we caught behind the scenes. Some threads to unravel the unspoken mysteries were put into our hands later by a suddenly talkative Yusuf, but the secrets of Taj are still safe with us!

Each one must unravel them for himself, for no traveller may tell when he has once crossed the threshold, not only of the great house on the cliff, but of the life of these people where each man's brain is an island in itself whose secrets are as jealously guarded as the oasis is by nature. The desert had paid us her debt. We had conquered her waterless desolation and her perilous dunes. We had won the right to her secret and generously she showed it, yet we knew she grudged us our triumph.

As the dark stone houses disappeared swiftly into the red sand and black rocks, so that, looking back after a few minutes one might believe one had dreamed of the wadi and its people, I wondered what price we should pay for our knowledge.

Behind the first ledge of rocks a gnome-like figure, green-hooded and cloaked, rose suddenly beside a microscopic grey donkey, while another, unrecognisably disguised by a scarlet handkerchief which left but an eye visible, appeared with a most unwilling sheep. They were the commandant, Saleh Effendi, sent to accompany us to our first camp, and a soldier to slaughter the sheep in our honour. Subdued greetings were hardly finished when a portly, panting figure, white jerd blowing wildly over a dark blue jubba, turban and spectacles slightly awry, hurried over the rocks. It was Sayed Ahmed es Senussi come to give us a last blessing with many injunctions to the guide to look after us well. After the "Fatha" had been gravely repeated, he clutched Yusuf's sleeve and murmured mysteriously, "Will you not halt your caravan round the next gherd, as I wish to send out to you food for your journey— meat, bread and rice!" In a still lower voice he explained that many of the friendly ekhwan had wished to feast us, but had been afraid of hurting the feelings of the kaimakaan, who looked upon us as his guests. Arab custom ordains that when a stranger comes to a town, any man who visits him afterwards sends food to him or feasts him in his house. Therefore, the ekhwan had been in some difficulty. Either they broke their laws of hospitality or they ran counter to the generous wishes of the kaimakaan, or they failed in respect to the Sayed by not visiting the guests in his house! We remembered that the sons of Sayed Ahmed Sherif and Sayed el Abed, boys between fourteen and seventeen,

had often waited to greet us as we left the house of
Sidi Saleh. "We wanted to see if the Sitt Khadija
wears the same clothes as our ladies," one had said
shyly, but they were frightened of being photographed,
the idea being that if one possesses a picture of a person
one possesses also his soul, or at least a certain hypnotic
power over him.

We were obliged regretfully to decline the delightful
offer of Sidi Ahmed, as speed was necessary. Therefore, we hurried north as fast as our odd little procession
—camels, donkey, sheep and foal—would go. The wind
dropped after the first three hours and a feeble moon
rose in a clear, translucent sky. It was a night of
colour so marvellous that it was unreal. I knew the
strange tricks moonlight could play in the desert, but
only once before had I seen such startling effects
and that was in *Chu Chin Chow!* White moonlight on white sand makes an iridescent silvery sea,
cold, almost cruel in its pale intangibility. But this
was a golden light on an amber-red world and, except
that one could not see so far, it was as clear as the
day. The palm trees were shades of sapphire, silvered
at the edge, and their shadows hot, clear-cut purple.
We rode through a world so wonderful that when
we had skirted the dreaming village of Hawari and
completely lost our way in the oasis beyond—the infalli-
bility of guides is a very brittle myth in Libya—we
hardly minded, but with jerds flung back we revelled
in unutterable stillness and colour onceivable. Even
after we had turned two complete circles and, with
a waning moon, unexpectedly discovered our camp
discreetly hidden in a hollow between great clumps
of palms and what looked like mimosa trees, we could
not go into the tent, though it was one of the
coldest nights we had had. We sat outside amidst

the violet and amber and, in spite of dates and
cinnamon bread, wondered how soon we should
wake up!

Our desire for a swift and secret departure from the
palm grove near Hawari was frustrated by the non-
arrival of our new camel till the afternoon of the following day. By this time, of course, most of the population
of the neighbouring village of Awardel was in our camp.
The Zouias were most friendly and terribly curious.
Their shrewd, suspicious eyes and pale, mean faces
encircled my tent all day, hoping to catch a glimpse
to satisfy their curiosity, but, out of sheer perversity, I
smothered my face in the barracan and then snapshotted
them when they were not looking!

Unfortunately, I had left behind something of a
reputation as a doctor, nature presumably having taken
my patients in hand after my departure, so all day
long my tent was thronged, by women with the most
mysterious maladies. The poorer ones crouched outside,
their scarlet woollen barracans an effective contrast to
their black tobhs, the most picturesque combination I
had yet seen. The wives of important sheikhs were
ushered into my tent and the flaps closed after them
by jealous male relatives. If they were young they
would not uncover their faces even to me, but, mute,
huddled bundles of voluminous draperies, with at least
three barracans of rich dark weaving one over the other,
they sat on my camp bed while an ancient crony translated their needs. They wanted me to *feel* skin diseases
through layers of garments, prescribe for invisible eyes
and generally guess at their ailments from the descriptions of their elderly relatives, who urged them at intervals, entirely without effect, not to be afraid. Their
jewellery interested me, for they wore bracelets like
gauntlets of thin beaten silver, reaching half-way from

wrist to elbow, and odd flat rings, big and thin as a five-shilling piece.

The day ended with a violent quarrel between Mohammed and Abdullah, who was to return with the soldiers to Jedabia, because the kaimakaan thought Sidi Idris would punish him more severely than he had power to do. The guide had told Mohammed he would beat his nose flat, apparently an appalling insult, for the uproar was prodigious and, in the middle of it, while everyone was shouting at the top of their voices, our trusted retainer wept like an infant! He was only comforted by permission to buy a slave-girl he coveted. "She has walked all the way from Darfur," he said, "so she can walk to Jaghabub with us." But we persuaded him to send her to Jalo later on. The caravan was already overloaded without the ebony maiden's food and water, though we were horribly tempted to take her when we heard she was a good cook. As camel-men were scarce at the moment in Kufara and fetched very high prices, we had taken Mohammed's follower, Amar, instead. He was a plucky and willing boy, a pupil from the Jaghabub zawia, but, alas, no cook! The way he ruined our treasured rice was little short of a tragedy.

The evening of January 24 was spent in a pursuit that was becoming habitual, that of sorting our rapidly diminishing baggage to see what could be left behind. This time the tent and camp beds had to go. There would be no time to put up a tent on the Jaghabub route. With our small and somewhat feeble retinue, after walking twelve hours a day, probably against a strong wind, by the time the camels were attended to and the rice or flour cooked, one would have no energy left to struggle with tent pegs. The most one could hope for would be a flea-bag on the ground sheet in the inadequate shelter of a zariba made of our food and

fodder sacks. We now had one suit-case, a sack of
provisions and two rolls of bedding. "We might put
the ground sheets in the bedding," I said casually, looking round the pathetically small pile of our belongings
to see if we could possibly do without anything else.
"Your flea-bag is the thinnest. We had better put
it in between the flaps." I thought there was a certain
nervousness in Hassanein's eyes as we undid the bulky
roll, but I did not quite understand it, even when a
bottle of amber eau-de-Cologne and an immense attaché
case fell out, scattering a complete manicure set in the
sand. I was quite used to this sort of thing by now,
but I was mildly surprised when a violent protest followed my efforts to insert the waterproof sheet. "Take
care! Take care! You will hurt yourself!" "What on
earth do you mean? Woollen flea-bags don't bite!" The
thought struck us both instantaneously that this was
hardly correct at the moment and we were both laughing when suddenly a pain that could hardly have been
inflicted by even the largest Libyan bug shot through
my hand. "What is that?" I gasped, and pulled
out a very large, sharp saw! For one horrible moment
I thought my companion had developed tendencies to
homicidal mania as I stood open-mouthed with the tool
in my hand. "I've hidden that damned thing in my
bedding for three months and whenever I turned over
it ran into my shoulder and I've cut myself on it three
times!" he said viciously. "But why, why, why?" I
could only stutter. "I thought it would be so useful,"
was the reply. Visions of the treeless desert, with no tuft
of moss or blade of grass, must have crossed both our
minds simultaneously, for almost before I could ask
feebly, "What did you mean to cut?" he said, "I don't
know. I just felt it would come in useful—to make things
with," he added hastily under my baleful eye. "But I

didn't want you to see it. I knew you would laugh."
"Laugh!" I exclaimed scornfully, sucking my finger-
tips. "After all, you needn't make such a fuss! It's
no worse than your bread!" and I remembered the days
on the way to Taiserbo when I had insisted on treasuring
a piece of ten-day-old bread in my knapsack with much
the same sort of feeling that "it might come in useful."
My companion, unlawfully in search of matches—the
only things we refused to share were matches and soap,
though we never used the latter—cut his hand badly on
the rough, sharp edge of my precious loaf and thereafter
spoke of food as the most dangerous element in the
desert!

CHAPTER XIII

THROUGH THE MOUNTAINS

LOADING the camels on January 25 was something of a difficulty. The whole male population of Hawari came out to help or to hinder, while various shrouded female forms lurked in the shadows of palm clumps hoping to exchange a few eggs for green tea, but we had left our last stores at Kufara, so could do no bartering. A young merchant from Wadai offered us crimson-dyed leather at three and a half mejidies for a whole goatskin. He would easily make his fortune among London boot shops! That morning was another revelation of Zouia character, for if we left anything out of sight for a minute it disappeared. I lost my pet woolly scarf which I used to roll round underneath my thin cotton garments, my only protection against the north winds. Mohammed politely spread his rug for two venerable ekhwan to sit upon. A few moments later they and it vanished altogether. Yusuf's bright-coloured blanket followed suit, with Hassanein's sleeping-helmet. It is not to be wondered at, therefore, that our farewells were somewhat chilly. Amar was venomous because some thrifty housewife had appropriated the grid on which he made his almost uneatable bread. We shuddered to think what it would be like without it!

By 8 A.M. we had received the last mixed blessings and warnings, the chorus of "Marhabas" and "Ma Salamas!" had died among the palms and an amazing

sense of peace had descended on us. For the first time
in three months we were a completely friendly party,
united to achieve a common object by dint of hard work
and endurance. It was a wonderful feeling! Everybody
was happy and nobody shirked. Even the plump Yusuf
forgot his plaintive whine, and with a fat smile gathered
hattab and urged on the camels. Unfortunately, our
great grey Tebu beast was suffering badly from his
first heavy date meal, just as the rest of the caravan
had done at Buttafal a month previously. At the last
moment, however, Sidi Mohammed el-Jeddawi, seeing
that the necessary dates for fodder took up three
complete loads, lent us one of Sayed Rida's foaling
nagas. We had no baggage saddle ("hawia") for her,
so we doubled across her back our thin, single fly-tent
which we had meant to leave behind. At the last
moment Yusuf, ever economical, stuck the three light
poles in somewhere.

We therefore started with a caravan of nine, but
they were distinctly overloaded, for we had to carry
water for six or seven days, since Suleiman, the guide,
was uncertain as to how long it would take to dig out
the Zakar well. That day we marched ten hours, with
a hot sun and a cold north-north-west wind. We left
the Hawari Gara a dark block to the west, with the
great indigo cliffs of the Gebel Neri far beyond it.
Gradually we drew away from the hot, red sands of
Kufara with their patches of strange black stones. In
the afternoon we emerged on to the pale, flattish country
sweeping up to the foot of the Hawaish mountains.
These, however, were still invisible when we camped at
sunset, because the two smallest camels refused to go
any farther. We missed the blacks while struggling to
unload our unruly beasts, two of whom were three-
year-olds and never could be barraked without a

prolonged fight. We built our zaribas with their backs to the persistent north wind, but nature played us a trick, for the temperature descended unpleasantly. We sat comfortably inside our flea-bags, however, cooking rice and coffee and watched a fading moon slowly dim our solitary candle.

Next morning Mohammed roused us long before the dawn and we were away by 7 A.M., but we were very under-staffed, for Amar and old Suleiman were both too feeble to lift the immense fodder loads and Hassanein and I were exceedingly inefficient! Nevertheless, complete cheerfulness still reigned. The Beduins invented and sang lustily doggerel rhymes of personal tendencies, such as,

> " If Sidi Yusuf won't walk to-day,
> A new little wife won't come his way."

We saw the Hawaish mountains, a long line of round peaks on the horizon, about 8 A.M., and at the same moment discovered that our new guide had deficient sight. He was a little, old, wizened Beduin, very poor but very shrewd for all his apparent simplicity. He was clad only in worn sandals, an ancient leather skull cap and a pathetically tattered grey jerd. He was quite illiterate and his rare speech was in a dialect which even Mohammed found some difficulty in following. He shuffled along all day, bent over his palm stick, untiring and unresponsive, though occasionally his cracked, hoarse voice joined in the lilting refrains of the retinue. Only when he failed to pick out a certain hill with a cleft top did he tell us that he had once rashly interfered in a private battle between two black soldiers and received a blow on the head which had permanently damaged his eyesight. After this admission I think we all expected to lose the way, but one becomes terribly fatalistic in the desert. "Allah alone knows" is repeated with complete simplicity by every traveller in the great wilderness.

By this time I could well understand the carelessness of the Beduins, their lack of forethought and their childlike trust in Providence. After all, what does it really matter on a twelve days' waterless route whether one overloads one's camel with a couple of extra girbas and a spare jarfa of fodder in order to ensure a day or two more of life? A few strong giblis may dry up all the water. It may go bad, or the skins may leak, or a load may be thrown on to sharp stones so that the girbas burst. On the other hand, the guide may lose his memory or his "instinct." Day after day without a landmark, with the ever-present knowledge that one slight mistake means destruction, is surely enough to trouble the most experienced. One day's bad march, owing to a mere trifle such as irregularly balanced loads, sore backs or unaccustomed date feeding, will endanger the whole issue, for the Zakar—Jaghabub or the Zakar—Siwa routes are the longest known stretches without water. The Boema-Farafra route is twelve days without water. The camels arrive completely exhausted and if an extra day be added to the march they probably do not arrive at all. The men may get sore feet or fever, but they cannot ride the heavily burdened beasts. The terrible north wind may blow day and night, making every step laborious, yet the daily average has got to be kept up. Therefore, the Beduins smile when one makes pitiful little attempts to arm oneself against nature, to forestall or prevent her rigours. "If Allah wills, we shall arrive," they say gravely and turn the conversation to lighter matter.

Fired by the example of Mohammed and Moraja, Yusuf began to wonder whether a wife or two would not satisfy his affectionate heart more than a camel. "A woman is so much cheaper," he sighed, and told us that among the ekhwan no dowry is paid to the bride's father. A small gift of silk or gold is given to the mother and sisters, perhaps a necklace or bracelet to the girl herself and there the expense ends. "Twenty-five mejidies are enough," said Yusuf; "but if one wants to take the daughter of a Beduin sheikh one must pay many camels." "How many?" I asked. "Oh, ten, twenty, fifty and one must give the girl silk and cloth for her clothes besides!" He dropped into meditative silence.

One by one we saw the landmarks of the Zieghen track to the west and learned that the north-westerly course we were following had been the original Zieghen route till one Mohammed Sherif established the present more direct way. First we saw the Gardia, a square block of dark cliff, then the Garet es Sherif, called after a traveller who shortened by a day the Kufara-Jalo journey, and late in the afternoon a conical hill called The Kheima (tent) by Mojabras and The Mohgen (funnel) by Zouias. One great advantage we had over our previous journey. This time the sun was behind us all the time. The difference was enormous. Riding or walking for twelve hours day after day straight into a blazing sun, without hat brim or umbrella, had been very trying to one's eyes and head. Altogether the absence of glare, the feeling that the larger part of our work was done, with no necessity to placate a constantly irritated retinue or to weld together the most inharmonious human elements, caused us to regard the dreary kilometres that lay before us as the most peaceful part of our journey.

"I want to see the white sands again," I said and urged my little expedition on into the rose-purple hills.

The Hawaish are not really mountains. They are an irregular mass of round, rocky hills, cliffs and cones and their direction would baffle even an experienced geographer. We spent any spare moments at dawn and at sunset sitting on the top of some abrupt hillock with binoculars, compass and a note-book, studying the complicated positions of the local mountains, but hair grew grey and tempers short in the task. Always there was a new wall of hills in the distance generally running at an unexpected angle and when we asked the retinue for explanations, all they could say was, "Allah alone knows!"

I wanted to camp within the first line of the Hawaish, for by now I was just as anxious to leave the mysterious, enchanted land as I had been to enter it. The circling horizon of strange hills seemed to shut us in with the hot coloured sands, but the cool white dunes beyond called us back to the open deserts of the north.

Just as Suleiman wavered as to whether we should turn right or left of a large cliff, sudden news brought by Yusuf and Amar, who had climbed a gherd we had just left, abruptly shattered our peace. Our fat retainer was actually running, a swift uneven little trot, which made him pant as he shouted, "There is a caravan behind us!" The idea was startling to say the least, for no one had travelled by this route for nearly four years and we knew that nobody was prepared to start when we left Kufara. At first we told Yusuf that he had dreamed his caravan. We were two days' march from Hawari, from where all travellers start, and when we left the oasis there had been no question of any-body else going north by any route. Amar, however, was equally positive. "We looked through the glasses," he said. "There are four or six camels and nearly a dozen men with them. They are travelling fast, about

OUR HOST AT JAGHABUB

SIDI IDRIS'S HOUSE AT JAGHABUB

MOSQUE AND QUBBA OF SIDI BEN ALI AT JAGHABUB

three hours behind us!" This was so definite that we had to believe it and Mohammed dotted the i's. "We shall be attacked to-night. It is a habit of the Zouias. They wait till a caravan is outside their country so that they cannot be blamed and then they eat it up!" "It is not the Zouias!" indignantly refuted the guide. "They have great respect for the Sayeds. It is the Tebus. They have swift camels. They attack in the mountains, where no travellers ever go and then they fly south to the French country before anything is discovered."

Intense gloom descended on the little party. Sunset light was fading and the one break in the purple stones ahead was a patch of vivid sand dotted with five camel skeletons. We had only three rifles and our revolvers!

Discretion in this case was certainly the better part of valour, so we decided on ignominious flight. We left the neighbourhood of the wide pass leading to Zakar and, in darkness, felt our way west, through curling defiles and over steep ridges, always driving the camels across the stony patches to avoid leaving footprints in the sand. When Suleiman thought we had gone far enough from our course to baffle any pursuers, we barraked in a convenient hollow out of sight of anyone who was not standing on the hills immediately surrounding us. "No fires," said Mohammed sternly. "No light at all! And we will put the camels a little way in front of us. They will move if anyone comes." "What shall we eat?" moaned Yusuf plaintively. "We must have a fire to cook," I agreed, thinking I should be much braver after some hot coffee, for it was very cold that night, but Mohammed was adamantine. He hung his revolver round Suleiman's neck, with strict injunctions to the guide to "Shoot straight and may Allah direct the bullet!" He then

suggested making a fortified zariba on the hill-side.
Yusuf and I, after furtive glances at the enormous
loads, with the very long march fresh in our minds,
thought it would be much better to perish comfortably
in the hollow. "It will only prolong the fight if we
defend the hill," said I plaintively. "I want to go to
sleep on that nice soft patch of sand." But, unfortunately, Hassanein and Amar were also against me.
Therefore, we were forced to drag the large fodder
sacks laboriously up the first ridge of the hill and push
them into a serried wall on a ledge. I have never been
crosser in my whole life, but it was a beautiful little
fort when it was finished. I felt that only a very
energetic bullet would get through those immense date
sacks and the position would certainly be impregnable
so long as any of the defenders were alive. The girbas
were arranged in front of us protected by stones, so,
sure of food and water, we could even stand a siege.
The camels were below us in the hollow. Yusuf and I
again suggested a very tiny fire, but Mohammed refused
and we contented ourselves with four-day-old bread and
tinned corned beef. After that I silently unrolled my
flea-bag preparatory to placing my revolvers, the aneroid
and the thermometer beside my pillow. "I shall not go
to bed," said Hassanein sternly. "We must take turns
to watch." "The right is with you," replied Mohammed with alacrity. "Is your rifle loaded, Amar, my
son? We will all watch." This, however, was too
much. Yusuf and I merely ignored the remark, but, as
I gave a last comforting wriggle to feel the thick,
woolly end of my flea-bag with my toes, I heard
Hassanein's voice somewhere above me, alert and
strained, "If anyone comes into sight shall I speak to
them first or fire at once? What is your custom
here?" Two simultaneous answers blended with my

sleep. "Speak first!" came drowsily from Yusuf. "Shoot quickly and shoot straight!" from Mohammed, "or you will never speak again!"

The only thing that disturbed my slumbers that night was a little yellow sand mouse. I woke up feeling something fluffy on my cheek and the absurd little beast was sitting on my nose. He scuttled to the other side of the zariba when I moved and Amar, bloodthirsty after a long, useless vigil, promptly killed and ate him! No Tebu warriors broke our peace, but unfortunately the fear of them made Mohammed wake me while the golden moon was still high and brilliant. I would not move without breakfast, so we hurriedly cooked rice and sweet tea in the unreal light almost as clear as noon and laboriously pulled to pieces our beautiful zariba of the night before. We rolled the heavy date sacks down the hill because the men were too tired after their hard twenty-four hours to carry them. One burst and scattered dates right and left. Thrift and fear mingled in the minds of the retinue, but caution for the long road before us was uppermost in my mind! We picked them up in silence and dumped the load on to the protesting camels with almost personal dislike. Then we took to the trail again and, still in moonlight, began picking our devious way round the irregular hills. When Suleiman finally led us back to the main pass we thought any pursuing caravan must be far ahead, for it was two hours after sunrise.

By this time we were all inclined to think that the four or six camels and the dozen men existed only in the imagination of Yusuf and Amar, but we had hardly turned into the wide sweep of sand that led north to the open spaces beyond the first range of Hawaish when we came upon fresh camels' tracks ahead of us. The plump one was delighted. "I was right! I was right!"

he exclaimed, "and now we are safe, for, when they do not catch us, they will think we have been warned and gone to Zieghen to avoid them." Perhaps his surmise was correct. We never knew. We found no more traces of the mysterious caravan. Its origin and destination remained a secret. It had travelled two days and a half on the route to Zakar far beyond the point where, long ago, travellers turned west to Zieghen. Then it vanished as completely as a mirage, but mirage does not leave footprints and camel dung!

In spite of the sleepless night the Beduins marched well that day. "If we reach those mountains to-night," had said Suleiman at 11 A.M., when we saw the second range of Hawaish, blue and mauve, beyond a wide expanse of pale sand waves and low dunes, "we shall say our Asr prayers to-morrow at Zakar." So we plodded on cheerfully. It was cool and cloudy, with the usual north wind and an incessant mirage that made pools and lakes in every hollow. The old camel I had ridden when we left Jedabia seemed to know the way. He made a bee-line for a certain cleft in the hills. Yusuf noticed this also and asked if I knew the story of the sand grouse and the camel. "They were arguing one day as to which was the cleverer," said the plump one, smiling. "I lay my eggs at random in the trackless desert," urged the sand grouse, "and then I fly far and wide in search of food, but I can always come straight back to hatch them." The camel sniffed scornfully. "If I drink at a well as a tiny foal trotting beside my mother, though I never see it again, I can find my way back to it even when I am very old and blind!" "No, no, he is cleverer than that!" interrupted Mohammed. "If a naga has tasted the water of a well when she is in foal, the camel she gives birth to can return to it surely." "Let us hope this particular camel has drunk of the well at Jaghabub," I suggested. "Insha-allah!" replied Yusuf devoutly.

We found a delightfully sheltered spot between two hills that night, so did not trouble to build a zariba. The thermometer registered a frost, but I think it had been affected by the mental atmosphere of the previous night because we did not feel very cold. I remember I drank so much coffee that I could not sleep, so I did not mind when the Beduins insisted on making a fire three hours before dawn and cooking their "asida," a sticky mass of damp flour flavoured with onions and zeit (oil). We must have been particularly inexpert with the loading for, in spite of this early breakfast, we started only just before sunrise. The new grey camel lay down almost at once, for he had not recovered from his greed. We had to divide his girbas among the others, for water is needed to harden the sand when digging the Zakar well. We watched the caravan anxiously as, leaving the second mass of the Hawaish hills, it crossed a rolling expanse of great flat slabs of stone, broken and slippery. However, it toiled slowly but safely across them and about 10 A.M. we were moving in sparkling white sand, blinding, dazzlingly clean in the hot sun. There was practically no wind for once, and Yusuf actually discarded his overcoat after he had climbed a mound to point out a square, solid, black gara among surrounding stony gherds. "Near that is the well," he announced. "We shall be there in one hour or perhaps four." As a matter of fact we saw the two tufts of palm scrub that mark the Zakar well at noon and they looked scarcely a stone's throw away among sands white as snow, but we only reached them two hours later.

The last caravan that passed must have suffered severely *en route,* for there were bits of broken baggage among scattered camel skeletons. Yusuf wished to ignore several legs complete with pads in building a zariba, but I hankered after ground less gruesomely reminiscent, so we compromised by turning our backs on the well and its immediate surroundings. "The animals always die at the end of this journey," said Suleiman calmly, "unless they are very strong. Then they drink so much water that one must travel very slowly, taking five days or even more to go from here to Hawari." The well, when we arrived, was a big mound of sand, but the guide told us it was properly made with stone walls, so it was only a case of digging. It is necessary to arrive at this well with a reserve of water as, before beginning to dig, one must carefully soak the surrounding sand to make it hold the stones like mortar. Otherwise they all fall in on top of anyone digging and it is most dangerous work.

Apparently the Zakar well was used in ancient days by Tebus, long before the Jaghabub-Kufara route was opened by the Mahdi. The latter never travelled over it himself, but he sent an exploring party to discover its possibilities and, later, his brother, Sayed Ahmed es Sherif, took a caravan across it. Since then it has been practically reserved for the use of the Senussi family, who make the journey with immense caravans with anything over fifty camels. They carry very large stores of fodder, casting several loads on the way if necessary. Sidi Idris and Sayed Rida have so far avoided the route, but Sayed Ahmed es Sherif used it several times. On one occasion some of his water went bad going south and his horse died of thirst four days out. He had to leave most of his stores and luggage behind and return hastily to Jaghabub with as many camels as possible. Three years later his luggage was recovered just as he had left it, which shows how little frequented is the route.

All afternoon the Beduins laboured at the well. It

was very narrow, about two and a half feet across, so only old Suleiman, thin and wizened, could get down to dig. It must have been a most uncomfortable task, for the water lay at a depth of 15 feet, but before he slept that night he had felt damp sand beneath his fingers. Next morning, January 29, the work was completed and our 14 girbas filled and ranged in two nice, fat rows ready for loading, but we could not start that day for a very bad sandstorm raged till 4 P.M. We could not light a fire or even go out to collect hattab for our journey. The camels moaned as they huddled in a miserable circle and we crouched under blankets and ate sand mixed with dates and stale bread. Hassanein devoted much labour to mending his primrose and scarlet boots with brass wire and was bitterly disappointed because he could not cut the latter with his saw!

In the evening the wind abated a little, but it was a gloomy sunset. The sun was a livid disk in a pale green sky seen through a drab blur of sand above grey desert. We sealed up our three precious fanatis with seccotine round the stoppers so that no one should be tempted to use them till the last possible moment. Then we re-covered the well with the old matting and skins we had found under the miniature dome which covered it. In four years the sand had filtered through them as if they were not there, but should any traveller be rash enough to follow shortly in our footsteps, our precaution might save him a repetition of old Suleiman's task.

On January 30 we began the long trek, leaving the well at 7 A.M. after a most careful adjustment of the loads. It was cold with a faint north wind which strengthened as we mounted the stony gherd north-east of the well. As we turned for a last look at the lonely clump of palms, a minute spot of green in a boundless stretch of undulating sand, a muffled voice came viciously

from the many-coloured kufiya which Hassanein had
wound over his nose and mouth. "The one comfort is
that we shall either be in Jaghabub in twelve days or
we shall be dead!" it said. "Are your boots very
painful with all that brass stuck in them?" I asked
sweetly!

For an hour we drove the camels slowly over rough,
stony ground with large loose slabs lying about. Then
the hills gave place to the white sands and we looked
down on to dunes like the turbulent breakers of a stormy
sea. Yusuf glanced solemnly at the last dark stones
behind us. "We are lucky to leave the red country
without exchanging gunpowder," he announced, "but
the friends of the Sayeds are always blessed. You have
been especially protected by Allah, for the Zouias are
a bad people." It was rare that the plump one was
really serious except when his food or sleep were
threatened, so we guessed that he knew more than he
would even tell us. The rising north wind, however,
prevented much conversation and before we had reached
the first line of dunes it had developed into something
resembling the sandstorm of the previous day. It was
bitterly cold. If one rode, the wind pierced through
every blanket that could be wound round one and one was
nearly blown off the camel. If we walked with a jerd
muffled over our heads, the sand poured through the
woollen stuff into eyes, mouth and nose and we literally
staggered as we mounted each succeeding ridge and met
the full force of the gale at the top. I used to struggle
on for a mile or two and then half bury myself under
the lee of a gherd till the stumbling, half-blinded caravan
caught up.

A weary day was passed in repeating this process,
until everyone looked upon the unfaltering guide as his
personal enemy who would never stop his slow, inter-

minable crawl over dune and hollow, which always kept
him just out of reach of our protests. Every time he
paused to look for the best place to cross a ridge we hoped
to hear the barraking cry, but always he shuffled on in
broken sandals, monotonously, untiringly. The wind
dropped at sunset, but we marched through the sickly,
grey light, with a faint lemon glow in the west and only
when the full twelve hours were completed did Suleiman
allow us to crawl into our flea-bags, half-frozen, half-
starved; for everyone was too tired to cook.

I believe I took off my boots, but certainly nothing
else, for I remember how bulky my red hezaam felt in
the narrow space; but I slept for nine blissful hours and
ate far more than my share of sardines and dates in the
morning. The rice was a strange, blackish grey colour,.
due to the girba water. The colour and smell of this
water after a few days are a great preventive of thirst.
We had gone back to the old ration of three cups of
water per day, with a. fourth for cooking. We soon
found that hot coffee made us too thirsty, but that cold,
strong, sugarless tea produced rather the opposite effect.
A much worse discovery greeted us that exceedingly cold
morning of January 31. Three of the girbas had either
dried in the sand-filled wind or leaked away. There was
scarcely the morning ration left in them. We spoke to
the retinue seriously when we found them drinking
copiously, but were baffled by their fatalism. We still
had a girba a day and two fanatis to spare, so they refused
to consider the infinite possibilities of delay, illness, loss,
leakage, or a camel needing water by the way. "What
is written is written," said Yusuf. "You cannot run
away from fate. That is what the eagle said to Suleiman." "What eagle?" I demanded suspiciously.

"The prophet Suleiman was sitting on a hill, from
which he could see many cities, when an eagle came to

him and said, 'You think you are wise because you know the wisdom of all these people, but I will take you all over the world and show you the wisdom of countries you have never heard of.' With that he took the prophet's girdle in his beak and flew north, south, east and west with him, showing him many marvels. When they had travelled far and wide the bird flew back to the prophet's own country and dropped his pupil in a field where a ploughman was setting snares. Before Suleiman could express his thanks he saw that the great bird was caught in one of the traps and was battering helplessly against the bars. 'Oh, thou who would'st teach me wisdom, where is thine own that thou who knowest all the world could not avoid one small trap?' 'What is written is written,' said the eagle resignedly. 'One cannot run away from one's fate.'" Yusuf looked at me expectantly. "The eagle might have looked where he was going," I said firmly, "and you will most certainly look at what you are drinking, my son."

Our start that morning was delayed because Suleiman's ear had to be doctored. A half-deaf, as well as a half-blind, guide was certainly a thing to be avoided, so we gave him all our spare under-garments, his ailment being entirely due to the fact that, with a temperature of zero, he slept on the cold sand in a ragged cotton shirt and a jerd transparently thin and tattered. He had started to walk more than a thousand miles (including his return journey after he had taken the camels back to Jedabia) with no other possessions than these and not one nickel of money! "Allah is great. He will provide," he said simply as he wound my knitted spencer on his head and tied a pair of Hassanein's breeches round his chest under his grimy shirt. The Arabs' one desire is to muffle every possible garment—no matter for what portion of the anatomy it is designed—round their heads and shoulders—the rest they leave to chance and the winds of heaven!

Nature was evidently determined to show us everything she was capable of in the way of climate, for that day not a breath of wind stirred and a torrid, aching sun beat down on us till our necks felt bruised and our heads heavy and unwieldy. We prayed for the night, almost as fervently as the day before, especially as a completely new range of the exasperating Hawaish mountains appeared to the east. "After a day you will see them no more," said Mohammed consolingly. "But they say the dunes go west all the way to Misurata—Allah alone knows!" After a three hours' march, about 60 kilometres from Zakar, the dunes stopped altogether and we crossed uneven, stony ground till, an hour before sunset, we came to a single long line of huge, heavy dunes running west to east. They rose suddenly, like clear golden flour, out of the dark stones which went right up to their base and though we followed them east for 14 kilometres that night and 24 the next morning, we never saw them merge into the rocky waste. Always they stood apart, immense, curly, ridged, like waves of a sunlit sea, a beautiful landmark which can be seen half a day's journey ahead.

It was warmer that night and we "fadhled" round a fire and ate Yusuf's "asida," the only thing he liked better than camels, he told us, and listened to Suleiman's tales of past journeys. As they contained every form of disaster that can assail humanity in the clutches of remorseless nature, we turned the conversation till he spoke of people living on this desolate stony ground "long, very long, ago!" "There used to be wood here and forage and there are stones stuck together with mortar and sometimes one picks up prepared milling stones, which have been used for crushing grain." I doubted his facts because in the afternoon he had pointed out traces of what he thought were walls constructed with mortar, but I thought they were merely a natural formation of the sandstone which takes so many odd shapes. I think his milling stones were due to the hand of nature in fantastic mood, for there could never have been water in the stony ground.

February 1 we started at 7.15 A.M. and barraked at 2.30 P.M. at the Mehemsa, a feeding ground, where it is customary to allow the camels a few hours' rest and a good meal before starting to cross the four days' waste in front without blade of grass or twig of firewood. A few camel skeletons mark the way below the towering dunes and, here and there, one comes across large stones set on end by preceding travellers. These impromptu landmarks are of great value and we religiously made them ourselves whenever possible. The Beduins are very good about this labour. I have seen Mohammed toil to the top of some hillock with a heavy slab of rock, after a long day's journey, to make a mark that might cheer and guide a chance caravan years hence perhaps.

We crossed the dunes where a wide channel of stony ground ran into a low, curly ridge and, immediately on the other side, found great shrubs and masses of dry grey brush, excellent fodder and firewood, but burning hot at midday. The dunes circled round west and north of an open space of some 4 kilometres. Beyond this again there was another track of hattab. Among this we camped and turned the camels loose to graze. They were disappointingly different. "Inshallah, we shall arrive at Jaghabub, but we shall leave two or three camels on the way," said Yusuf. We were very anxious about our animals. The two young nagas were terribly thin, the big blond camel was obviously ill and two of the others were feeble and overworked. They should all have been rested and fed up at Kufara for at least another fortnight. We knew this at Taj, but the complicated politics of the place necessitated our precipitate departure. Yusuf told us that generally when a caravan travels the Kufara-Jaghabub route it spends a month at least in preparation. Forty or fifty camels are taken and these are all fed up for weeks beforehand, till they are very fat and strong. During that time they do no work, but are gradually trained to last thirteen days without drinking by ever-increasing waterless periods. When our camels arrived at Kufara they had done a hard 800 miles of journey, including one stretch of ten days without water and twelve without sufficient food, during the last three of which they were practically starving. After nine days' rest they had to start to cross one of the hardest routes in North Africa, overloaded and at a bad period of the year, when the climate is at its worst. We had, therefore, reason for our fears, and when the animals turned away from the plentiful fodder of the Mehemsa our little party lost something of its high spirits.

CHAPTER XIV

THE ELUSIVE DUNES

NEAR the feeding ground are two large cisterns erected by order of Sayed el Mahdi. When any of the Senussi family wished to travel by this route, water was sent on ahead and stored in the cisterns, near which there is a small shanty falling into disrepair. As a matter of fact, there should undoubtedly be water at the Mehemsa. It is the same sort of ground as at Buttafal and Zakar and green bushes are plentiful and healthy. There is no rainfall and no dew to account for their existence otherwise. We also noticed a number of birds, conspicuous among them a grey and black variety larger than the "abu fasada." In the time of Sidi el Mahdi slaves dug for water to a depth of 20 feet at the Mehemsa without coming to wet sand, but since then no one has tried.

On February 2 we started north at 6.30 A.M. after a violent argument as to the best way of saving the camels. I wanted to follow the summer plan, start an hour before sunset, walk all night and camp two hours after dawn. One can do much longer marches this way, but the Beduins were reluctant to face the cold of the night. On the other hand, Mohammed was desperately afraid of another sandstorm, which would inevitably delay us. He therefore wanted to walk at least 15 hours a day. It is an unfortunate fact that a camel does 13 hours, at a pace of 4 kilometres, infinitely easier than 10 hours at 5. He is capable of plodding along evenly

without halting for an indefinite time, but the slower
he goes the longer he will last. Mohammed was a bad
camel-man. Frightened of the desperately long route
in front of him, which had to be traversed in 12 days,
he was anxious to push on at first in order to have something up his sleeve; yet the loads, chiefly fodder and
water, would grow lighter every day. I refused, therefore, to do more than 12 or 13 hours a day, especially
as our camels would not feed properly when it was dark
and cold. The best way of travelling is to start at
5 A.M., barrak for a few hours at midday, feed the
camels as the afternoon grows cooler and walk late into
the night. But it means a double loading and we had
not enough men or energy for that, so our beasts had
to accustom themselves to feeding by starlight night and
morning.

That first day we had a cool wind, so we all walked
cheerfully across the unbroken stretches of monotonous
fawn sand. The world had become a level disk again,
infinitely flat, its smoothness polished by the glaring
sun till the mirage broke the edges, which seemed but
a few yards away. I asked old Suleiman how he knew
the way. "You put Jedi over your left eye and walk
a long way—thus. Then you turn a little toward the
kibla[1] and walk still more and then, if Allah wills, you
arrive." It was not exactly a reassuring answer after
Abdullah's vagaries, so I asked him where Jedi was at
the moment. "I don't know," he replied with engag-
ing frankness. "Where is she?" I showed him by
the compass and he trudged on perfectly placidly,
nibbling a date from the little store he kept tied up in
a corner of his tattered jerd.

When the sunset had painted our narrow world
flame-red and, one by one, the stars had come out to

[1] The *kibla* is turned towards the *ka-aba* at Mecca.

show how infinitely remote is "that inverted bowl we call the sky," Mohammed pleaded for an extra spurt. "Let us just put that star out," he urged, pointing to the brightest point in the west. Having noticed, however, that all the camels were stumbling and swinging out of the line, I thought a race with the evening star would be a mistake, so I insisted on barraking. We made no zariba, leaving the loads ready coupled for the morning. We had taken very little hattab from the Mehemsa because of the weight, so our fire was of the smallest description and we should have been asleep in an hour, but for a prolonged dispute between Mohammed and Suleiman as to the necessity of agaling the camels. "They will not move, my son," said Suleiman. "They are tired, like me, and I am an old man." "Old, too, in experience," replied our polite retainer, "but make my heart at peace by agaling them." And he related a lurid story of how 70 camels had stampeded midway on the Zieghen route. They all reached Jalo safely, but some of the men, unexpectedly left to carry their food and water, died on the march. Suleiman was already rolled like a dormouse between two hawias, so he appealed to me for support. "Know you the saying of the Prophet, Uncle Suleiman," I asked, "how a man came to him and asked whether he should agal his camel or put his trust in Allah? 'First place the agal on the camel and then your trust in Allah,' was the reply."

Various grunts and roars, mingled with my sleep, told me that the guide had been impressed by my theological learning and it seemed only a few minutes later that I woke to the sound of Yusuf's voice, "Allah make you strong! Are you ready for rice?" Protesting that it must still be the middle of the night, I poked my head out of the flea-bag, dislodging a shower of sand from its folds, and a few yards away was one of

MY LONELY PICNIC IN KUFARA WADI

A GLASS OF MINT TEA ON THE WAY TO SIWA

DOCUMENT OF WELCOME AT BUSEIMA (TAJ)

DOCUMENT OF WELCOME GIVEN AT KUFARA (TAJ)

the odd, vivid little pictures that flash suddenly into one's life and that one never forgets. A crackling, scented fire, criminally large in the circumstances, threw a wavering golden circle in the midst of flat, shadowed sand, interminable, bourneless. Against the brilliant stars a tall, white-robed figure was silhouetted, hands raised to heaven, white hood framing the stern, dark-featured face, intoning the dawn prayers. "Allahu Akhbar!" rang out with undaunted faith, with undimmed courage, to the one Guide whom the Beduin trusts to lead his labouring caravans through desert and dune to the desired oasis. Beside the glowing brushwood, Suleiman, bent double over a huge cauldron, monotonously pounded the morning's "asida," his long pestle moving to the rhythm of his quavering chant, while Amar, huddled under his coarse jerd, stirred red sauce flavoured with fil-fil. Yusuf's plump face was set in immobile discontent against the flames, as, muffled in every conceivable garment and wrap, he methodically fed the fire, twig by snapping twig. White robes, a fire and the paling stars, with a circle of camels looming formless and dark in the background. That was my picture and then Yusuf's cross voice spoiled it. "The girba water is very bad," he said. "The rice will be black!" "Maleish! I shall not see it!" I said, shivering; but a few minutes later we *tasted* it, when the plump one, sleepy-eyed, shuffled across with a grimy frying-pan. He had sand on his nose and forehead to show that he had said his morning prayers, but, whereas the rest of the retinue devoutly bowed their heads to the earth three times a day at least, I always suspected Yusuf of calmly dabbing a little shingle on his face as he went along.

The hard-boiled eggs gave out that day, so we had to drown the taste of the girba rice with sardines. Our midday meal now consisted of dates and a handful of "bucksumat," for we had been given a couple of bags of these hard, unleavened biscuits, slightly sweetened and flavoured with carraway seeds, by the kindly ekhwan of Taj. In the evening we shared a tin of corned beef, but, alas! our great support of the Taiserbo journey had failed us, for the dates we had brought from Hawari were too fresh and they stung our mouths, blistering our gums and reducing us to agonies of thirst. The water allowance was too small to allow of our drinking except in the morning and the evening, so we had reluctantly to discard our dates. Yusuf insisted on eating one only each day, because there is an Arab proverb, "A date by the way or a young girl smiling makes a fortunate journey."

We started at 6.30 A.M. on February 3 and walked till 7 P.M., when the whole party, men and camels alike, sat down and groaned. It had been absolutely torrid, without a breath of wind. The girbas began to look distinctly thin and the clank of the water in the fanatis showed that a good deal had evaporated. Unfortunately, it had been very cold after the sandstorm the evening before our departure from the Zakar well and the camels had not drunk properly. Yusuf had made gloomy prognostications most of the day and when we came to a mound of sand, which had drifted over a few old hawias thrown away by a former caravan, he poked them viciously. "How many of our own shall we throw in this way?" he asked of fate.

There is no logic in desert weather. After midday heat we had a very cold night. I remember I ate my chilly dinner with my gloves on and was not surprised to find there was frost, when a sudden storm of shouts and roars brought me rapidly out of my flea-bag and I fell over the thermometer in the dark. The camels apparently had gone wildly mad, for in spite of their agals they were all hobbling and hopping wildly round making immense noise, which the retinue were exceeding in their anxiety to drive the beasts away from our neatly arranged girbas, protected, as usual at night, by a hedge of baggage saddles.

February 4 saw us away by 6.15, a good effort, chiefly due to a loading race between Amar and Yusuf against the guide and Mohammed. I think the former couple won, but all the loads were a little wobbly that day. A black duck flew low across our path, heading north. "It has gone into the upside-down country," said Suleiman, pointing ahead; and there, on the far horizon, we saw pale dunes and ridges, clear-cut, with violet shadows below peak and cliff. They looked but a few hours' march away and we were all immensely happy, though we knew they were more than a day's journey away.

Again it was very hot, but Yusuf, who always enjoyed a burning sun, took it upon himself to cheer up the whole party. When a camel lay down and groaned, he carefully made a row of toy "asidas" in the sand, modelling the little hole at the top for a sauce with infinite trouble. "These are for him to eat, then he will be strong again," he said smiling. When Suleiman complained of his eyesight the plump one cried: "I will ride ahead and see the way." And, mounting his stick, he gambolled round, imitating every trick and gesture of horsemanship with perfect art. Finally, when the rest of us were so oppressed by the heat that we only wondered what we could take off next, we saw Yusuf solemnly fill the skirt of his shirt with sand and begin sowing it like grain right and left. "What on earth are you doing, you man?" exclaimed Mohammed. "The next traveller will find a patch of green grain and will be happy," he said placidly. Nevertheless, that night, when the elusive dunes had failed to materialise even as shadows on the horizon, anxiety spread. Hassanein balanced himself perilously upright on the back of the Tebu beast, but could report nothing in sight, so consoled himself by re-mending his yellow shoes.

All the afternoon there had been disputes as to whether we should go east or west of certain invisible dunes, and the retinue disagreed violently as to how soon we ought to see these landmarks or in what direction they were. Therefore, I was not surprised when I heard a bitter argument behind me. Reproaches were being hurled at Suleiman, who replied that he was old and could not see: "He has lost the——" wailed Mohammed. "We must stop. We cannot go on." Yusuf joined in. "Is he sure he has lost it? Think, you man! Let him think, I tell you!" Expostulation and suggestion followed in loud chaos. I had coped with one such dispute on the morning when there should have been a ridge to the left and there wasn't! I determined that Hassanein should struggle with this. Slightly deaf, he was nodding over his shoe—making far ahead on the grey camel. I rushed up to him crossly. "Get down at once," I urged, seizing the beast ruthlessly by the neck and feeling angrier than ever at the sight of Hassanein's mildly surprised and protesting face, as he desperately clutched his boots and the nearest supporting rope in preparation to being forcibly barraked! "Pull yourself together! Suleiman has lost the way. They are all fighting desperately. If it's an important landmark he's missed we had better wait till the morning. For heaven's sake hurry!"

One anguished glance at the angry group in the rear, who were all pointing backwards, was sufficient to make Hassanein swing off without question. I watched him literally propel himself into the argument, heard "Wallahi!" furiously repeated, saw hands flung sky-

wards and then, surprised, saw him extricate himself
from Mohammed's detaining hands and walk slowly back
to his camel, methodically picking up the possessions he
had ruthlessly scattered at my peremptory request.
"Well, what is it? What has he lost?" I shouted impatiently. Hassanein waited till he was quite near and
then he gave me a withering look and said very slowly,
each word enunciated separately: "It—is—a—small—
leather—bag—which—the—kaimakaan — gave — him —
to—sell—in—Jaghabub. Suleiman— has — left — it —
behind!"

On February 5 we broke camp at 6.30, singularly
indifferent to coffee mysteriously mixed with candle-
grease and rice, hairy with girba fur, in our anxiety to
see the morning mirage. This time the dunes looked
even nearer. One could see the wavy furrows along the
ridges and every separate golden hillock, yet an hour later
everything had vanished and the flat, fawn disk stretched,
drab and monotonous, on every side. Suleiman was
confident, however, that we should sleep in the dunes
that night. Yusuf was cheerfully certain that, as we had
not yet seen the Mazul ridge to the west, we should not
"see land" for another day. When Beduins are
travelling across a big, trackless desert, they always
speak of any known country as "the land." It is rather
like a long sea voyage with the guide as pilot. He
keeps the caravan's head turned in the right direction by
the stars and waits to pick up a familiar landmark before
making directly for his oasis. At 10 A.M. the old guide
uttered something nearly resembling a shriek and threw
himself on Yusuf's neck. "I see the Mazul!" he exclaimed, "and it is near, very near." Leaving the pale
line of distant hillocks to our left, we headed directly
north towards other dunes which began to appear, a faint
blur on the horizon. The two little nagas edged away to

the west all day in the most determined way. Yusuf said they knew that their mothers, from whom we had separated them at Taj, were now travelling on the Zieghen-Jalo route and instinct was driving them towards the soldier-slaves' caravan.

The plump one's character always appeared to greater advantage in really hard times. When things were going easily his scowl was a marvel of discontented endurance. His eyes shut into little slits and his voice became a plaintive whine. When big difficulties arose, when camels were failing and everybody was over-tired, Yusuf cheered up the whole caravan. His absurd little songs trickled out hour after hour, he told long fairy stories about giants and princesses, he made elaborate jokes which we daily received with new interest. Thus, if anyone lagged behind they were always greeted when they rejoined the caravan as if after a long absence, upon which they replied that they had come from Jedabia or Jalo in two or three days, were congratulated on their walk, and asked minutely for news concerning every person in the place. This particular game never wearied and we all grew most inventive at the expense of the good folk at Jedabia.

One would think that in a thirteen hours' walk each day one would find time for much conversation, but the desert breeds reserve. It is so big that one's own plans and projects seem too little to be talked about. Also, there is so much time to say anything that one continually puts it off and ends by never saying it at all. We used to walk for hours without a word, till Yusuf broke the silence by some reflection on his approaching marriage or the sickness that he saw in some camel's eye. By this time I had learned how to make myself understood in Libya. The nouns are nearly all different, but after one had learnt a list of those one gets on very nicely with but two verbs. To express any more or less peaceful occupation like travelling, stopping, loading, unloading, letting fall, starting, etc., *ad infinitum,* one employs the word "shil." If one wishes to imply any more vigorous or offensive action, like fighting, attacking, climbing hurriedly, eating, burning, becoming angry, "akal" seems to be elastic enough to express it.

We finally arrived at the dunes nearly two hours before sunset, luckily hitting two very big dunes that were well-known landmarks. Yusuf wanted to turn in behind them. Suleiman insisted on going to the right, which brought us into a wide, flat stretch some 12 kilomeres long. We barraked at the end of it in a rising wind, which soon put out our little folding lantern, so that we lost everything, including the tin opener, in the dark. It was rather a miserable night, for the hattab we had brought from the Mehemsa was exhausted and our efforts to make tea over a little fire of "leaf" torn from one of the hawias were not very successful.

The water from the girba we opened that night was really bad. Its colour and taste alike were extraordinary, so we regretfully decided to use it only for cooking. Suleiman looked at it with interest. "We have enough water, Hamdulillah!" he said. "In any case I can live for a week without drinking." When we questioned him as to this amazing statement he told us that Sidi el Mahdi habitually sent out caravans to explore the country round Kufara. Suleiman, an old man and a boy, had formed one of these parties, and they had wandered as far afield as Merg, thirteen days south-east of their starting-point, when one dark night their camels were stolen by a band of brigands. Presumably something happened to the girbas and provisions, for in the morning the exploring party found themselves with enough water and dates for a day and a half and they were six days' journey from the nearest well, the Oweinat. However, the three started off to walk to it, actually carrying their rifles. The old man got ill after one day and insisted on being left behind. After two days his erstwhile companions discarded their rifles. After three, Suleiman got fever and lay down to die, but the boy went on and arrived safely at the well. Our guide unexpectedly recovered from his fever after twenty-four hours and started off again, walking only at night and lying down all day. He arrived at Oweinat on the seventh day so exhausted and so parched with thirst that he could not get the liquid down his throat, so he lay in the water in the well for a whole day and was then able to drink. Luckily a caravan had thrown away some dates, and with a small store of these and the little water he could carry, Suleiman calmly walked on to Kufara, another week's journey! The old man who had been left to die on the road arrived a day later *with his rifle*. The feat seems inconceivable, but Yusuf vouched for the truth of the story and Amar told how he had drunk only once in 72 hours when the water in the girba went bad. Then Mohammed, not to be outdone in endurance, related how he had travelled from Jalo to Jaghabub in four days and four nights, without sleeping, eating as the camels went along, because the girbas were all leaking and he was afraid of running short of water.

By this time we felt that our own little effort to draw a new red line across a survey map was very small and insignificant and that we should certainly be able to walk to Jaghabub carrying a fanatis and a tin of corned beef if necessary! We were much less confident of it next morning, however, when all the camels turned up their noses at the date food offered them and deliberately ran away. There was nowhere for them to run to among the dunes, so we got them back after a laborious half-hour, but I felt that the word "agal" and not Kufara

would be written across my heart in future! There was
no fire that morning, and uncooked soaked rice is not
appetising. I remember I was tying the remains of my
stockings round my feet when I heard a gloomy voice
say: "We ate the last box of sardines last night because
you lost the beef-tin-opener in the sand and the rice is
coal black. I wish you would not be so miserly with
the fanatis water!" I didn't pay much attention as I
hadn't any more stockings. Evidently the primrose and
scarlet boots which I had bought for four mejidies (sixteen shillings) at Jof were not suited for walking, for I
had been wearing two pairs of woollen stockings one
over the other and now they all hung in shreds round
my feet. However, I did look up when the plaintive
tones continued. "I've found one sardine. He must
have fallen out when you upset the canteen in the sand."
With horror I saw a soddened, dark mass and on the
top of it a minute yellow block shaped like a fish, but I
did not like to be discouraging. "Are you sure that there
is a sardine inside that sand?" I asked diffidently. Hassanein was offended. "Will you carve him or shall I?"
he asked majestically.

On February 6 we plunged right into the dunes. On
the whole they ran north to south in great wavy ridges,
which would be impossible for camels to cross. In between were wide stretches of rolling ground, rising
gradually to lower dunes through which Suleiman confidently picked his way. The little old man was very
calm. "I have never been this route before, but if I
keep Jedi in my left eye we shall arrive, Insha-allah!"
he said, and when Yusuf complained violently that there
was no hattab—the retinue had eaten raw flour and water
that morning—he answered simply, "Allah will bring
provisions." A few minutes later we came upon a
camel skeleton, a most welcome sight, for it proved

we were on the right track; inside the ribs were some large slabs of dried dung. Mohammed pulled this out triumphantly. "A fire! A fire! Hamdulillah!" And therefore everyone was cheerful till Amar brought the news that Yusuf was ill. We had seen the plump one lie down some way in the rear, but thought he was only resting for half an hour, a thing we all did in turns, only the difference between the nature of East and West showed at these moments, for whereas the Beduins slept peacefully in the rear and then ran after the camels, I used to toil on ahead and lay myself across the path of the caravan, so that I must wake at its approach. It appeared that Yusuf had fallen down and then lost consciousness for about an hour; it was very lucky that he managed to catch up the caravan at all. We mounted him on the Tebu camel, which was the strongest of the caravan but was already showing signs of thirst, and toiled on.

It was much harder walking in the dunes, for the sand was soft and deep in patches, but the great curly ridges, golden as Irish butter, which Yusuf always looked at affectionately, because they reminded him of his beloved "asida," were friendly spirits after the dreary disk of the preceding four days. It was always a thrilling moment when one mounted a high gherd, for there was the possibility of a view. Logically one could expect to see only waving yellow crests, a sunlit expanse of sand valley and mountain in every direction, but the impossible might always happen. One might espy a caravan or an oasis—or at least some hattab!

For this reason we always hastened ahead up the big rises to look down on wind-tossed ranges, and towards the evening we were rewarded for our energy by the appearance of little black specks in one of the hollows. "Hattab," said Suleiman laconically and Yusuf recovered at the word—or perhaps it was the quinine which

we had given him earlier in the day! We raced down
to the brittle stalks of twisted coarse-grained wood that
meant fires and hot food that night, and everyone began
to talk of what they would eat!

Just after sunset we came to an almost perpendicular
dune which the camels refused to descend. We had to
dig a sloping trough down it and push the beasts into it
one by one. Everybody was tired and the camels were
incredibly stupid. The young nagas simply rolled down,
flinging their loads in front of them, at which Mohammed
lost his temper and made matters worse by violently
beating the animals, still hesitating at the top. They
stumbled forward in a huddled mass, and I saw the
girbas threatened. Luckily the Tebu beast was carrying
most of them. He plunged solidly down on his great
splay feet and I had just enough energy left to seize his
head-rope and drag him out of the chaos. We barraked
before our short-sighted guide could lead us over another
such precipice and, because it was a joy to be wasteful
of anything on that journey, we made no fewer than three
fires and recklessly poured everything we could find into
the frying-pan together—rice and corned beef and tinned
turnips—so that we ate a hot, very hot, meal. We even
drank our one cup of tea hot, debating the while whether
coffee were not preferable, for, though it made one thirsty,
it somewhat hid the taste of the girba water.

Everything by now tasted slightly of wax, for, in the
hot days, all the candles had melted in the canteen. It
is certainly possible to clean pots and pans beautifully
with sand, but it needs a great deal of energy to do it
and I defy anyone to have any superfluous energy after
loading and feeding camels before a twelve to thirteen
hours' march, unloading and feeding the tired and smelly
beasts at the end of it, agaling them while they persistently tried to escape, preparing some sort of a meal

and then, worst of all, oh! intolerably worst, the sand-rash that tortured our nights! Let no one who dreams of a poetic, Swinburnian desert come to Libya! We had not washed anything but our hands since leaving Hawari thirteen days before and not even these since the Zakar well; since then we had had a sandstorm which had filled every pore with minute grit, so that by day the irritation was just bearable, but at night, in the warmth and the restricted space of the flea-bag, it was a torture beyond belief. I used to feel that never, so long as I lived, would I able to bear seeing water spilled or wasted.

Fate had been cruel to us in one respect, for the day at the Zakar well, when we had dreamed of sandy baths in the canteen lid behind a friendly palm tree, she had sent us the first of our two sandstorms, so washing had been confined to a teacup for our fingers. One lay at night, sleepless and burning, and looked up at the aloof peace of the stars and wondered vindictively how one could get even with the desert for this last trick of hers. Yet, in the cold, still dawn, the desperate tiredness vanished and one made a huge, unnecessary fire to breakfast by and ate black rice with immense relish. Yusuf was very proud of his skill as a cook, so we did not like to tell him of all the foreign bodies we found in our food—bits of leaf and straw from the baggage saddles, grit, hair, pebbles and sand—it was the Libyan sauce and I think Hassanein suffered much in silence, for it was his first desert journey and he still hankered after cleanliness. I used to find him desperately and secretly rubbing a plate with a corner of his muffler or his best silk handkerchief and, whenever he was late for breakfast, I knew it was because he had been unwise enough to look at his cup or fork before using them!

On our second day in the dunes the flat spaces grew

rarer, so that we climbed up and down ridges most of the time. The camels began to show signs of wear. One of the nagas trailed her head most of the time. The big blond beast had to be relieved of his load. They were all very smelly, which is the first sign of thirst. Luckily, we found patches of green hattab, the prickly, juiceless bush of the Mehemsa, scattered under the dunes and the animals raced to it, fighting for the freshest tufts. Amar got fever and had to be allowed to ride, while I was so tired that I found a way of festooning myself over the pegs of the baggage saddles, my knees wound round one and my neck round another. In this extraordinarily uncomfortable position I actually dozed, while Yusuf wandered beside me doubtfully. "You are very long," he said politely. "I think you will fall." And he tried to double up a dangling foot much as if it was a piece of baggage slipping.

I could not understand the presence of green bushes till I found my pillow that night wet with a heavy dew. Then I realised that we had left the southern lands behind us and next day, February 8, there were a few little clouds in the sky, just specks of fluffy white, but we had become used to the molten blue that roofs the red country of Kufara and her encircling wastes. That was for me the worst day. The little camels persistently threw their loads, ill-balanced because the fodder had become so much lighter. There was a cold east wind, which blistered one's skin on one side, while the sun scorched it on the other. The camels would not keep together, but strayed off to each patch of green. The dunes seemed steeper than ever and the sand softer and heavier. No one was sure of the way. Even Suleiman was a little depressed at not picking up any of the landmarks he had known on previous journeys. He insisted on keeping his course due north, though we knew

Jaghabub lay north-east, and his only explanation was that it was easier to approach the place from the west. Logically, I thought it would be easier to strike east, so that if one went past Jaghabub one would at least reach Siwa. To the west lay only the seven days' waterless stretch to Jalo.

However, Suleiman was immovable and we plodded wearily on, placing one foot in front of the other with desperate firmness and flinging ourselves flat on our faces for a few minutes' blessed sleep whenever the camels lingered to feed. I remember wondering, as I dragged myself up after one of these short respites, how many separate and distinct aches one's body could feel at the same moment. I was getting quite interested in the problem when Hassanein's bronzed face—it seemed to have grown hollow these last few days—appeared beside me. He was painfully shuffling on blistered feet after a twelve hours' walk the previous day. "When we get to Cairo everyone will say, What fun you must have had!'" he said drearily. Even this idea could not make me speak. I had discovered it was easier to walk with my eyes shut and so, mutely, I shuffled after the guide, dragging my stick till I dropped it and was too tired to pick it up again.

Yes, it was a bad day, but it ended at last with a few patches of black pebbles, sure sign that we were nearing the northern edge of the dunes. Even the sand rash, combined with a most remarkable tasting dish produced by Hassanein's efforts to clean the frying-pan, could not keep me awake that night and I slept soundly till Yusuf's plaintive voice, saying all in one breath, "Allah-make-you-strong-the-fire-is-ready-for - the - rice!" roused me to a starry world and an exceedingly damp one, but I imagine these very heavy dews helped the thirsty camels considerably, so I didn't regret a wet barracan which twisted itself reluctantly round everything but me!

February 9 was memorable, for on climbing the high dune under which we had camped we saw a long, faint ridge, blue on the north-east horizon. "Land at last!" exclaimed Mohammed. "It must be the mountain between Jaghabub and Siwa!" Even this reassuring suggestion would not turn our guide from his northerly course, but signs that we were leaving the great desert abounded. So far the only living things had been large, unpleasant beetles, mottled black and fawn creatures, some nearly four inches long, which looked like scattered stones till they suddenly raised themselves on long legs and scuttled away. That morning, however, we saw many black and grey birds and at last, when the green patches of hattab had developed into large brown-like shrubs and neat little dwarf trees, leafless and but two or three feet high, we came across gazelle traces. We also found two complete skulls with the tapering horns in perfect condition. The country was changing noticeably. The previous day there had been a few patches of the Jaghabub grey stone among the sand, the sight of which filled the retinue with delight. On February 9 great blocks of it appeared in fantastic masses rising suddenly from dune and hollow. We noticed scattered pieces of fossilised wood, some of which appeared to have been part of the trunks of big trees. Stretches of what looked like black pebbles shimmered dark beyond the farthest ridge.

Finally, Mohammed, mounting an immense curly backed sand peak at noon, tore off his turban, tied it round his staff and, waving it bannerwise above his head, shouted wildly, "I see my country! The land is near!" The camels were the only indifferent beings in the caravan. They were too tired to quicken the pace, which had dropped to two miles an hour during the last day or two. They had got very thin, with dull eyes, but luckily there was a slight breeze to relieve the intense heat which scorched us whenever we stopped for grazing in a hollow. There were streaks of white cloud in the pale sky and I imagined a breath of salt flavoured the northern breeze, so that suddenly I was desperately home-sick for the great free desert, lawless and boundless, that we were leaving. Ahead were the comfortable lands where the nomads camp in their tattered "nuggas" and the Beduins pasture their herds, the Gebel Akhbar and Cyrenaica, the welcome of the tent-dwellers for all caravans who have travelled the "big routes."

Somewhere, "east of us," said the compass, "north of us," said Suleiman, lay the last outpost of the wilderness, if not the birthplace, at least the training ground of Senussi-ism, but the lure of space dragged one's mind back. The claw of the desert was tearing away the peace that should lie at a journey's end. I do not think I ever felt mentally flatter than when, just before 2 A.M., we passed through the last little hollow where green and gold were mixed and the mighty belt of dunes lay behind us. In front was a most desolate country of grey slate and streaks of white chalky sand and pebbles, with here and there a dull madder gherd or stony cliff. A faint thrill of interest was given to the moment by the fact that none of the retinue knew where we were, but as I was determined that east we should now go, whatever they said, it did not much matter.

Suleiman climbed one dune and said we were between the hatias of Bu Alia and Bu Salama on the Jalo road. Mohammed climbed another and said that both these places were to the east of us. Yusuf lay down firmly on a soft spot and said that all known country was still to the north and he was going to sleep till the guide found his head again.

The happy-go-lucky Beduin spirit had completely got possession of us, so no one was particularly surprised when, after an hour on the course insisted on by the compass and myself, we picked up a definite trail with some slabs of stones stuck upright as landmarks. As a matter of fact we had struck the Jalo-Jaghabub route, rather more than a day's journey west of the latter place, but at the time nobody was certain as to our exact position. Amar, however, announced that undoubtedly Bu Alia lay behind us, and no sooner had the whole retinue agreed on that one point than the beginning of the hatia of that name became visible a few hundred yards ahead! "Hamdulillah! We shall camp to-night in our own country!" exclaimed Mohammed, and hurried on the caravan in spite of Yusuf's expostulations. Gazelle tracks were now plentiful and we tried to track down four in the hope of getting a shot, but Suleiman was nearly dead-beat. "The last word is in your hands," he said, "but I am an old man and very tired. Let us barrak here."

The hatia was really a wadi stretching about 5 kilometres north to south, with a breadth of 4 kilometres. The whole space between the white shale and sand banks was filled with mounds and shrubs of hattab, mostly green, while here and there massive blocks of greyish sandstone stuck up in strange shapes. As one wandered slowly through the low bushes far away to the north a long purplish ridge with a mound at the end shaped exactly like the dome of a mosque caught the first red of the sunset. "That is the gherd of the qubba," exclaimed Yusuf, his round tired face lighting up, "and look, in front of us is the Gara of Sidi el Mahdi!" At the farthest end of the hatia was an immense block of red sandstone flung up by the hands of some forgotten giant upon a mighty base of polished white, so that it looked like a primeval altar to the gods of earth and sky. Here the Mahdi used to halt his immense caravans on the Jalo journey and under the shadow of the rough natural sanctuary pray for a prosperous venture or give thanks for a safe return.

Even Suleiman spoke no more of barraking. Without a word spoken, everyone felt that the Maghrib prayers must be said where the spirit of the Mahdi would surely welcome travellers from the far-off oasis, whose red and amber he had changed to wealth of grain and fruit and flowers. The weary camels were hurried from their indifferent nibbling among the dry shrubs. When the full glory of the golden west lit up the strange altar, balanced between heaven and earth, and the faint silver crescent of a new moon glowed pale amidst the flame, we came round the corner of the rock and saw the simplest kibla that ever the faithful turned towards the Ka-aba. It was but three grey, rough boulders, with a circle of stones to mark the shape of an imaginary mosque, yet it was holy ground and we left our worn shoes outside, before we bowed our faces to the desert sands. What prayers the stern Mohammed mixed with his, "In the name of Allah compassionate and merciful," I know not. What simple thanksgivings were murmured by our weather-beaten guide, if the young zawia student, Amar, grasped the perils from which he had been protected, if Yusuf's mind realised for one fleeting moment that there was something beyond his comfortable practicality, I cannot guess, but I know that never in my life have I offered more whole-hearted gratitude to the Power that, called by many different names in many different cities, is omnipotent in the deserts!

CHAPTER XV

THE END OF THE JOURNEY

WE camped that night at Bu Salama, the next hatia on the way to Jaghabub. The wood was too green to make really good fires, though Mohammed and Hassanein laboured manfully in the sand. The rest of us were too tired to care what happened, provided we could lie down and not move for hours and hours. The grey camel evidently shared our feelings, for he had fallen in barraking. Amar, hopping round him distressfully without making the slightest attempt to help the rider, called repeatedly on the name of Sidi el Mahdi. It is amazing the complete faith every Senussi has in the spiritual and mental power of the Sayeds. Whenever the young nagas ran away old Suleiman used to stand perfectly still and repeat urgently, "Influence of Sidi Idris! Influence of Sidi Idris!" While once, while sleeping perilously in a more than usually odd position, I nearly fell as my camel stumbled down a dune, Yusuf muttered the name of every Sayed living and dead to ensure my safety.

I have never travelled in any country so united in devotion to its ruler as Libya. Presumably Sidi Idris is somewhat less powerful than Allah in the eyes of the Senussi, but he is nearer at hand! Their confidence in his capabilities is so unbounded that it must occasionally embarrass the Sayed himself. From curing a camel a thousand miles away to stopping a sandstorm, from conquering the world to producing a well where there

291

is no water, all are within the power of the son of Sidi el Mahdi. Our own prestige as friends of so important and puissant a personage was, therefore, considerably lowered when we humbly suggested that the retinue had better leave their varied armoury in Jaghabub as we could not guarantee that the Egyptian frontier authorities would allow them to enter Siwa. Yusuf looked blank. "But you will write a letter——" he suggested. He knew the all-powerful, almost magical effect of a missive from Sidi Idris in Libya, and reasoned that his guests could surely arrange the simple affair of the rifles in their own country by putting pen to paper. When we confessed our impotence he entertained the gravest doubts as to our position and respectability!

We had decided to send Mohammed on to Jaghabub before sunrise so that we might sleep next night in a house. Therefore, long after I had retired into my flea-bag, I saw Hassanein and Yusuf struggling to shave our delightful retainer by the light of the camp fire with a safety razor blade held in a pair of pliers. Suleiman and Amar offered interested suggestions interspersed with remarks on the number of grey hairs which had resulted from the journey.

In spite of the eight hours' journey ahead, Mohammed donned his best clothes to present himself at the zawia where he had been educated. Therefore I was surprised when Yusuf started next morning in his ragged white shirt and patched waterproof. "I always ride the last day of a journey," he announced firmly, depositing himself on the least weary camel.

We broke camp at 7 A.M. and straggled slowly by dreary grey gherds and uneven stretches of colourless sands and stones to a small hatia, Bahet Hafan, where a few palms grew among more fantastic boulders. The heat was intense as we entered a country of low white

hillocks, with slabs of shale that made the camels stumble
more than ever; but the end came with unexpected
rapidity, for, after the guide had told us under a noon
sun that it was a long day's march to Jaghabub, Yusuf
spied the white qubba of the zawia from a friendly gherd.
In a few minutes the whole round wadi spread before us,
with its strips of scattered palms and brushwood, and
beyond a line of square sandstone cliffs the white walls
of Jaghabub that looked so near and that took us more
than two hours to reach.

The home of Sidi Ben Ali is by far the most picturesque of the Senussi oases, for it is blinding white in
the sunshine—a smooth, polished cupola and tall madna,
with the open-arched gallery of Sidi Idris's house rising
above the massive, fortress-like walls of the zawia, all
white—white as the windmills that look like marble
pillars in the distance or the pale sand brick of the few
big houses that surround the zawia.   Jaghabub is not a
town in the proper sense of the word.   It is one immense
building with thick, windowless walls, surrounding a
maze of courts, passages, schools, lodgings for students,
the big houses of the Senussi family and the large mosque
and qubba of Sidi Ben Ali.   It stands on a cliff from
which flights of steps lead down to palm gardens and the
one big well that supplies water to the whole settlement.
Outside the massed, many-storied buildings of the zawia
are a few scattered houses, but Jaghabub is a university
pure and simple.   When Sidi el Mahdi removed his headquarters to Kufara he freed half a hundred slaves, giving
them the gardens that they cultivated and ordering that
their rights should be respected by his successors; so now
there is a colony of these liberated blacks who live among
the palms in the wadi. They work hard in their vegetable
gardens, which are irrigated by an excellent system of
channels and reservoirs dependent on the spring below

the zawia, and they sell their dates and produce to the
college.

Two of the students met us half-way across the wadi
with a note from Mohammed saying that rooms were
being prepared for us in the zawia and Yusuf promptly
proceeded to change his clothes. He tore off his tattered
shirt, baring a muscular brown torso to the public gaze,
produced a mysterious bundle from a sack on my camel
and shook from it embroidered waistcoat, silk jerd,
yellow shoes and immaculate white linen, all of which he
donned as we walked along. When the white walls were
very near we fired our revolvers into the air to announce
our arrival and Mohammed came out to meet us, smiling
broadly. We passed through a big, white arch into a
wide, open space with a well in the middle, round which
were clustered groups of students who gave us warm
greeting. To the right rose the solid, castle-like wall of
Sidi Idris's house, whose gallery on the other side looked
down on to a beautiful square court of the qubba with
its wide-arched and columned arcades. The façade near
the square is pierced by a few shuttered windows and
the carved main door through which one goes to the
qubba court. To the left the square was bordered by a
row of neat little round-lintelled doors, each with a slit
of window above it, the lodging-houses for the students.
A big, two-storied house rose beyond and, at the door
of this, we were met by a delightful old man with pale,
thin face, a long beard as white as his woollen jerd or
the colourless walls behind him.

"Greeting to you and the peace of Allah!" he said,
and led us into a dwelling more complicated even than
the kaimakaan's house of many courts at Taj. We
went up and down little flights of steps which seemed to
exist without reason, under low arches, by odd little
passages and mud-floored yards, till a longer staircase led

us to a flat roof, across which we followed our host to
a large high room, matted and carpeted, but devoid of
furniture.   For the first time I lived in an Arab house
which had a view from the windows, for here there was
no yard to shut one into a mysterious little world of
secluded privacy.   From the cross-barred windows with
swinging shutters one looked down on the big square
and the white figures gossiping round the well or across
to the group of our weary camels, literally bulging after
their enormous drink, to students seated at the doors of
their rooms with Koran and rosary.

Our host, Sidi Yadem Bu Gemira, one of the important ekhwan, was so anxious to hear the complete
story of our journey that he would not leave us before
we had drunk sweet coffee, seated on his best carpet,
and answered all his questions as to why we had come
from Kufara by such a hard route.   Before we had
satisfied his kindly curiosity, Sidi el Fagil, plump and
ebony-faced, with greying moustache, the Imam of the
mosque, and other ekhwan, had hurried to visit us.   I
was so tired I could hardly hold up my head.   My nose
was blistered and peeling, my face burning, my eyes
watering.   I was intensely hungry.   Every nerve seemed
to be throbbing and aching and, above all, I was conscious
of dirt.   I felt completely vague as I leaned against the
wall and, when a murmur of voices below suggested the
possibility of other visits, I basely left Hassanein to
entertain the venerable ekhwan and crept down a discreet
little stairway to a quaint-shaped room that lurked under
one of the innumerable archways, forgotten, I think,
by the architect, who must have had a most tortuous
mind.   It was full of dust and clay, but I felt a little
more dirt did not matter, and here I was found by the
kindly Yusuf, when the last visitor had gone, fast asleep
on Hassanein's grimy jerd.

"The Sitt Khadija must eat," he said. "The wakil of Sidi Idris has sent you dinner." The magic word roused me and the sight of a gleaming brass tray set on a little table 6 inches high in the middle of our unbroken sea of carpet finished the cure. When we lifted the palm-leaf covers from the bowls we found eggs, pigeons and vegetables cooked in wonderful savoury sauces, with piles of most delicious bread, brown and flaky, but, alas! every cunning sauce was so impregnated with red pepper that we had most gingerly to remove the pigeons and dust them carefully before eating, after which we regretfully deposited a just proportion of the rest of the meal in a carefully prepared hole in a back-yard lest the feelings of our host be hurt. We had just removed all traces of our villainy when he appeared to drink tea with us.

Sidi Hussein, the wakil, was, of all the hosts who generously entertained us on behalf of the Sayeds, the most delightful because he was the most simple. Jaghabub is not a political or mercantile centre, like Kufara or Jalo. It has all the dreaming peace of a little university town, only its dons are reverend, grey-bearded sheikhs in flowing white jerds over grass-green or indigo-blue robes. Its undergraduates are graver figures, with books and beads, than those of Trinity or The House, while the scouts, I suppose, are the black slaves of hideous aspect who live in a special court of the zawia, but I feel sure they are more industrious and certainly more frugal than their English counterparts on the banks of the Isis and Cam.

Sidi Hussein made tea with a formality as deliberate as that of the kaimakaan at Taj, but his conversation was much less ceremonious. There was no rigid etiquette observed in series of questions and answers. For once the undercurrent of suspicion and unrest was

absent and we curled up our mental antennæ with a
feeling of complete peace. The little town, so aloof
from the world in its secluded wadi, yet the nursery of
a great confraternity where still is nourished a force
whose influence is felt all along North Africa, wished us
well. A very intimate friendliness pervaded the gathering in the semi-gloom of the candle-lit room. The
wakil's huge beard flowed grey and soft over dark
jubba with a many-coloured waistcoat beneath, but theré
was no lavish display of silk or embroidery, because the
ekhwan of Jaghabub are more devoted to learning than
to luxury. "We are poor men who spend our time in
prayer," said one of them with the utmost simplicity
and a dreamy look in his faded old eyes. Their great
pride is their qubba, and a reflection for this homage
showed in Yusuf's face when, the night of our arrival,
just as I had finished scrubbing off the first layer of
grime and was wondering if I could decently ask Amar
to heat another quart or two of water, he arrived with
a guttering candle to suggest that I should go at once
to see the sanctuary. "There will be no people there
at this hour," he said, but, when we had crossed the
starlit square and left our shoes inside the first arcade
of the mosque, we heard a low, monotonous chanting
coming from the shadows beyond the great white court!
It was in keeping with the solemn spirit of the night
and the scene and the proud happiness in Yusuf's face,
as he led me through long, dim ways which he trod
unfaltering, back again in imagination in his boyhood's
days, when perhaps he had been as earnest and devout
a learner as the grave-faced students who passed us in
the square.

Through a fine carved and painted door we passed
into the mosque, very quiet, white and dignified, the
dark carpets on the floor the only rich note to break

its utter simplicity. The silence began to beat on my ear drums with the impression of so many prayers, hopes, resolves, fervently uttered by youth in these low aisles, remembered again by age when it revisited the earliest centre of its faith. Yusuf did not break it. Eyes bright with a light I had never seen in them before, he beckoned me on into the qubba itself and we stood in a painted chamber, ornate with gold and many colours, below the big dome, hung with huge, finely moulded glass lamps. I murmured swift Arabic prayers before a square grid of carved bronze that surrounded the tomb of the great Senussi. I was afraid even the whisper of the "Fatha" might hurt the silence, for our footfalls were muffled by thick, piled carpets, but the man whose mind I had always imagined fixed on things of the earth, earthly, shattered it with a sudden sound, half cry, half groan, as he bent passionately to kiss the rail and afterwards the hand with which he had touched it!

In the morning, after an excellent but peppery breakfast brought by Mabruk, a hatchet-faced slave whom we used to watch running across the square with a bowl into which he poked a surreptitious finger at our door to see if it were still hot, I went again to the mosque and saw other Senussi tombs. I found the wide, white arches had much charm by sunlight, but I never again caught the mystic spirit of the night when the living force of Islam had flamed for a second before my eyes.

Yusuf proved an excellent guide to Jaghabub. With intense pride he took us through the maze of college buildings, pointing out the house of each of the Senussi, Sidi Rida, Sidi Idris, Sayed Ahmed Sherif, Sayed Hilal and Sayed Safi ed Din, which make a massive block round the white qubba. In the big open square, where the pupils of the zawia lodge, he announced, "We each of us have a house here. Amar has one. I have one. We can come back whenever we like. It is our own country." Thus the zawias hold their pupils long after they have gone out to the cities and deserts. The portly ekhwan, the prosperous merchant, the Beduin sheikh or the wandering scribe may turn into the zawia where he has been educated, sure of finding a room and a welcome. Even the chance traveller may claim the three days' hospitality of the Senussi and the poorer he is the more generous it will be.

We spent two days in the high tower above the square, talking simply about simple things with the ekhwan, doctoring some of the students with pathetically inadequate remedies, exchanging the gossip of Kufara for that of Egypt with a few west-bound merchants. Then we set out on the last stage of our journey, determining that for once we would travel slowly and peacefully, grazing the camels as we went, riding a little by night for the sheer joy of the stars and barraking to make mint tea wherever a haita tempted us with its wood and shade.

Fate must have laughed in her sleeve, but no echo of her mirth reached us as we loaded our four camels inside the zawia walls or paused beyond the first gherd while Sidi Hussein said the "Fatha." I only realised that this was the last Arabic blessing that would attend my journey and suddenly I felt heartsick for the land I was leaving. The white, clustered walls, the white qubba behind, stood for the effort we had made, the object we had struggled for, far more than Kufara itself had ever done. Mohammed was really broken down by the journey and unable to come on with us, so, with this little land of hope and fear, success and failure, with these winter months of high-pitched excitement and tense endurance, we were losing a friend! An odd pain possessed me as we finally parted in fine, whirling sand and a wind which blew his jerd wildly about his face and when Yusuf said complacently, "The Sitt Khadija is happy. She will be in her own country soon," I knew the desert had won after all. Those who are initiated into her secrets are for ever held in her thrall. I think my voice was rather wobbly as I answered, "No, no, I am sad because I am leaving the Senussi country behind!" So quick is Arab sympathy, so responsive is their instinct, that Yusuf's face reflected my woful expression. "My heart was touched," he confided to Amar. "I would have wept with the Sitt Khadija because she has many feelings."

There was a strong north-west wind that day, but it was behind us, so we rode slowly and placidly through the distorted country of sand and shale that lies east of Jaghabub. I do not know whether sportive giants dig for treasure or young gods build play castles and entrenchments in that desolate land, but on every side rise fantastic shapes of wind-blown sand. Reddish layers drip over polished white bases that look like chalk. Ridge after ridge of storm-polished gherds shut one into a maze of strange hillocks that give way occasionally to welcome green of hatias. The retinue had shrunk to three, Yusuf, Amar and a new guide, one Abu Bekr Manfi, who looked exactly like the wicked Caliph in Dulac's illustrations to the Arabian Nights, for he had a huge beaked nose which, under an immense loosely rolled turban, curved to meet his pointed beard and nut-cracker jaw. His curious eyes were for ever asking questions, but his dialect was almost beyond my comprehension.

We proceeded very slowly because all the camels were tired and the retinue had surreptitiously added to their loads immense earthenware jars to fill with oil at Siwa, but it did not matter, for this was a friendly desert, generous of her wood and water. We halted at El Amra, where the Mahdi had built two great cisterns some fifty feet long with domed roofs, through holes in which the water drips into the immense chamber below. Abu Bekr made tea with a swiftness suggesting that his Caliph ancestor had bequeathed to him the services of his familiar genii. Then we proceeded slowly, walking and riding alternately another 12 kilometres to Maktuh, where we turned the weary camels loose to graze and cooked our rice and "asida" respectively under a delightfully sweet-scented bush, while inquisitive blackbirds with impertinent white patches over their bills hopped cheerfully around us. In red mist of sunset we started to reload, noticing that Abu Bekr carefully joined his "Asr," "Fagr" and "Aisha" prayers into one unending stream in order to avoid having to do any work.

A golden crescent lighted a white world as we left the hatia, labouring through the sabakha with great dunes looming on our right. I felt infinitely at peace in the shimmering, silvery stillness, the silence only broken by the soft pad-padding of the camels or Yusuf's sudden wailing chant in praise of his beloved qubba, "white as the breast of a virgin." The desert was in her most magical mood and I longed to turn south again and ride back into her bourneless country by the pale light of Jedi and Suhail. Then a strange murmuring sound arose in the dunes. It was as if a great wind bore the humming of a myriad monstrous bees. "The jinns are awake to-night!" said Yusuf fearfully. "Something evil will befall us. They are making a great noise in the sands!" I laughed at him and wondered if it were the throb of the breeze reverberating

in the empty oil jars or if we were so near civilisation
that an aeroplane had become a possibility. Then I
remembered the desert drums of the French Sahara, for
which no human fingers are responsible, and I wondered
if, when one is very near akin to the Spirit of the Earth,
one can hear the beat of her pulse.

I turned on my big blond beast to ask Hassanein
what he thought of the strange throbbing and instead
of a crouched figure swaying monotonously on the grey
Tebu, I saw a heap pick itself briskly from a patch of
stones. "I think I have broken my collar-bone!"
said a calm, laughing voice. "You wouldn't say it
quite so happily if you had!" I grunted, with memories
of hunting falls. "Perhaps not," replied my companion,
clambering back on to his camel. "All the same,
there's a most enormous lump. I believe I have."
And, though the voice still laughed, I grasped suddenly
that it spoke disastrous truth! Camels were roughly
barraked. Yusuf, for once bereft of speech, stumbled
round, mutely offering most of his clothing as bandages.
Abu Bekr, practical and brutal, wished to massage the
lump as a sprain. I blessed for once the cumbersome
length of the red hezaam. Bandages and sling it made
at the same time and left an end over to fix a cushion
under the armpit.

All the time Hassanein was cheerfully explaining
that the Tebu had thoughtlessly stumbled just as he was
practising gymnastics, in order to extract a blanket from
some mysterious recess among the baggage sacks, but
we gave him short time for talk. We hustled him into
a roughly made "basoor" and a pitiful little procession
started off again, for suddenly the silver night had
become desperately lonely, the drumming of the jinns
sinister and the trail to Siwa, with half-exhausted camels
and none too willing men, a thing of intolerable length.

Thereafter our journey was just the chronicle of a very gallant feat of endurance. The golden sickle died behind us, but we plodded on. No longer were the 85 kilometres in front of us a friendly desert to be traversed slowly and comfortably. At all costs we must reach Siwa and a doctor before the fractured bone broke the skin and set up mortification. The greatest difficulty was the retinue, who could not believe that the "Ahmed Bey" who laughed at them and urged them to sing could really have a broken bone. "It is a little sprain," said Yusuf hopefully. "We will make a fire and massage it with oil of jasmine and it will be cured." But I drove them on unrelenting till the rough ground west of Kusebeya made the camels stumble hopelessly in the darkness. I hated Abu Bekr when he calmly lit himself a fire and, warming his feet at the blaze, started chanting the Koran in a loud, exasperating voice.

We could not get the unfortunate Hassanein into a flea-bag and no position we could devise could give rest to his shoulder, already jarred by the unending bumps and jerks of a camel's pace. All we could do was to pile our cushions and blankets under him and cover him with the sleeping-sacks. Yusuf toiled nobly and, in the cold night which followed, during which Abu Bekr was the only one who slept, I heard him come shuffling several times to see if he could help.

Never was a dawn more welcome, but as we helped my infinitely plucky companion on to a camel, waiting for no breakfast except coffee, made overnight in a thermos flask, I wondered whether human endurance could last out another forty-eight hours like this. The shoulder was already inflamed and the ground terribly rough, so that every few minutes the rider was jerked and jolted painfully. We passed the blue salt lake of Kusebeya, a strip of colour on our left, and clambered down into the hatia, where the camels had to be turned loose to graze. We found a palm clump and cooked rice in the shade and Hassanein's smile grew a little more twisted, in spite of my best efforts with bandages and sling.

I would hardly allow the retinue to finish their noisy gulps of tea. "What does it matter if you are tired?" I flung at them. "That bone has got to be set to-morrow night!" "Three and a half days from Jaghabub to Siwa," said Yusuf mournfully. "We would walk with you all night, but the camels will not go." "They have got to go," said I sternly, but I knew that our animals were very nearly exhausted. They had come more than a thousand miles, with periods of overloading and insufficient food. For nearly three months they had had no rest but the eight days at Kufara, and we had always hoped to leave them at Jaghabub to recuperate. Unluckily, there was not a single beast of burden in the zawia to take us on, so we had to pick out the four least weary camels and trust once more to luck.

That afternoon was one of the longest I have ever spent. When I saw Hassanein put away his compass I knew that things must be pretty bad and the fantastic hills were a tortuous maze through which we wandered eternally! Yusuf pointed out the "Grid," a group of three gherds which might serve to support the cooking-pots of the largest giants. "We shall camp at Zaizeb," he said and I prayed that it might be near. "Allah alone knows how far it is to that hatia," said Abu Bekr placidly as we mounted, it seemed to me for the millionth time, a little rise and saw nothing below but reddish sand over hard, white blocks, in monstrous forms that suggested beasts and edibles to the fanciful Amar. Hassanein was the last of us to fall into silence.

The sun set without showing any signs of the promised hatia. The camels were obviously incapable of going much farther. Yusuf said pathetically, "I have walked seventeen days from Kufara on these legs and now they are very tired." But Hassanein said nothing. Only when I climbed a huge mound of stones beside the track and saw the hope in his face as I looked across a great expanse of broken country I could not resist the impulse. "I see the hatia," I lied. "It is quite near." Darkness came as we jolted down into the wadi and every rolling stone, every sudden drop made me realise that two more days of this would be impossible. The swift appearance of the hatia almost justified my impulsive speech, but it was very dark as we barraked behind a convenient mound. I insisted that food should be eaten quickly and that we should then walk till the moon went down. The retinue expostulated violently. "You must leave some of the loads," said Yusuf; and Abu Bekr so firmly ensconced himself in his blankets that I thought a concerted mutiny was probable. However, after a forlorn meal, for even my companion's unfaltering courage could not hide his pain, I literally pushed the retinue on to their feet and, by dint of doing half the loading myself, forced them to prepare for another march.

Hassanein dragged himself mutely on to the grey Tebu, still far the strongest of the hamla, but when I saw the party crawl away from our camping ground I knew that I could not force the pace any longer. On the morrow I would put up the tent and leave my companion there with Yusuf and Amar. I would take the Kufara camel and Abu Bekr who, for love of heavy mejidies, would guide me in one long march to Siwa, from where I could bring back help. "This is the end," I said to Yusuf. "Pull up your energy!" And then,

Hamdulillah, a dog ran out barking and figures loomed in the shadows. "Friend," came the answer to Amar's challenge. "No friend walks thus at night," said Yusuf decidedly and to me, "Get ready your revolvers!" But I had heard an English voice! Rushing forward, unheeding of ungirdled barracan, of Moslem custom, of anything in the world but that the hands of my own countrymen could help as no other hands in the world, I met a Camel Corps Patrol which the Frontier Districts Administration had sent out to look for us!

I have absolutely no recollection of what I said to the calm-eyed shadow in khaki who drew away from the dark figures in close-rolled turbans and the precise, double row of neatly barraked hejin, but, oh! the efficiency of England! I have railed at her so often and with so much justice. I have run away from her powers-that-be when I have wanted to penetrate to particularly unauthorised and impossible places, but that night I valued her as never before! In so few minutes the situation changed. Did I relinquish my command or was it unconsciously taken from me by Beneficent Khaki? I do not know, but the retinue's grumbling sank to awed silence at the power which had leaped to meet us. The hamla were driven on to camp at a given place and the swiftest hejin went back to Siwa, untiring through the night, to fetch a doctor and car to Girba, only half a day ahead.

Fate had played against the kindness of an English Governor then at Siwa, for the rescue party had camped but a couple of hundred yards from our distressed dinner, and she had lost, because the wandering dog had heralded our approach. Otherwise we might have drifted on into the night.

Almost before I realised how life had changed I found myself on a white trotting camel with a specially

immense sheepskin testifying to very gracious forethought. Beneficent Khaki was beside me and, behind
me, a swiftly broken camp, the still-glowing ashes of the
fire and then a line of dark figures on the slender hejin
of the Camel Corps. It seemed so small a thing now,
the distance that lay before us, and even the long trail
behind us was suddenly of no account, for we talked of
world wars, of nations still in the melting-pot. How
eagerly I asked for news! Governments had fallen, a
new republic had sprung into existence, a famous general
had vanished with a great army! Long before I had
filled the gap those desert months had made in newspaper
knowledge, we had overtaken the hamla and Beneficent
Khaki was looking out for convenient shelter. "The lee-
side of a gherd, I think," he said firmly. "That big
fellow over there will do," and he wheeled his tall, white
beast sharply under the hill.

So swiftly the camp was made! I felt ashamed of our
clumsy loading, our lumbering halts, when I saw the ease
with which each tall hejin barraked in its own place in
the double line. "What a good thing it is to belong to
such a Government," said Yusuf enviously. "What fine
camels and what a good turn-out!" There was no
grumbling at making a zariba that night. A meek retinue
bestirred themselves mightily to little effect, but Beneficent Khaki took charge. Marvellously soon, it seemed,
Hassanein was tucked into a wondrous flea-bag, complete
with sheets, a real pillow propped up his shoulder, a
thoroughly wind-proof zariba shut out northern blasts, a
fire blazed cheerfully before us and, as I tugged my own
roll of bedding nearer its happy crackling, a voice said
reproachfully: "You mustn't do that! Do remember
that you've got lots of people to do it for you
now!" I smiled, for I had almost forgotten the ways
of England.

"Hot tea," said the same voice. "With milk."
And I noticed an enormous kettle on the fire. Mugs
came from a magic picnic basket filled with all sorts of
good things. Rugs and sheepskins appeared from the
spare camels brought for our riding. Was there anything
the Frontier Districts Administration could not produce
at a second's notice? Then someone said "Sausages"
and even Hassanein was enthusiastic. We cooked them
with tomato sauce on the scented brushwood fire and ate
them steaming hot, with white new bread from the hospitable basket and then—how we talked! Beneficent
Khaki smoked a pipe and we, blissfully indifferent to
the stern Senussi laws which had forbidden us tobacco
for so many weeks, saw visions and dreamed dreams in
the blue haze of our first cigarettes.

It must have been nearly 2 A.M. when we finally
buried ourselves in our flea-bags, but no one slept—
Hassanein because of his broken bone, Beneficent Khaki
because he had been too recklessly generous in the disposal of his own blankets and I because the Great
Adventure was ended!

I lay on my back and looked at the stars, weighing
the balance of success and failure and, suddenly, I felt
that this was not really the end. Some time, somehow,
I knew not where or when, but most assuredly when
Allah willed, I should come back to the deserts and the
strange, uncharted tracks would bear my camels south
again.

For those who like to know the end of every story be
it said that the efficiency which had taken possession of
us did not relinquish its grasp until it had deposited us,
bewildered and hopelessly out of place, in the hotel at
Alexandria, after a 430-mile motor drive from Siwa. It
was complete to the last detail.

Hot tea steamed beside our flea-bags before the dawn

brought us out of them. At a pace which would have made light of the long trail to Zakar we trotted on to the hatia at Girba, where, under the largest palm, waited a doctor complete with aluminium fittings. The cars arrived exactly at the correct moment. The road to Siwa was unexpectedly smooth and oh! how hot and plentiful was the bath water at the rest house!

There I discarded my worn barracan with a sigh of relief, yet, as I wandered through the honeycomb of old Siwa, with its close-piled houses one upon another and its labyrinth of dark tunnels that serve as streets, I was ashamed before the gaze of Arabs. It seemed to me intolerable that a Moslem should see my face unveiled. Instinctively I pulled at my hat brim and my flying cloak, for, curiously, the soul of this people had become mine and I resented the lack of privacy till I remembered that the Sitt Khadija was no more!

Once again we spent a night in the desert, but this time in the shelter of a tarpaulin hung between two F.D.A. cars, which were to take us to Matruh, and it was a tame desert with friendly caravans passing and newly sunk cisterns to prove the enterprise of its Governor. Yet the silvery moon was the same that turned the Hawari sands to molten amber, scarred with the sapphire of her palms, and I crept beyond the shelter and the comfort to watch the setting of the star that Mohammed had always wanted to "put out!"

"Warm congratulations on your success," said generous-hearted officialdom at Siwa and Matruh and the more than kindly welcome was our best reward.

"So you have been to Kufara," said a civilian on the coast. "It is an island, isn't it, but I always thought it was spelt Korfu!"

Then I met a pretty Englishwoman. The stripe in her skirt matched her French sweater and faint scent of "Mille Fleurs" drifted from her rose-petal skin. My nails were broken, my nose blistered. My only European dress had been hidden for months at the bottom of a sack of bully beef tins, yet was I sincere when I echoed Hassanein's vicious "Civilisation, Hamdulillah!" as he stuffed his kufiya into a corner of his knapsack and pulled out a fez!

DABA-A, *February* 19, 1921.

APPENDIX A
ROUTE HISTORY

Date	Start	Halt	Distance	Direction	Weather	Temperature Highest	Temperature Lowest	Altitude	Country	Wells	Zawias and Qubbas
Dec. 8th	6.0 a.m. 11.30 a.m.	9.30 a.m. 2.0 p.m.	24 kils.	140°	Strong, cold E. wind. Sun.	26° Cent.	2.77° Cent.	40 metres	Flat. Gravelly sand. Thick, coarse grass.		At Jedabia. Modern zawia. Sheikh Mohammed Qurinyim and some 40 ekhwan. Disused Madeni Zawia of Omar Zafr.
Dec. 9th	8.0 a.m.	5.0 p.m.	36 kils.	165°	Rain at 9 a.m. Cloudy.	43° Cent.	5.55° Cent.	60 metres	Flat. Sandy. Much grass. Two faint rises.	Wadi Farig, long depression running E. and W. No vegetation or palms. One large well (spring) 15 ft. deep. Perennial water, very salt in summer and always slightly bitter.	
Dec. 10th		Farig.			Hot sun.	32° Cent.	3.88° Cent.				
Dec. 11th	At Wadi.				Strong S. wind.	44° Cent.	6.66° Cent.		Wadi Farig.		
Dec. 12th	1.30 p.m.	3.0 p.m.	8 kils.	170° and 175°	E. wind a.m. N. wind p.m.	30° Cent.	5.55° Cent.	30 metres	Undulating E. to W. Vegetation scarce.		

Date	Start	Halt	Distance	Direction	Weather	Highest	Lowest	Altitude	Country	Wells	Zawias and Qubbas
						Temperature					
Dec. 13th	8.40 a.m.	2.40 p.m.	24 kils.	170° and 175°	Shower 10 a.m. Sun. N. W. wind.	40° Cent.	3.88° Cent.	30 metres.	Flat Sand. Slight ridges E. and W. No scrub.		
Dec. 14th	6.15 a.m. 1.30 p.m.	8.45 a.m. 4.0 p.m.	22 kils.	155°	Sun. No wind.	42° Cent.		000 metres. Sea level by well.	Tableland, sudden square ridges. No vegetation. Drop to plain. El Arida Hill in sight.	Bir Rassam. 1 well in soft flat sand. Tufts, palms. Perennial bitter water. 1 well, Sahabi, 4 kils. S. W., bitter.	
Dec. 15th	7.30 a.m.	2.30 p.m.	30 kils.	155°	Cold S. wind. Gibli at night.	24° Cent.		30 metres.	Rolling sand. Rare vegetation. Sharp square hillocks. El Arida Hill 8.30 a.m.	One bitter, bad well. Bir Mareg E. of route, 10 kils. El from Rassam.	
Dec. 16th	7.30 a.m. 5.30 p.m.	3.30 p.m. 9.0 p.m.	38 kils. 16 kils.	160°	S. wind. Cold. Sun.	22° Cent.	5.55° Cent.	90 metres on hillock nr. Garet el Melh.	Very flat. No vegetation except in Hatiyet Buddefar. 2 p.m. Rolling sand.		
Dec. 17th	8.30 a.m.	3.30 p.m.	30 kils.	135°	Strong S. W. wind. Sun.	32° Cent.	5.0° Cent.	70 metres on highest swell.	Deep sand. Flat. Occasional swells.	Msus Oasis. Many wells. Bir Sibil in wadi.	Zawia built 1872, with mosque. Eight smaller mosques. Saleh Bu Fatma square tower on hill. 30 to 40 ekhwan.

Dec. 18th At Aujela.					Very hot. No wind.	45° Cent.	3.33° Cent.		Oasis with palms and acacias.	Aujela. Many wells. Good water.	Sheikh Abdul-Kassim. Mohammed's clerk Abdullahi Sahabi Qubba.
Dec. 19th	9.30 a.m.	3.30 p.m.	24 kils.	110°	Cool. Cloudy.	32° Cent.	4.44° Cent.		Flat. Fine gravel. No grass.	Jalo. Wells, bad water at Shurruf.	
Dec. 20th At Jalo. Dec. 21st					Hot. Cloudy. No wind.	42° Cent.	5.0° Cent.	80 metres on highest sand ridge near town.	Large straggling oasis. Palms. Acacias. Cultivation.	Wells at Manshia, El Erg, Lebba, and water 5 ft. below surface in most parts of oasis.	Zawia El Erg. Sheikh Mohammed es Senussi, modern. 40 ekhwan. 7 mosques. 2 unimportant qubbas, Sidi Saleh and Sidi Mukhtar. Zawia Lebba founded by Sidi Ben Ali, Sheikh Omar. 80 ekhwan. 150 boys.
Dec. 22nd	11.30 a.m.	12.30 p.m.	3 kils.	115°	Sandstorm.	21° Cent.	6.66° Cent.				
Dec. 23rd	7.30 a.m.	1.30 p.m.	24 kils.	115°	Sun. Strong N. wind.	30° Cent.	6.66° Cent.	60 metres	Flat. No vegetation.	Bir Buttafal. 1 well often has to be dug. Excellent water.	
Dec. 24th At Buttafal. Dec. 25th Do.					Strong N. wind. Cloudy. No wind. Sun.	26° Cent. 38° Cent.	6.66° Cent. 5.0° Cent.		No vegetation or palms. Rolling sand. Firewood 5 kils. E.		

Date	Start	Halt	Distance	Direction	Weather	Temperature		Altitude	Country	Wells	Zawias and Qubbas
						Highest	Lowest				
Dec. 26th	8.30 a.m.	7.30 p.m.	46 kils.	180°	Cloudy. N. Wind. Sun.	39° Cent.	3.88° Cent.		Desolate, flat waste, unchanging. Kelb el Metemma to E. on Zieghen route. *See note A, page 322.*		
Dec. 27th	8.0 a.m.	7.0 p.m.	44 kils.	180°	Cloudy and sun. N. wind.	28° Cent.	7.77° Cent.		Desolate, flat. No vegetation. Unchanging. Hameimat to E. on Zieghen route.		
Dec. 28th	7.40 a.m.	7.10 p.m.	46 kils.	180°	Cloudy. Sun. N. wind.	30° Cent.	6.66° Cent.		Flat waste. No vegetation. Unchanging.		
Dec. 29th	6.40 a.m.	6.5 p.m.	46 kils.	165°	Hot sun. N. wind. Shower at night.	34° Cent.	7.22° Cent.		Flat waste. Wadi Farig imaginary depression running E. and W.		
Dec. 30th	7.0 a.m.	6.35 p.m.	46 kils.	180°	Very hot.	46° Cent.	6.11° Cent.	220 metres	Flat with faintest sand-waves. El Mazul to E. on Zieghen route.		
Dec. 31st	6.30 a.m.	7.0 p.m.	46 kils.	190°	Cool. Sun. N. wind.	36° Cent.	6.11° Cent.		Flat. No vegetation. Patches of black pebbles.		
Jan. 1st	7.0 a.m.	7.0 p.m.	48 kils.	30 K. M. 220° / 18 K. M. 180°	Hot. Cloudy.	42° Cent.	5.55° Cent.	240 metres	Flat. Patches larger black stones.		

Date	Time	Time		Distance	Direction	Weather	Temp.	Temp.	Altitude	Description	Remarks
Jan. 2nd	8.0 a.m.	6.0 a.m.		40 kils.	170°	Fog a.m. Hot. Cloudy.	40° Cent.	5.0° Cent.	240 metres	Slight rises. Mounds. Big dunes 60 ft. at 4 p.m.	El Atash well near dune 60 ft. high N.E. to S.W., disused well, good water. Few shrubs. No fodder.
Jan. 3rd	8.30 a.m.	2.0 p.m.		18 kils.	130°	Mist a.m. Sun. No wind.	42° Cent.	4.44° Cent.		In Hatia, near Zieghen, few palms. Mounds. Small dunes.	El Harrash. Wells can be dug in bed of Hatia near vegetation. Good water. Fodder very scarce.
Jan. 4th	7.30 a.m.	6.0 p.m.		40 kils.	180°	Mist a.m. Sun. S. wind.	37° Cent.	3.33° Cent.	280 metres	After Hatia, barren sand in slight waves. Saw Buseima Gebel at 10 a.m.	
Jan. 5th	7.30 a.m.	2.30 p.m.		28 kils.	180°	Cold S. wind. Hot Sun.	26° Cent.	4.44° Cent.	300 metres	Buseima. Black Nubian sandstone, impregnated iron oxide and magnesian cliffs. Big dunes.	Many wells. Nasrani well best water, clear, but flavoured magnesia sulphate.
Jan. 6th	At Buseima.					Cool. Bright. No wind.	32° Cent.	2.77° Cent.	380 metres (on dunes)	Oasis with salt lake 8 to 10 kils. long. Palms. Mountains 15 kils. long. 1 fresh spring. Salt marsh. Figs. Tamarisks. Acacias. Tebu ruins. Sandstone (Nubian). Flints and little quartz on sub-layer of limestone.	No zawia. Sheikh Mohammed el Madeni is chief of Senussi.
Jan. 7th	Do.					No wind. Hot.	43° Cent.	3.33° Cent.			

Date	Start	Halt	Distance	Direction	Weather	Temperature		Altitude	Country	Wells	Zawias and Qubbas
						Highest	Lowest				
Jan. 8th	8.30 a.m.	5.0 p.m.	25 kils.	130°	Hot. No wind.	45° Cent.	3.88° Cent.	460 metres (on dunes)	Large dunes. Two black sandstonecones E. of route called Gor Sibb el Abid or Saar el Khaddama.		
Jan. 9th	8.0 a.m.	3.0 p.m.	28 kils.	130°	Cold N. E. wind.	30° Cent.	3.33° Cent.	500 metres (on dunes)	Large dunes, highest Seif el Birem.		
Jan. 10th	6.30 a.m.	6.0 p.m.	44 kils.	130°	Very hot.	45° Cent.	3.88° Cent.	520 metres (on dunes)	Dunes gradually smaller. Gebel Neri S. Hawaish mountains W.		
Jan. 11th	6.30 a.m.	4.0 p.m.	38 kils.	130°	Hot. Still.	43° Cent.	5.55° Cent.	500 metres (on dunes)	Mountains. Rocky waste. Stony ridges. Black sand-balls and tubes. Passed W. of Hawari Gara 12 noon.		
Jan 12th	In Hawari				Torrid.	112° F. in tent.	5.0° Cent.	440 metres (on dunes)	Long strip oasis. Palms. Vegetation. Gardens.	Hawari. Wells. Good water.	Small zawia. Sheikh Musa Sqaireen. 1 mosque.
Jan. 13th	Do.				Cool.	30° Cent.	4.44° Cent.	Do.			

Jan. 14th to Jan. 23rd	11.0 a.m. At Taj.	4.0 p.m. Kufara.	20 kils.	140°	Cold. E. wind. Sun. Occasional cool N. wind.	23° Cent. Average 35° Cent.	5.0° Cent. Average 2.22° Cent.	490 metres Taj.	Kufara. Taj on cliff overlooking wadi. No palms or vegetation. Wadi 68 kils. long and 15 to 30 kils. wide, surrounded N. S., and E. by cliffs & gherds about 100 to 160 ft. high. On W. and in places S. W. wadi runs out into flat sand. Palm groves at Buma, Boema, Zuruk, Jof, Tolab, and Tolelib. Also some belts "hattab" with mounds up to 20 ft. high. In cultivation, barley, some wheat, vegetables, grapes, peaches, olives, figs, tamarisks, acacias. Thorns wild. Salt lakes Buma, Jof and Bahr el Azra. Large salt marshes at Jof and Buma with Tebu ruins.	Wells at Taj 120 ft. deep. Good water. No springs in Wadi, but water 9 ft. under soil. Wells everywhere. Jof, Talakh, Zuruk, Buma, Boema, Tolab, and Tolelib. System of artificial irrigation by shadouks and channels.	At Taj, Zawia El Asyad. Qubba of Mahdi. Important mosque. No sheikh. Sidi Saleh el Baskari acts as sheikh. 30 ekhwan. At Jof, ancient original zawia. Sheikh Mohammed el Basama. Qubba daughters of Mahdi. Large mosque. 20 to 25 ekhwan.

Date	Start	Halt	Distance	Direction	Weather	Highest	Lowest	Altitude	Country	Wells	Zavvias and Qubbas
Jan. 24th	To Hawari 5.0 p.m.	(Awardel village) 11.0 p.m.	23 kils.	N. W. to Hawari, then E. N. E. 3 kils. to Awardel.	Cold. N. wind.	36° Cent.	2.77° Cent.		Uneven rocky waste. Sandstone ridges. Stones give way to sand on approaching oasis.	Wells at Awardel. Good water.	
Jan. 25th	8.0 a.m.	6.0 p.m.	40 kils.	345°	Cold. N. wind.	30° Cent.	—1.11° Cent.	500 metres	Gebel el Saraia and Hawari-Gara to W. 26 kils. Red sand; then white sand. Occasional stony ridges. Passed E. of three landmarks on Zieghen route—Garet el Gardia, Mohgen, and Garet es Sherif; small hills.		
Jan. 26th	7.0 a.m.	8.30 p.m.	45 kils.	345°	Cold. N. wind.	33° Cent.	—2.22° Cent.	480 metres	Camped in Hawaish mountains. Rocky, steep hills, 100 to 180 ft. high. In Hawaish mountains.		
Jan. 27th	4.30 a.m.	5.45 p.m.	45 kils.	345°	Cold. N. wind.	32° Cent.	—1.66° Cent.	400 metres	Flat sand 16 kils, between 2 ranges. Black pebbles. Stony ground.		

Date	Time	Place	Distance	Bearing	Wind	Temp.	Min. Temp.	Elevation	Remarks	Well notes
Jan. 28th 6.0 a.m.,	2.0 a.m.		32 kils.	345°	N.W. breeze.	43° Cent.	−1.66° Cent.	360 metres	Beyond second Hawaish range large flat stone slabs. Sand waves. Saw third Hawaish range to E.	
Jan. 29th		At well at Zakar.			Strong sand-storm.	16° Cent.	−2.22° Cent.	250 metres	Two clumps of palms. Small mounds, hat-tab. Rolling sand. Stone gherds to N., which are possibly continuation of third range of Hawaish.	Zakar well. Good water. 14 ft. deep, 2½ ft. across. Stone-made walls, filled in with sand. *Note.*—Before digging, water must be used to damp surrounding sand and prevent walls falling in.
Jan. 30th	7.0 p.m.		50 kils.	60°	Cold. N. wind. Sandstorm.	12° Cent.	−1.66° Cent.	340 metres	Dunes wide, flat-backed and rolling. A few ridges. Probable continuation of dunes between Zieghen and Gedel Fadil, which join the Buseima dunes.	
Jan. 31st 7.30 a.m.	8.30 p.m.		52 kils.	60°	Torrid. No wind.	50° Cent.	−2.22° Cent.		Dunes for 12 kils., then uneven, stony country. Milling stones occasionally found. Mehemsa dunes seen half-day away N. E.	

Date	Start	Halt	Distance	Direction	Weather	Temperature		Altitude	Country	Wells	Zawias and Qubbas
						Highest	Lowest				
Feb. 1st	7.20 a.m.	2.15 p.m.	28 kils.	60°	S. W. wind.	43.33° Cent.	0.0° Cent.	280 metres	Mehemsa—two stretches "hattab" between large dunes running S. W. to N. E. Empty cisterns.		
Feb. 2nd	6.30 a.m.	7.30 p.m.	54 kils.	360°	N. W. wind.	40.55° Cent.	—1.11° Cent.		Flat, unbroken fawn sand. Minute pebbles. No vegetation.		
Feb. 3rd	6.30 a.m.	7.0 p.m.	52 kils.	360°	Torrid.	52.22° Cent.	—0.55° Cent.	Aneroid stolen. Heights were taken from highest points near camping ground.	Do.		
Feb. 4th	6.15 a.m.	6.45 p.m.	50 kils.	360°	Very hot. Slight breeze.	50.55° Cent.	3.33° Cent.		Do.		
Feb. 5th	6.30 a.m.	7.0 p.m.	54 kils.	360°	Slight breeze.	47.77° Cent.	—1.11° Cent.		Mazul dunes visible W. 10 a.m. Entered N. dunes 4 p.m.		
Feb. 6th	6.0 a.m.	6.30 p.m.	54 kils.	360°	S. E. wind.	46.11° Cent.	—1.66° Cent.		Large dune ridges N. to S. Flat stretches between. Dry "hattab."		
Feb. 7th	6.30 a.m.	7.0 p.m.	48 kils.	360°	N. E. cold wind.	26.66° Cent.	—2.22° Cent.		Dunes closer together. Occasional green "hattab."		
Feb. 8th	6.30 a.m.	6.30 p.m.	42 kils.	360°	E. wind.	32.22° Cent.	—2.22° Cent.		Dunes with green "hattab"		

Date	Time start	Time arrive	Distance		Bearings	Wind/Weather	Max.	Min.	Description	Arrival	Notes
Feb. 9th	6. 20 a.m.	6.25 p.m.	48 kils.	{ 10 kils. 28 kils. 10 kils.	{ 360° 42° 80°	Torrid. No wind.	51.11° Cent.	1.11° Cent.	Dunes. Much "hattab," patches black stones and grey rocks. Hatias Bu Alia 4.30 p.m., and Bu Salama 5.30 p.m. Garet el Mahdi, large rock at E. end of Bu Alia.	Bu Salama Hatia, much brushwood and fodder. Filled-in well.	
Feb. 10th	7.0 a.m.	3.30 p.m.	34 kils.	{ 29 kils. 5 kils.	{ 84° 48°	S. E. wind.	48.88° Cent.	0.0° Cent.	Grey sandstone gherds. Uneven, rocky country. Hatia Bu Battal with vegetation, 11 a.m.	Arrived Jaghabub	Large zawia of Sidi es Senussi with his qubba and the qubbas of his family.
Feb. 11th	At Jaghabub.								Circular Wadi of Jaghabub. Scattered palms. Cultivation below zawia. Massive blocks and cliffs of sandstone.	Wells in Jaghabub Wadi brackish and water near surface. System of irrigation with reservoirs and artificial channels in gardens.	Large mosque. Colleges and lodging-houses for 200 students. Post of Sheikh el Zawia filled by Imam Sidi el Fagih.
Feb. 12th	Do.										
Feb. 13th	Start for Siwa.										

For Notes see page 322.

NOTES TO ROUTE HISTORY

NOTE A.—The three little hillocks of sand, Kelb el Metemma, Hameimat and el Mazul, should not be taken as definite land-marks, as there is much discussion among the Beduin as to their exact identity and situation.

NOTE B.—The Oasis of Jedabia is inhabited by the Mogharba tribe, with a few Zouias, that of Aujela by the Aujela tribe, that of Jalo by the Mojabra, and those of Taiserbo, Buseima, Ribiana and Kufara by the Zouia with a sprinkling of Tebu. At Zuetina are the Fawakher, and at Solluk and Ghemines the Auwaghir.

It is estimated that the population of Kufara and Buseima is about 3,000 Zouias and 100 to 150 Tebu. In addition to these there are large numbers of negroid slaves from Wadai and Darfur. In Jaghabub there is no tribe. It is a religious centre of the Senussi ekhwan.

NOTE C.—The mileage recorded is the actual distance marched. Occasionally in dune country it was necessary to make a small détour which would reduce the distance traversed in a straight line on the map.

NOTE D.—Our failure to reach Taiserbo on the southern journey was partly due to the fact that we failed to allow for the variation between the Magnetic North and the True North, while we probably over-estimated the distance marched. At the same time, as may be seen by comparing the map published in this book and the 2 million Egyptian Survey printed 1912 and reprinted 1915, we walked through the green cultivated area and passed Kusebeya as charted in the latter, without finding any signs of Taiserbo. Our compass traverse showed an error of 20 miles in the final closure on Jaghabub. The total distance travelled, ex-clusive of the ride round Kufara Wadi, was 1,009 miles, so the error of 2 per cent. was distributed throughout the whole journey.

APPENDIX B

NOTES ON THE HISTORY OF THE SENUSSI CONFRATERNITY

SIDI MOHAMMED BEN ALI ES SENUSSI was born near Mastaghanem in Algeria in 1787. He was of the Ulad Sidi Yusuf, Berbers, yet descendants of the prophet through Idris, founder of the Moroccan dynasty. It is generally supposed that the grandfather of Ben Ali derived his name from a holy man who died in 1490—Sidi Mohammed ben Yusuf ben Amr ben Shat es Senussi of the Beni Snus—but it has also been stated that it referred merely to the Gebel Snus where his family lived. Mohammed Ben Ali, having quarrelled seriously with a cousin, went to Fez in 1821 and studied at the famous Karuim University. Morocco in those days was the birthplace of many religious confraternities and, during the seven or eight years he spent there, Ben Ali joined those of el Gadria, esh Shadelia, ej Yazula, en Nasria and ed Dergania, while at the same time he seems to have won some renown as an ascetic who wished to amalgamate every Moslem sect on a basis of a pure and simple Islam in strict conformity with the teachings of the Koran, but shorn of every modern digression and addition.

Mulai Suleiman, Emperor of Morocco, offered him preferment, but he refused it and, returning to Algeria in 1829, he taught grammar and jurisprudence at Laquat. At Mesad he married a woman of the Beni Tuaba, a gift from the faithful, which would prove that already he had gathered a certain number of disciples. He left Algeria on the eve of the French occupation and, undoubtedly, his fanaticism was strengthened by the sight of his native land in the hands of unbelievers, for, though technically Turks and Christians were equally condemned by his teaching, he reserved his fiercest hatred for the latter.

Having divorced his wife at Bu Saada, he wandered along North Africa preaching his mystic doctrine of a purer Islam till he reached Cairo, where he proposed to continue his studies at the El Azhar University. Here, however, his asceticism, intolerance and hatred of innovation made him many enemies among the

323

Ulema and, in 1831, his teachings were solemnly condemned by the Sheikh el Hamish, a noted Alim.

He therefore went on to Mecca where he became the pupil of a famous theologian, Sidi Ahmed ibn Idris el Fasi, head of the confraternity of El Khadria, of much influence in Morocco. Here at last Sidi Ben Ali found a mind akin to his own. Master and pupil travelled together to the Yemen, during which missionary journey the former died, having left instructions to his followers to transfer their allegiance to his favourite pupil, who thus found himself the head of a definite group of fervent ascetics—the Tarika el Mohammedia. His teachings met with their greatest success among the Beduin tribes of the Hejaz and the Yemen, for many of the Meccan townsmen preferred to follow another pupil of Idris, one Mohammed ibn Osman el Mirgani, Sherif. Sidi Ben Ali, therefore, having founded his first zawia at Jebel Abu Cobais made a second journey to the Yemen where he came in touch with the Wahabis, a puritanical confraternity founded in 1746. At all times his hatred of Christian and Turks alike, his opposition to the modern spirit of compromise, appealed more to the nomad tribesmen than to the settled inhabitants of the towns.

Therefore, when the opposition of the older sheikhs, who expressed doubt as to his orthodoxy, forced him to leave Mecca in 1838, he definitely formulated his policy of keeping away from centres of civilisation, and thus avoiding contact with those countries which were under European rule or protection, while uniting the various Beduin tribes in an immense religious organisation which should eventually include the negroid races of the south and stretch in an unbroken line from the Hejaz to the Tuat Oases.

Passing through Cairo, he went to Siwa, where he was ill with fever for eight months, to Jalo, and to Skekherra where he first came in touch with the Zouias, who were destined to play such a large part in his scheme for the regeneration and the unity of Islam, for this warrior tribe was feared throughout the Northern Deserts, and, having conquered the Tebu in the oases of Taiserbo and Kufara, they were a possible link with Darfur and Wadai.

In 1844 the first African zawia was founded at El Beda in the Gebel Akhdar, where Ben Ali's eldest son was born the following year, and from it the ekhwan (brothers of the Order) went throughout Cyrenaica and Tripoli, the Fezzan and even as far south as Tibesti, founding zawias and preaching the doctrine of their leader.

The Senussi are sometimes wrongly spoken of as a sect, but at
no time have they been other than an ascetic confraternity, opposed to all forms of luxury or of ceremonial, intolerant of any
intercourse with Jew, Christian or infidel. Since spiritual and
temporal power in Islam are inevitably synonymous, Sidi Ben Ali,
towards the end of his life, was looked upon as the actual ruler of
the Cyrenaican hinterland, but his aim probably did not go further than a Moslem Freemasonry, primarily religious but depend-
ing for its wealth and political power on the mercantile organisation of the ancient Saharan trade-routes by which the commerce
of the Sudan came north to the Mediterranean ports. Thus his
zawias were always built at strategic points where passing caravans must stop at the wells. While camels were watered, the
merchants were entertained by the Senussi sheikh, who was thus
afforded the best possible opportunity for propaganda. The
zawias, which were colleges and marts at the same time, gave three
days' hospitality free to any traveller and, gradually, as the fame
of the Senussi spread among the tribes, ekhwan were appointed to
accompany the more important caravans to prevent attacks from
Beduins. Thus the doctrine of Sidi Ben Ali was eventually carried to Kanem and Borku, to the Comalis and Senegambia without the existence of any written dogma. There is, in fact, no special Senussi ritual, nor have I heard any unusual prayer or rite
used in their mosques. The use of gold or jewels or any form of
luxury was forbidden, as were tobacco and alcoholic stimulants.

The fundamental ideas of the brotherhood were equality, simplicity, and complete detachment from all outside influence. The
sheikhs of the zawias had considerable temporal power because
Sidi Ben Ali's appeal was primarily to the Beduin, who were encouraged to bring their disputes to be settled at the nearest zawia,
but they were also responsible for education and to this day a
diploma of learning from Jaghabub or Kufara is highly valued in
the Moslem world.

In 1852 Sidi Ben Ali returned to Mecca where he was able to
disseminate his doctrine among pilgrims from all parts of the
world and where he met Agil the Zouia.

II

Having founded six zawias in the Hejaz and Jedda, he returned via Egypt and Akaba to Ezziat, where he remained till

1855; thence he sent ekhwan to build the zawia at Jaghabub. Doubtless this was a precautionary measure in accordance with his habitual policy of avoiding any open conflict with existing governments, for Turkey was growing nervous with regard to the Senussi power in North Africa. At first she had supported the order, according it important privileges such as grants of land and exemption of the zawias from taxation. Sidi Ben Ali, however, was not to be won over from his condemnation of Turkish unorthodoxy and in 1852 he had excommunicated the Sultan. It was therefore obviously necessary for him to remove his headquarters from the territory nominally under Ottoman jurisdiction. He went to Jaghabub in 1856 and, according to Duveyrier, he made the small and uninteresting oasis into an important centre of political and mercantile activity. A deputation of Zouias headed by Abdel Kerim Helayig, Jaballa and Agil visited him there offering the allegiance of the tribe. Sidi Ben Ali must have realised the strategical importance of Kufara as a base of propaganda from the Sudan to Lake Chad, for he instantly despatched four ekhwan to disseminate his doctrines throughout the four oases. The letter written at this time to Wajanga, of which the interpretation is given in Appendix D, page 338, is typical of his missionary methods.

It is probable that Sidi Ben Ali contemplated a further withdrawal from the zone of Turkish activity for he caused two zawias to be built near Ghadames, but his death in 1859 occurred suddenly at Jaghabub.

His two sons Mohammed el Mahdi and Mohammed es Sherif were aged 16 and 14 respectively, so most of the ekhwan were in favour of electing Sidi Abed el Ali Ibn Ahmed Ibn Idris el Fasi as their head. A decision was finally made in favour of Mohammed el Mahdi because it was remembered that Sidi Ben Ali had once bidden his eldest son resume his shoes upon entering a mosque, himself handing the boy the slippers he had put off, which menial act was interpreted to mean that he had already chosen him as his successor.

An ancient prophecy foretold that the Mahdi who would reconquer the world for Islam would attain his majority on the first day of Moharram in 1300 Hegire, having been born of parents named Mohammed and Fatma, and having spent several years in seclusion.

On November 12, 1882, after a minority spent in the charge

of Sidi Omran and Sidi Ahmed er Rifi, who afterwards remained his most valued counsellor, the son of Sidi Ben Ali fulfilled all these conditions.

At this time there were 38 zawias in Cyrenaica and Syrte and 18 in Tripolitania. Others were sown broadcast through Algeria, Tunis and Fezzan, but in Morocco there were only five, probably due to the opposition of another great religious order, the Moulai Tayyeb. By way of the Western Sahara and Timbuctoo, where they built a zawia, the Senussi ekhwan had penetrated to Senegal where they must have found fertile soil for their doctrine, as in 1879 Senegalise pilgrims travelled 4,500 kilometres across Africa to visit the Mahdi at Jaghabub and returned to their own country without troubling to continue the journey to Mecca. From Air to Gonda, from Lake Chad to Wajanga, as well as among the three millions in Wadai, it may be supposed that the Senussi influence was preponderant.

The Sultan of Wadai had been wont to entrust his north-bound caravans to the care of his "brother and fellow-ruler," Sidi Ben Ali, and immense gifts of slaves and ivory cemented the friendship between the two potentates.

In Egypt the influence of the confraternity was never very strong, though, in 1882, there were 17 zawias within its borders, exclusive of the mother house of Jaghabub. At the same date there were zawias at Jedda, Mecca and Taif and at least nine others in the Hejaz and Yemen. Duveyrier estimates the number of brothers of the Order as anything between 1,500,000 and 3,-000,000 at the time when the Mahdi's minority was ended. Each of these ekhwan was a more or less active missionary agent and each was ready, at the bidding of his superiors, to turn himself into a soldier to fight the hated infidel. Thus the power given into the hands of the young Mohammed el Mahdi was great. He might have declared a Holy War and had as amazing and meteoric a career as the humble carpenter of Abba Island in the Nile, but he preferred to strengthen his position at Jaghabub and to carry on his father's policy of holding aloof from centres of civilisation and avoiding all open rupture with European Powers. Doubtless Sidi Ben Ali was responsible for the stubborn resistance of Laghuat in Algeria in 1852 under Mohammed ibn Abed-Allah, who had joined the confraternity on a pilgrimage to Mecca, as well as for much of the oppositon to the French occupation of Nigeria and Senegambia. It is possible that the Mahdi had in view, if not an empire, at least a sphere of influence among the negroid races between Wadai and Lake Chad, for which reason he was prepared secretly to oppose the French penetration of Nigeria, but, in his withdrawal to Kufara in 1894, is seen his determination to avoid any declared hostility.

Mohammed el Mahdi was the great figure of the confraternity, and under his rule the Senussi attained the zenith of their power. Since the acceptance of his tenets meant the payment of tithes, the leader of the confraternity had by this time considerable wealth at his disposal. Having established a profitable trade in slaves and arms between south and north, he also possessed the nucleus of a negroid army, yet the Mahdi aimed at peaceful penetration rather than at military occupation. His zawias were neutral meeting-places where difficulties—tribal, commercial, legal or religious—could be settled by an unbiassed authority. His ekhwan were judges as well as missionaries. They defined tribal areas, settled water and grazing rights, as well as meting out the justice of the Koran to those who infringed the code of Islam.

In view of the undoubted influence and prestige of such a confraternity, it is not to be wondered at that wholly exaggerated ideas of its importance were brought to Europe by rare travellers who, impressed by the dangers they had escaped from, overlooked the fact that the Order must necessarily lack cohesion, disseminated as it was through countries differing in race, tongue, custom and form of government and hemmed in on every side by gradually encroaching European Powers.

During the 13 years of his rule at Jaghabub the Mahdi resolutely held aloof from the spirit of revolt which animated the Moslem world.

When the Sudanese Mahdi sent a deputation to ask for his help in driving the English from Egypt in 1884, he replied, "Tell your master we have nothing to do with him. He must write to us no more for his way is wrong. We cannot reply to his letter."

His move to Kufara isolated him in an almost impregnable position where he could command the trade routes of half a continent. His chief counsellors were his old tutor Ahmed er Rifi, his brother Mohammed es Sherif and Mohammed ibn Hassan el Baskari. His nephew Mohammed el Abed was left as wakil at Jaghabub.

Kufara under the rule of the Zouias had been the most noted centre of brigandage in the Sahara. Sidi el Mahdi substituted a regular system of Customs duty on all merchandise passing through.

He built the towns of Jof and Taj, each with a large zawia, and in the course of a few years developed the oasis into an entirely self-supporting centre of civilisation and the headquarters of the confraternity, visited by large numbers of "Brethren" from all parts of Africa.

Nevertheless he had to acknowledge that, temporarily, the north offered no further field of expansion for his teachings. Any trial of strength with France, Turkey or Egypt could have but one issue. Therefore he concentrated his energies on Borku, Wadai, Kanem and the Western Sudan. He sent his ekhwan throughout these districts with instructions to settle disputes between the tribes, thus inducing them to acknowledge Senussi authority and to build zawias in such places as would control the wells and markets. Intending to follow in the wake of his disciples, he left Kufara in August, 1899, after receiving a deputation from Ali Dinar expressing the Sultan of Darfur's devotion to the Order. After 63 days' travelling by slow stages, he reached Ghiru, from where he directed the opposition to French penetration from Lake Chad.

This step was notable because it was in direct contravention of the policy initiated by Sidi Ben Ali and previously adhered to by the Mahdi.

At no time a military power, the Senussi depended for their wealth and influence on the stability of their mercantile organisation.

The French were the first Europeans who seriously imperilled their profitable trade in slaves and arms. The former merchandise came from Constantinople and was disembarked at Tobruk or Benghazi.

Since its principal markets were between Darfur and Kanem it was essential that France should not advance farther towards Wadai. Tuareg rebels, flying north from French Nigeria, came in touch with Sidi el Barrani at Kanem, were converted to the Senussi tenets, and joined with Arabs from Kufara in fortifying the zawia at Bir Allahi.

The victory of Zugiba on August 23, 1901, relieved the French from further pressure from the south and they were able to establish themselves firmly at Massacori. An advance party, however, was attacked and defeated by Tuaregs from Bir Allahi and this zawia remained a centre of opposition until it was taken in January, 1902.

By this open aggression Sidi el Mahdi apparently pledged himself to a definite campaign against France, yet he had no regular army. His policy was to unite the tribes against the Christian, himself supplying arms, ammunition and money. Borku was virtually under his rule. He had a wazir in Wadai and zawias in Nigeria and the Cameroons.

Mohammed es Sunni, one of the most famous Senussi ekhwan, who had undertaken many missionary journeys in the Sudan and West Africa, was adviser to the Sultan of Wadai, for whom he had obtained the financial support of the Tripolitanian merchants.

The sudden death of the Mahdi, however, on June 1st, 1902, removed the motive force of the order. As his sons were then minors at school at Jaghabub, his nephew Sayed Ahmed es Sherif was nominated as his successor.

The new Sheikh es Senussi remained at Ghiru, from where he continued to oppose the French advance, till a bad defeat in December, 1902, decided him to retire to Kufara.

For some years he moved his headquarters between this oasis and Jaghabub so that he was able to keep in touch with his northern zawias without relinquishing the hold gained by the Mahdi on the negroid races of the south.

Since the Anglo-French Treaty of 1904 ceded the Zinder-Chad route to France, the advance of the latter power has inevitably involved the ebb of the Senussi influence throughout the occupied districts.

The Ulad Suleiman tribes, who had been among the strongest adherents of the Mahdi, submitted in 1905.

The following year Bilma was occupied in spite of determined attacks by Tuaregs and Kufara Arabs.

In March, 1907, the principal zawia in Borku, Ain Malakka, was captured and its sheikh, Sidi el Barrani, the virtual ruler of Borku, killed.

In June, 1909, Abeshe, the capital of Wadai, was entered.

Turkish troops occupied Tibesti in May, 1910, and Borku in September, 1911, but were recalled at the outbreak of the Turco-Italian war in 1912, leaving the Senussi free to continue the propaganda that was finally put an end to by the French advance into Tibesti and Borku, in the winter of 1913-1914.

Meanwhile, Cyrenaica and Tripoli having been acknowledged

an Italian sphere of influence, Sayed Ahmed was fully occupied in the north.

When the Italians landed in Libya in 1911, there existed a kingdom within a kingdom and the Turks were only masters in name. They were almost as much despised as the Christians by the ascetic confraternity of Sidi Ben Ali, who held themselves entirely aloof from the Ottoman Government.

Therefore when Sayed Ahmed definitely allied himself with Turkey, he departed from the fundamental principle of his Order. He was persuaded by Enver Pasha to allow the tribes to take part, under Turkish leadership, in the long-drawn-out guerilla warfare which was so successfully carried out that, in 1914, Italy was left in possession of the coast towns of Tripoli and Cyrenaica only, while the interior was in the hands of the Senussi.

This material success was counter-balanced, however, by the dissolution of Senussi entity. The principle of religious detachment for which the Order had originally stood had disappeared and the confraternity had resolved itself into a political weapon in the hands of Turkey. From this standpoint it was but a short step to the declaration of war against Egypt.

At no period was Sayed Ahmed really anti-British, because he knew that Britain had no interests to serve in Libya. Moreover, she facilitated his trade with Egypt, a vital point for the welfare of the Beduins, for the Cyrenaican ports were already closed to them.

Mannismann and Nouri Pasha, respectively German and Turkish agents, provided arms, ammunition and money, while holding before the Senussi sheikh the idea that the Egyptian Beduins would all join him, and that he would be the ruler of Egypt, yet, in spite of Teuton organisation and of a widely preached Jehad, it is doubtful if the Senussi could ever have put in the field more than 4,000 men.

Sayed Ahmed established his headquarters at Bir Waer and the Egyptian Coastguards, under Mohammed Saleh, were persuaded by religious fanaticism to join him.

Jaafer Pasha, a keen and capable soldier, an Arab from Baghdad, trained in German methods, was in command of the Senussi troops.

The *Tara* was sunk on November 5, 1915, and her crew sent as prisoners to the desert.

Sollum, under the command of Colonel Snow Bey, of the Egyptian Coastguards, was evacuated in the same month, and as the garrison went down the coast in a cruiser, they could see Sidi Barrani in flames.

British Headquarters were established at Mersa Matruh and in December the outlying garrisons were collected there.

Colonel Snow Bey, whose name with that of Major Royle Bey is famous throughout the Western Desert, was shot in a reconnaissance on November 11.

On Christmas Eve the Senussi were defeated at Medwa and on December 29 at Jerawla, but the first decisive battle was at Halazin, where Sayed Ahmed had gathered his main force.

On January 23 he was attacked with complete success, and forced to retreat precipitately towards Sollum, leaving 700 dead on the field.

A further victory on February 26 at Agazia resulted in the capture of Jaafer Pasha and the flight of Sayed Ahmed, with the subsequent opening of the road to Sollum, which was occupied on March 14.

The following day the Duke of Westminster made his famous dash to Bir Hakim on the Tobruk-Jaghabub route, some 60 miles inland, and 120 from Sollum, to rescue the *Tara* prisoners.

Sayed Ahmed retired through Siwa to Dakhla, while the remaining portion of his force went to Baharia. Kharga was immediately evacuated by the British and then, with a successful army occupying the post, a beaten enemy practically cut off from all supplies in two isolated desert oases, a disaffected and half-starved Cyrenaica, heartily tired of its ruler's policy and already turning to Mohammed Idris, whose pro-British attitude was obvious from the beginning, was initiated the scheme for fortifying Egypt at an expense of some 60 million sterling against a foe who numbered perhaps 2,000.

The three armed camps of the Ulad Ali which lay behind the British line from Matruh were rapidly disposed of, but the whole summer of 1916 was spent in fortifying the line of the Nile Valley and in October the Senussi were driven out of Dakhla and Baharia by Camel Corps and Light Car Patrols. Sayed Ahmed retired through Farafra to Siwa, where he had left Mohammed Saleh in command.

In February, 1917, after a sharp engagement at Girba, where, east of Munasib Pass, some 20 armoured cars sustained a 24 hours' enfilade from 800 Senussi hidden in the rocks above them, the latter were finally driven out of Egyptian Territory.

For 18 months Sayed Ahmed spent a precarious existence in the hinterland of Cyrenaica and, in August, 1918, retired to Constantinople by submarine.

Meanwhile, in 1916, an Anglo-British Mission under General (then Colonel) the Marchese di Vita and Colonel Talbot had approached Sidi Mohammed Idris es Senussi at Tobruk and Zuetina with a view to arranging a *modus vivendi* in Cyrenaica.

Sayed Idris had taken no part in his cousin's campaign against Egypt. On the contrary, he threw all his influence as the son of Mahdi into the opposing scale.

As soon as Sayed Ahmed decided to attack, the younger Senussi retired, with his brother Sayed Rida, to Jedabia, writing to General Maxwell to say that he did not support his cousin's policy. He continued firmly in this course, though when Sayed Ahmed was defeated Mannismann came west with some Turks and Egyptian Coastguards to try and persuade him to continue the war. Sayed Idris refused, and Mannismann was killed on his way to Tripoli, a journey he had undertaken in direct opposition to the Senussi's advice.

It was thus natural that both Cyrenaica and Italy should turn to the eldest son of the Mahdi for help in the work of re-organisation, necessitated by Sayed Ahmed's disastrous policy.

A dual agreement was drawn up in 1917 between the British and Italian Governments on the one side and Sayed Mohammed Idris, as the head of the confraternity, on the other, by which it was agreed that:—

(A) The Italian Government will retain the coast towns, and certain already occupied posts a short distance inland, but will create no new posts.

(B) Commerce is to be unrestricted between the interior and Benghazi, Tobruk and Derna.

(C) Courts according to Sharia Law and schools for the education of natives will be built and maintained by the Italians who will also restore zawias and zawia property not still required for military purposes and be responsible for the salaries of sheikhs el zawia appointed by Sidi Idris.

(D) Material assistance will be rendered to Mohammed Idris by the Italian Government supplying him with arms, ammunition, equipment and food for a limited number of men. For the moment 4,000 is the number fixed. These are to be used partly against the enemy and partly for the purpose of maintaining public security in the interior of Cyrenaica.

(E) Personal allowances to certain members of the Senussi family are to be paid monthly.

(F) In return for this, Mohammed Idris will make himself responsible for the maintenance of peace in the interior, but will form no new posts, will gradually disarm the population, will place no obstacles in the way of the Italian Government for the forcible disarmament of hostile groups, will allow Italian delegates to enter the interior for the settlement of affairs with his local representative while the Italian Government may at any time send a representative to discuss matters with him in person.

Since then an excellent understanding has been arrived at, chiefly owing to the personal influence of H. E. The Governor of Cyrenaica, Senator de Martino and Sayed Mohammed Idris under which Cyrenaica bids fair to have a prosperous commercial and agricultural future.

By the accord of Regima in November, 1920, Italy and the Senussi ratified the Italo-British Agreement before quoted.

Sayed Idris was given the hereditary title of Emir with jurisdiction as "an independent ruler on behalf of Italy" over the oases of Kufara, Jaghabub, Jalo, Aujela and Jedabia. He is to disband his "karakols" and armed camps in Cyrenaica, and the Italians are to find employment for the men thus left without work in a regular police force. The terms of the new Constitution granted to Cyrenaica provide that five members, out of the 44 constituting the Legislative Assembly, shall be elected from the oases of the interior. It is expected that a port will be built at Zuetina and that the trans-Saharan trade from Wadai and Darfur will pass through Kufara, Jalo, and Jedabia on its way to this Mediterranean outlet.

At the present moment Sayed Idris rules by means of kaimakaans at Kufara, Jalo, Jaghabub, Jedabia, el Abiar, Takness, Merawa and Kholaf. Under each kaimakaan is a *Qadi* (judge), and a *Mahkama Sharia* (Religious Court) consisting of two clerks, a *Mudir Amual* (Head of the Financial Department), a Treasurer and Clerk, and a *Mamur Tahsil* (Head Tax-collector).

The justice is that of the Koran and "Onshur"—a tenth part —is paid yearly on palms and live-stock. Five per cent. Customs dues is levied on all goods entering the Senussi country and a small sum on the sale of a camel, sheep or goat, but it is expected that, in view of the friendly relations at present existing between the Italian Government and the Emir Idris, a system of customs will be organised to encourage trade between the interior and the coastal districts. In the future it will be interesting to observe in what direction the Senussi will develop.

The organisation has departed from the basic elements of its inception. Begun as an isolated religious confraternity, it has expanded by way of mercantile and political influence into a dynastic entity whose desire for civilisation must necessarily force it along lines widely divergent from those contemplated by its founder. It is certain that the Emir Idris will have the whole-hearted support of the country in whatever course he chooses to pursue, and with the present sympathetic co-operation of the Italian Government it is probable that he will lead the march of Arab progress in North Africa.

APPENDIX C

Translation of Arab Document of the Welcome given at Buseima.

IN the name of God, the Compasionate, the Merciful.

On the blessed day of Friday, 28th Rabia eth Thani, 1339, there came to our town Buseima, the honourable Ahmed Abu Mohammed Hassanein, the Egyptian, son of Sheikh Mohammed Ahmed Hassanein el Bulaki, the professor of the sacred Azhar and the lady Khadija and they are carrying the orders of His Beatitude our Great Prince, Sayed Mohammed Idris, son of Mohammed el Mahdi es Senussi. We met them with great honour and hospitality and congratulated them on their safe arrival to us. We hoped that God may be exalted, would grant success to their efforts, and return them safe and victorious in the best conditions for the sake of the Prophet, his friends and his family.

Signed.

Mohammed Ali el Mardini
Saad Ibn Ahmed Faqrun
Yunis ibn Mahi
Suleiman ibn Khalid Faqrun
Omar Ibn el Gaid
Saleh Ibn Ahmed Faqrun

Translation of Arab Document of Welcome given at Kufara (Taj).

ON the blessed day of Friday the 3rd of Jamad el Awal, 1339, there came to our town in Kufara the honoured Ahmed Mohammed Hassanein Bey, the Egyptian, son of Sheikh Mohammed Hassanein el Bulaki, professor of the honoured Azhar and the lady Khadija. They were carrying the orders of our great prince Sayed Mohammed Idris el Mahdi es Senussi and, according to the exalted orders we met them with all honour and respect and thanked God for their safe arrival to us, and hoping of Him their safe return.

Signed:

The Second Adviser of Kufara, Ahmed es Sussi, May God forgive him.

The Judge, Osman el Barassi, May God forgive him.

The Adviser, Sayed Mohammed Ibn Omar el Fadhil, May God forgive him.

The Wakil of the Sayed at Kufara, Mohammed Saleh el Baskari, May God guard him.

APPENDIX D

Translation of original MS letter of Sidi Ben Ali es Senussi, founder of the Senussi Confraternity, to the people of Wajanga. Seen in Kufara.

In the name of God, the Compassionate, the Merciful, May God pray on our master Mohammed, his family and his companions, and may He give them peace!

It is from the chosen of his God, Mohammed ibn Ali ibn El Senussi El Khatabi El Hassani El Idrissi to the noble and learned and brilliant Sheikh Farag El Ginghawi and all the people of Wajanga, old and young, male and female, may God save them all and give them their wish of this world and the next! Amen.

Peace be upon you and the mercy of God, His blessings, His salutations, His forgiveness and His approval.

Our intention and our wish is, first to enquire after you and all your affairs, may God guide them and make them conform with His Book and the tradition of His Prophet Mohammed.

Secondly, we wish to ask you in the name of Islam to obey God and His Prophet. He, praise be to Him, said in His dear Book, "Oh, ye, who are believers, obey God and obey the Prophet!" He also said, "He who obeys the Prophet has also obeyed God." He also said, "He who obeys God and His Prophet has won a great victory." He also said, "Those who obey God and the Prophet, they are with the prophets whom God has rewarded."

We wish to ask you to obey what God and His Prophet have ordered, making the five prayers, keeping the month of Ramadan, giving tithe, making the Haj to the sacred home of God and avoiding what God has forbidden, of telling lies, abusing people behind their backs, taking unlawfully other people's money, drinking wine, killing people unlawfully, giving false evidence and other things which God has forbidden.

In following these you will gain everlasting good and endless profits which will never be taken from you.

Some men of your country had asked us to send with them

338

some of our ekhwan [brothers] in order to remind them of God
and teach them what God and his Prophet have ordained and guide
them rightly. We decided to do this because it is our profession
[mission] for which God has put us, i.e. to remind the negligent,
teach the ignorant and guide him who has gone astray. But at
that time we were in the sacred "Haramain" [Mecca]. When we
arrived in these parts we occupied ourselves with guiding the people to the paths of God and we did not find anyone of your country
with whom to send those who would teach people this religion.

Now our sons of Zawaya, who are the inhabitants of Tazerr,
which you know, have come to us and repented and asked us to
build a zawia at the mentioned Tazerr.* Our intention is to become your neighbours and teach you and your sons of the Book of
God and the tradition his Prophet, Mohammed. May God's
prayers and peace be on him! Also we intend to make peace between you and the Arabs who invade you and take your sons and
your money. In doing this we will be enacting what God has said,
"If two parties of believers fight, make peace between them."
Also his saying, "Fear God, make peace between one another and
obey God and His Prophet if you are believers." He also said,
"Give an order for alms or a good deed or making peace between
people. He who does this for the sake of pleasing God will gain
a great reward."

In this way there will be co-operation for doing good and for
piety, as God has ordained by saying, "Co-operate for doing good
and for piety and do not co-operate for vice and assault." The
Prophet said, "People of God, be brethren and help one another in
religion."

As to rebellion and dispute, no good comes out of them and
God has forbidden them in his dear Book by saying, "Do not dispute or you will fail and be dispersed; be patient, for God is with
the patient."

Inshallah, if you obey our orders and accept our advice, then a
few of our sons will come to you to teach your sons the Book of
God, and your men the tradition and ways of His Prophet. You
will then not fear anyone and you will have much of God's bounty
and mercy, Inshallah.

Give our salutation and this letter of ours to all who are round
you, those who wish for the obedience of God and His Prophet and
who wish to follow the Book and the Tradition.

* Tazerr was the old name for Kufara.

May God, may He be praised, make you of those who guide
and who have been guided and of those who point out what is good
and who follow it!

May you remain in endless peace and health!

Dated the fourth day of Moharren, 1266.

GLOSSARY

"Adaryayan!" A cry used when halting camels. "We have arrived, oh sick ones."

Agal. A rope used to tie a camel's legs or the thick cords worn on the head above the *kufiya.*

Alaf. A measure of fodder.

"Allahu Akbar." God is great.

"Aselamu, Alaikum, Marhaba, Marhaba." Greetings to you. Welcome!

"Ash hadu illa Illaha ill Allah wa ash hadu inna Mohammed an rasul Allah." I confess there is no God but God, and I confess that Mohammed is His Prophet.

Asida. Sticky mass of damp flour flavoured with onions or oil.

Azzau. The act of calling to prayer.

Barracan. A long cotton garment worn by the women.

Basoor. Camel saddle in which women travel.

Bayid. Far.

"Beit esh shar." Camel's-hair tent.

"Beit Ullah." The house of God.

Belad. Village.

"Bisilama." With safety.

"Bismillah." By the name of God.

"Bismillah arahman arahmim." By the name of God the merciful and compassionate.

Burnus. Arab garment.

Ekhwan. Brothers. Used colloquially in Libya to mean "a brother."

"El Fagr." Dawn.

"El Maktub Maktub." What is written is written.

"En nahs teyibin hena. Ana Mabsut." The people are good here. I am happy.

Fadhling. Sitting down and talking.

Fanatis. Tin water-carriers.

"Fatha." The first sura (chapter) of the Koran.

Fatta. An Arab dish of carrots, bread and eggs.

Feisha. A gourd used as a charm to keep a husband's affection.
Fil-fil. Red pepper.
Gara. A tabular hill.
Gebel. A mountain.
Gherds. Dunes.
Gibli. Sand-laden south wind.
Girba. Dried goatskin water-carrier.
Haji. A man who has made the pilgrimage (Haj) to Mecca.
Hajin. Trotting camels.
"Hamdulillah." Thank God.
Hamla. Baggage camels.
Hatia. A depression containing brushwood.
Hawia. Baggage saddle.
"Haya alla Salat! Haya alla falah." The Moslem call to prayer.
Hejab. Charm.
Hezaam. Sash or belt.
Hubz. Bread.
"Inshallah ma temut illa Islam." If God wills (or I hope) you
    will die a Moslem.
Jaafa. A large leather sack.
Jelabia. Wide native coat.
Jerd. Native garment—a strip of woollen or silk stuff.
Jubba. Arab under dress.
Kaftan. Long Arab inner coat.
Kaimakaan. Governor.
"Keif halak?" How are you?
"Khallas." Finished.
Khoor. Saddle-bag.
Kibla. The direction of prayer (towards Mecca).
Kufiya. Arab head-dress.
Laghbi. Fermented palm-juice.
Leaf = palm leaf.
Ma-araka. Skull cap.
"Maasellam." With safety.
"Mabsut." Happy.
Madna. Tower.
Mamnum. Grateful.
Mandil. Handkerchief.
"Marhaba." Welcome.
Megliss. Council.
Mejidie. A Turkish coin worth 3s. to 4s.

Mihrab. Praying-niche.

Mimbar. Pulpit.

Morabit. As an adjective "Holy." As a noun "The tomb of a holy person."

"Min da?" Who is that?

Naga. A female camel.

"Nahs Taibeen." Good people.

Nugga. A Beduin tent.

Oke. A measure.

Qubba. A domed holy tomb.

Qurush. A small Turkish coin.

"Raqa-at." Positions or stages of prayer.

"Rahmat Allah!" The peace of God.

"Rahmat ullahi Allahim." "The peace of God be on him."

Sabakha. A salt marsh.

"Salamu aleikum wa Rahmab Allah." Greetings to you and the peace of Allah.

Sederiya. A short shirt.

Serg. A saddle.

Shadouk. Well.

Shamadan. A certain kind of wind-proof candlestick.

Shehada. The Moslem profession of faith, "There is no God but God," etc.

"Shey latif." A pleasant thing.

Sitt. Lady.

Suq. Market.

Sura. Chapter of Koran.

Tobh. Woman's dress.

Tukel. Round hut.

"Ulla-la een." Women's cry of rejoicing.

Wakil. Representative (steward or lieutenant-governor).

Wazir. Minister.

Zawia. College.

Zeit. Oil.

Zemzimaya. Felt-covered water-bottle.

INDEX

Slave farms, 213
    trade, stringent French law
        against, 213
Slavery in the East, 39
Slaves, smuggled, 109
Smoking prohibited by the Sen-
    ussi, 4, 14, 220, 308
Snakes, fearsome, 235
Soluk, 7, 63
Squaireen, Sheikh Musa, ix, 176
Stecker, surveyor to Rohlfs' expe-
    dition, ix, 16
Stockley, Cynthia, 58
Sudan, the, Senussi influence in,
    119
Sudanese, quixotic valour of, 166
    ruthlessness of, 83
    tiffs with the Beduins, 130, 135,
        151
    voracious appetite of, 51
Sudani slaves of Zuruk, 211
Suleiman Bu Matar, Sheikh, 206,
    207, 218
    as guide and host, 230, 231, 241
    on the Mahdi, 228
Suleiman (the guide), 230, 241,
    244, 252 et seq., 260 et seq.,
    271 et seq., 285 et seq.
    a remarkable feat of, 279
    loses a leather bag, 276, 277
Surur, 225

TABAWAYEIN, the, houses of, 154
Taiserbo, 15, 91
    a start for, 126 et seq.
    Madeni at, 158
    Moraja's opinion of, 144
    reached by Rohlfs, 17
    Rohlfs and, 154, 156
    topography of, 157
    villages of, 157
Taj, 16, 177
    a council at, 204 et seq.
    city's formal farewell to author,
        240

Taj, exploration of, 222
    first sight of, 191
    flight from, 222 et seq.
    fortress sanctuary of, and its
        builder, 228
    meaning of, 214
    qubba of Sidi el-Mahdi at, 191
    translation of Arab document of
        welcome given at, 336-337
Talakh, a visit to, 214
Tawati Halfan, 208
Tazerr, 211
Tea-drinking, ceremony of, 71
Tebu camels, thin coats of, 242
    houses, exploration of, 161
    oasis, Hornemann on, 174
    ruined villages and houses, 15,
        154, 157, 210, 218, 223
    tombs, 154
    village, visit to a, 220
Tebus, tribe of, 91, 151
    ousted from Kebabo, 15
    their old-time sultanate, 205
Theft, punishment for, 227
Thermos flask, a, in the desert, 78
Tobruk, 120
Tolab, 158, 192
    gardens of, 236
    why so named, 214
Tolelib, 158, 192, 233, 236
Treachery, punishment for, 227
Tribal bands, savage, 91
Tripolitania, 16
    Italians at bay in, 120
Tuaregs, the, 20, 52, 104
    slave farms of, 213
Tuggourt, 52, 219
Tunisi, 157

UAU, Szerir, 16

VITA, General di, ix, 3

WADAI, desert of, 14
    Mahdi institutes regular cara-
        van route to, 228

Some of the other titles in the Adventure Travel Classic series
published by The Long Riders' Guild Press.
We are constantly adding to our collection, so for an
up-to-date list please visit our website:
www.thelongridersguild.com

The Rob Roy on the Jordan	John MacGregor
In the Forbidden Land	Henry Savage Landor
From Paris to New York by Land	Harry de Windt
My Life as an Explorer	Sven Hedin
Elephant Bill	Lt.-Col. J. H. Williams
Fifty Years below Zero	Charles Brower
Quest for the Lost City	Dana and Ginger Lamb
Enchanted Vagabonds	Dana Lamb
Seven League Boots	Richard Halliburton
The Flying Carpet	Richard Halliburton
New Worlds to Conquer	Richard Halliburton
The Glorious Adventure	Richard Halliburton
The Royal Road to Romance	Richard Halliburton
My Khyber Marriage	Morag Murray Abdullah
Khyber Caravan	Gordon Sinclair
Servant of Sahibs	Rassul Galwan
Beyond Khyber Pass	Lowell Thomas
True Stories of Modern Explorers	B. Webster Smith
Call to Adventure	Robert Spiers Benjamin
Heroes of Modern Adventure	T. C. Bridges
Death by Moonlight	Robert Henriques
To Lhasa in Disguise	William McGovern
The Lives of a Bengal Lancer	Francis Yeats-Brown
Twenty Thousand Miles in a Flying Boat	Sir Alan Cobham
The Secret of the Sahara: Kufara	Rosita Forbes
Forbidden Road: Kabul to Samarkand	Rosita Forbes
I Married Adventure	Osa Johnson
Grey Maiden	Arthur Howden Smith
Sufferings in Africa	Captain James Riley
Tex O'Reilly – Born to Raise Hell	Tex O'Reilly and Lowell Thomas

The Long Riders' Guild
The world's leading source of information regarding equestrian exploration!
www.thelongridersguild.com

Printed in the United Kingdom
by Lightning Source UK Ltd.
106058UKS00005B/25